PENGUIN ENGLISH LIBRARY

MEMOIRS OF MY LIFE

EDWARD GIBBON

Betty Radice read Classics at Oxford, then married, and in
the intervals of bringing up a family, tutored in classics,
philosophy and English. She became joint editor of the
Penguin Classics in 1964. As well as editing the translation of Livy's *The War with Hannibal*, she has translated
Livy's *Rome and Italy*, the Latin comedies of Terence,
Pliny's Letters, *The Letters of Abelard and Heloise* and
Erasmus's *Praise of Folly*, and has also written the Introduction to Horace's *Complete Odes and Epodes*, all for the
Penguin Classics. She has edited and annotated her translation of the younger Pliny's works for the Loeb Library of
Classics, and translated from Italian, Renaissance Latin
and Greek for the Officina Bodoni of Verona. She is
collaborating as a translator in the Collected Works of
Erasmus in preparation by the University of Toronto,
editing an eight-volume production of Gibbon's *Decline
and Fall of the Roman Empire* for the Folio Society, and is
the author of the Penguin reference book *Who's Who in
the Ancient World*. Betty Radice is an honorary fellow of St
Hilda's College, Oxford.

EDWARD GIBBON

MEMOIRS OF MY LIFE

*Edited with
an Introduction by*
BETTY RADICE

PENGUIN BOOKS

Penguin Books Ltd, Harmondsworth, Middlesex, England
Penguin Books, 40 West 23rd Street, New York, New York 10010, U.S.A.
Penguin Books Australia Ltd, Ringwood, Victoria, Australia
Penguin Books Canada Ltd, 2801 John Street, Markham, Ontario, Canada L3R 1B4
Penguin Books (N.Z.) Ltd, 182–190 Wairau Road, Auckland 10, New Zealand

Published in Penguin English Library 1984

Made and printed in Great Britain by
Richard Clay (The Chaucer Press) Ltd,
Bungay, Suffolk
Filmset in 9/11½ pt Monophoto Photina by
Northumberland Press Ltd, Gateshead

CONTENTS

PREFACE AND ACKNOWLEDGEMENTS

The text of this edition of Edward Gibbon's *Memoirs of My Life* is based on G. A. Bonnard's arrangement of the drafts Gibbon left unfinished, but with a major difference. His was a text which meticulously reproduced Gibbon's uncorrected manuscripts. I have tried to standardize the punctuation and the variable use of capitals, and to follow conventions in italicizing names of books and foreign quotations and in abbreviations (M. for Monsieur, not Gibbon's Mr), while adding (or correcting) accents on French words and putting breathings and accents on Greek quotations. I have also divided long continuous passages into shorter paragraphs, and made some changes in Gibbon's spelling, which can be idiosyncratic and influenced by French forms. Rightly or wrongly, I hope by so doing to remove any feeling of outmoded quaintness from what is so candid and direct a work; and to break down any further barriers between Gibbon and his modern readers I have provided translations in notes of all his quotations from French, Greek and Latin.

I have drawn on Bonnard's notes, many of which are simple directions to the standard reference books, as well as on the editions of Gibbon's other works listed in the Bibliography, but the notes are my own. In attempting to solve the problem of the great numbers of persons and authors cited by Gibbon, I have put their names in a comprehensive index; though I have not included all the details of Chapter I, which I believe Gibbon would have removed on revision (see Introduction, p. 15). This has reduced the notes, and left the reader free to follow up names or not, undaunted, I hope, by lists such as that of the members of the Literary Club (p. 177) or of the reading matter which Gibbon thought essential preparation for the Grand Tour (p. 140). Many of the authors and their works feature in the footnotes to *The Decline and Fall of the Roman Empire*.

My thanks for encouragement and help on special points are to Mrs Gwynydd Gosling and the library of the Highgate Literary and

Preface and Acknowledgements

Scientific Institution, Dr Colin Kolbert, Lieutenant-Colonel Patrick O'Kelly de Conejera, I. de Lisle Radice, Dr P. J. S. Whitmore and L. P. Wilkinson.

EDITOR'S INTRODUCTION

On 27 June 1787, Edward Gibbon wrote the last sentence of the sixth and final volume of *The Decline and Fall of the Roman Empire*:

It was among the ruins of the Capitol that I first conceived the idea of a work which has amused and exercised near twenty years of my life, and which, however inadequate to my own wishes, I finally deliver to the curiosity and candour of the public.

Nearly four years later he recalled the details: the time, between eleven and midnight; the scene, the summer-house in his garden by Lake Leman; his emotions, as he laid down his pen and paced the acacia walk – joy at recovering his freedom, satisfaction at the prospect of fame, mixed with sober melancholy at having taken 'everlasting leave of an old and agreeable companion', and the thought that at the age of fifty the best part of his life was over.

He was in fact to live another six and a half years, but felt no great urge to embark on further large-scale writing. Some essays survive, but there was much to distract him from concentrated application. He was rich and famous, with a wide circle of correspondents; he led a full social life in Lausanne, and entertained an increasing number of visitors as the refugees from the Revolution arrived from France. He also returned from a year (July 1787 to July 1788) spent in England arranging for the publication of his final three volumes, to find that Georges Deyverdun, the friend of thirty years whose house he shared, had suffered a series of strokes. Deyverdun lingered on for a year, during which Gibbon found it impossible to recover his 'studious ardour', and his bereavement was keenly felt for some time. Moreover, though Gibbon's mental energy never seriously flagged and he always insisted that his health was generally good, his friends were increasingly worried about his unhealthy corpulence and the plainly visible rupture or hydrocele which he was still determined to ignore. His letters also mention severe attacks of erysipelas in 1790, and another crippling bout of his old enemy, gout.

Gibbon did not return to England until May 1793, and then only when he heard that Lord Sheffield's wife had died suddenly in April and he wanted to be with his friend. He set out on his fifty-sixth birthday, bringing with him no less than six incomplete drafts of autobiographical memoirs. Doubtless he intended to continue working on the final one and to show the memoirs to Sheffield, who was the only person to know that he had been working on them intermittently since soon after the completion of *The Decline and Fall*. There is nothing to indicate that Sheffield knew of Gibbon's plans before he brought his family on a visit to Lausanne in the summer of 1791, and Gibbon's letter of 28 December after Sheffield's return insisted that he should keep what he had been told secret: 'People must not be prepared to laugh: they must be taken by surprise.'

The summer of 1793 was spent at Sheffield Place, the autumn was taken up by visits to Bath and Althorp. It was clear to everyone that Gibbon was not well, but it was November before he called in a surgeon and wrote to Sheffield about the rapidly increasing hydrocele. This had started with a rupture as far back as Gibbon's militia days in 1761, when he had seen a surgeon but ignored his advice to return for further examination. Three surgeons now conferred and agreed that the fluid must be tapped. This was successfully done twice, while Gibbon continued to dine out and visit his friends, returning to Sheffield Place in mid December. He was then feverish and in pain, and set off back to London on 7 January – a journey by carriage over 'hard, frozen, long and cross ruts' which must have been agonizing. Once home in St James's Street his optimism returned, another tapping on 13 January was apparently successful, and he talked of complete recovery. Then inflammation set in, and he died on the 16th, before Lord Sheffield could be with him. The sudden collapse suggests that lack of antiseptic precautions had led to streptococcic peritonitis.

Lord Sheffield brought the body home, and on 23 January the coffin was placed in the family mausoleum built on to the north transept of Fletching Church, just outside the gates of Sheffield Park. The Latin inscription (see p. 34) commissioned from Dr Samuel Parr can still be read, set amongst inscriptions to the Sheffields on the Gothic-style stone screen; the mausoleum is now sealed. Sheffield then had to cope with Gibbon's will and with all his papers, including the six drafts of memoirs, to which Gibbon had added nothing during his eight months in England and for which he left no instructions. But by 6 August 1795, thanks to Sheffield's unflagging energy and devotion to his friend, and with the help of his elder daughter, Maria Josepha (later Lady Stanley of Alderley), he had sent to the printers two quarto volumes of *Miscellaneous Works of Edward Gibbon, with Memoirs of his Life and Writings*. A third volume was added in 1815, and a new edition in five volumes octavo came out in the same year (but dated 1814), with the Memoirs revised and occasionally augmented.

Lord Sheffield's task of editing the six drafts plus 'notes and memoranda on loose unconnected papers and cards, all in Mr Gibbon's handwriting' was indeed formidable, although the beautiful writing is always clear. He said in his own preface to the first edition that 'it is difficult to discover the order in which these several pieces were written. From all of them the following memoirs have been carefully selected and put together.' The *Miscellaneous Works* were reprinted in 1837, but not subsequently, though the Memoirs were printed separately in 1827 and several times in the nineteenth century, when they acquired the name of Gibbon's Autobiography. No further revisions were possible, however, as Lord Sheffield wished no additional publication from the Gibbon papers during his lifetime, and left the following clause in his will when he died in 1821:

And I request of my said trustees and my heirs that none of the said manuscripts, papers, or books of the said Edward Gibbon be published unless my approbation of the publication be directed by some memorandum indorsed and written or signed by me. And I also request the person entitled for the time being to the possession thereof not to suffer the same to be out of his possession or to be improperly exposed.

It was not until the centenary of Gibbon's death in 1894, which the Royal Historical Society celebrated by an exhibition in the British Museum, that the third Lord Sheffield felt that 'it is a duty I owe to my ancestor and to the public to give to the world all the remains of the historian which for more than a century have been preserved in the strong-room of Sheffield Park'. Of his grandfather he wrote:

Lord Sheffield executed his editorial task with extreme judgment, singular ingenuity, but remarkable freedom. He was assisted in preparing the manuscripts for publication by his wife and by Lady Maria Holroyd, his eldest daughter, who became by marriage the first Lady Stanley of Alderley. This very able and remarkable woman, of whose abilities the historian expressed in letters his great admiration, evidently marked the manuscripts in pencil handwriting (now recognised as hers) for the printer's copyist. These pencil deletions, transpositions, and even additions, correspond with the Autobiography as published by Lord Sheffield. Quite a third of the whole manuscript is omitted, and many of the most piquant passages that Gibbon ever wrote were suppressed by the caution or the delicacy of his editor and his family.

The result is a problem of singular literary interest. A piece, most elaborately composed by one of the greatest writers who ever used our language, an autobiography often pronounced to be the best we possess, is now proved to be in no sense the simple work of that illustrious pen, but to have been pieced together out of seven fragmentary sketches and adapted into a single and coherent narrative.

The Gibbon memoirs were then placed in the British Museum, bound in a single volume (Add. MSS 34874); John Murray was entrusted with the copyright, and set about preparing his *Autobiographies of Edward Gibbon, printed verbatim from hitherto unpublished MSS*, to be published in 1896. Two people had seen the papers since the first Lord Sheffield. Dean H. H. Milman, when preparing his twelve-volume edition of *The Decline and Fall* in 1838–9 had edited the *Autobiography* and been allowed to see the original manuscripts 'on condition of not publishing any new matter'. And Dr William Alexander Greenhill, physician and man of letters, was lent the box of papers by the second Lord Sheffield in 1871. He would have liked to edit a new edition, but was prevented by the embargo; he did however arrange the six drafts in what, on internal evidence, he judged to be their chronological order, and left a paper with them, listing them as A to F and giving his reasons for doing so:

A was started 'in the fifty second year of my age', and so was written in 1788–9, but went no further than a lengthy account of the Gibbon family.

B was written in 1789–90, and is a straightforward account of Gibbon's life up to his setting out for Italy in 1764.

C was written before the death of his aunt Hester Gibbon in 1790, and covers his life up to 1772, when he moved to London after his father's death.

D was written in 1790–91, and is a short factual account of Gibbon's life up to 1772.

E is dated at the end 'Lausanne, March 2 1791', and covers ground beyond its predecessors, up to the death of Georges Deyverdun in July 1789. It also has expansive notes added later, after the arrest of Louis XVI of France but before his execution (see Gibbon's Note 48, p. 183).

F was written 'after forty years' from Gibbon's leaving Oxford (i.e. in 1792–3), but goes no further than his enforced departure in 1753. It is presumably the format Gibbon intended to continue, taking material from the discarded drafts. F had been made the basis of Lord Sheffield's *Autobiography*, and was printed first by John Murray, whose order is F, B, C, E, A, D.

Murray's edition was reprinted in 1897, but not again. It remains an indispensable source-book, but it did not 'catch on' with the general public, and is not particularly enjoyable reading. The drafts inevitably repeat each other; the passages omitted by Lord Sheffield are enclosed in heavy, unattractive square brackets; the notes mingle Gibbon's own with those of Lord Sheffield, Dean Milman and of Murray himself; and the claim that it is a facsimile printing of Gibbon's drafts 'in the exact form in which he left them at his death' is not strictly true: Gibbon's spelling is retained but not his (admittedly rather arbitrary) use of capitals. It sadly lacks the charm of the Sheffield *Autobiography*, which had long been popular with its readers. George Birkbeck Hill made little use of it when he brought out his *Memoirs of the Life of Edward Gibbon* in 1900, saying in his Preface: 'Respect for Mr Murray's copyright has made me sparing in emendations. My text, with the exception of a few words, is Lord Sheffield's.' Again, it was the Sheffield revised text of 1814 which was included in the World's Classics series in 1907 and in the Everyman Library in 1910, and which remains in print and available today.

A great deal of work has been done on Gibbon during this century: new, comprehensive editions of his letters and journals, bibliographies of his writings and the contents of his library, as well as studies of his historical method and D. M. Low's standard biography (see Select Bibliography). But it was only in 1966 that Thomas Nelson & Sons published 'Edward Gibbon: *Memoirs of My Life*', edited by the late Georges Alfred Bonnard, Professor of English language and literature at the University of Lausanne (1916–56) and already the editor of Gibbon's French journals. This book is now out of print and not easily accessible.

Following Sheffield's example, Bonnard used the six drafts of memoirs to create a continuous narrative in Gibbon's own words. A scholarly apparatus on each page made it immediately clear where his fuller account differed from Sheffield's, and also where the latter had made verbal changes in what he took from the drafts. Bonnard made draft F his basis (as Sheffield had done), but prefixed it by introductory paragraphs from A and B and from a loose sheet bound up with the MSS; when F gave out (in 1753) he used B, and when B stopped (in 1764) he moved on to C as far as 1772, and thence to E. He divided the whole into chapters (see Contents, p. 5), as was evidently Gibbon's original and final intention (chapter headings appear in drafts A and F). Gibbon's Notes to E were retained as end notes to Bonnard's Chapters VII and VIII; Sheffield had printed selections of these interspersed with his text, thus destroying the composition of E planned by Gibbon; Murray had transferred them to footnotes, a system which Gibbon personally disliked (see Gibbon's Note 64, p. 187).

Bonnard discussed the reasons for Gibbon's false starts before he settled down to the format he was working on when he died. One obvious reason was his own perfectionist view that 'The style of an author should be the image of his mind', when the right style was not easy to capture. He tells us himself (p. 158) that he wrote the first chapter of *The Decline and Fall* three times and the second and third twice before he was 'tolerably satisfied with their effect'. The important Chapters XV and XVI on the Christian Church were also revised and reduced three times. Then the very thing which probably prompted him to write memoirs at all proved a red herring. In late 1786 or early 1787 Ernst Langer, the Duke of Brunswick's librarian, gave him the short Latin *Introductio ad Latinam Blasoniam* ('Introduction to Latin Heraldry') published in 1682 by John Gibbon, Bluemantle Poursuivant, who included an account of the Gibbon family of Kent and their descent from a John Gibbon who was architect (*marmorarius*) to Edward III, and from a Lord High Treasurer, the Baron Saye and Seale mentioned in Shakespeare's Henry VI Part II (see p. 45). Gibbon wanted to believe that his own ancestors belonged to this family. When he was in England in 1789 he made inquiries at the College of Arms, but had to return to Lausanne before the answer was given – that he and the Bluemantle Poursuivant belonged to different branches of Kentish Gibbons. Lord Sheffield was told but, not knowing that Gibbon was embarking on memoirs, failed to pass on the message.

Meanwhile Gibbon had written some thirty-nine pages of A, incorporating all the family history of the *Introductio*, plus a digression on his father's sisters. He must then have realized he was being too discursive, and he still needed confirmation from the College of Arms; he broke off and started at once on a plain account of his own life (B) which he might well have carried further but for the death of Georges Deyverdun. It was some months before he had the heart to resume writing, and then he chose to make a fresh start, reducing the length of the last draft but copying some of it into draft C. This is planned in sections and carefully written, but in its turn was abandoned on 9 February 1790, when Gibbon was 'seized by such a fit of the gout as I had never known' (letter to Sheffield, 15 May 1790). Several months later he could hold a pen again, and made another start on a brief record (D) of the main events of his life, but stopped after thirteen pages at 1772. He changed his style in draft E, which is written in the form of notes with marginal dates, completed in nineteen pages, and dated 'Lausanne, March 2 1791'. The further amplifying notes may have been written before Lord Sheffield's visit to Lausanne with his family in July, when he was told of the project; but when Gibbon wrote to him in December, swearing him to secrecy, he was still diffident and dissatisfied, saying 'as you do not think it ridiculous I believe I shall make the attempt'. Soon afterwards the annalistic form, dates and notes were all scrapped, and Gibbon began on the more relaxed and fluent draft F. Again there were frustrations. The first chapter on the Kentish Gibbons must have been written before he read an article in the *Gentleman's Magazine*, signed N.S., which gave definite proof that he must give up any idea of being related to the herald John Gibbon. Gibbon wrote to the editor of the magazine, John Nichols, on 24 February 1792, to ask for the name of N.S., and getting no reply wrote to Lord Sheffield in May and September, as well as to his publisher and twice more to Nichols in January and April 1793. Then he had to hurry to England, with only three chapters to show for over a year's work, and the first of these still awaiting revision. The fact that he brought all the five discarded attempts suggests that he intended to incorporate passages from them into his final version, as he had sometimes done before: see, for example, Chapter VI, p. 152 and note 33, and Chapter VIII, p. 175 and note 13.

But it was not only the social life of Lausanne, worry over the Revolution in France, and the death of his Swiss friend M. de Sévery which delayed his progress and prompted him to write to Sheffield on 6 January 1793: 'Of the *Memoirs* little has been done and with that little I am not satisfied ... I much doubt whether the book and the author can ever see the light at the same time.' The nagging knowledge that he had based an argument on evidence which was subsequently shown to be inadequate and misleading would surely inhibit him from moving confidently forward as long as errors remained uncorrected and his first steps were not soundly based. The historian had set the example of logical progress through his great work, and the autobiographer would demand of himself the same high standards.

Lord Sheffield devoted twenty years of a parliamentarian's life to the pious duty of presenting the unpublished works of his friend to the public, confident (as he wrote in his advertisement to the first edition of 1796) that 'the author of them cannot be made to appear in a truer light than he does in the following pages'. In a later paragraph he wrote:

Few men, I believe, have ever so fully unveiled their own character, by a minute narrative of their sentiments and pursuits, as Mr Gibbon will here be found to have done; not with study and labour – not with an affected frankness – but with a genuine confession of his little foibles and peculiarities, and a good-humoured and natural display of his own conduct and opinions.

All lovers of Gibbon must admire his conscientious 'discharging this latest office of affection'. But the fact remains, as his grandson wrote in the passage quoted above (p. 11), that Lord Sheffield made many changes, and today we need not be inhibited by his caution or delicacy from publishing anything relevant to the life of a writer who died nearly two centuries ago.

We also have a better idea of the order in which Gibbon wrote his drafts and, believing that the later ones reflect his final intentions, are chary of 'piecing together' one with another. Readers accustomed to the early *Autobiography* may sometimes regret changes in wording; they will look in vain for the words describing Gibbon's renunciation of Suzanne Curchod ('I sighed as a lover, I obeyed as a son'; see p. 105 and note 18) which Sheffield took from draft C and inserted in the narrative of B. Again, his account of Gibbon's being on the Capitol on 15 October substitutes a sentence taken from draft E for the C version of this edition (p. 143), to give the familiar sentence:

It was at Rome, on the fifteenth of October 1764, as I sat musing amidst the ruins of the Capitol, while the barefooted friars were singing vespers in the temple of Jupiter, that the idea of writing the decline and fall of the City first started to my mind.

Sheffield's more substantial omissions are Gibbon's drily humorous account of his father's sisters (p. 52 'The union ...' to p. 55 '... the Saint') and several pages (121–4) on Gibbon's general ideas on the formation of a militia and its status in England during the Seven Years' War; his own militia service is also given in a shortened version. The splendid final sentences of Chapter VIII (which include Gibbon's theory on why time seems to pass more quickly as we grow older) are relegated to a footnote, perhaps because Sheffield wished to gloss over the ironic self-depreciation of 'the vanity of authors'. Where twenty lines are dropped here, a whole paragraph there, or a sentence is curtailed or re-phrased, the reason seems generally to be a reluctance to print anything which might detract from Gibbon's dignity or reputation or offend his relatives and friends. Thus the whole passage on Gibbon's relations with Mme Bontems (18 lines on p. 137) is omitted, as well as two passages giving details of his attacks of gout (14 lines on pp. 127–8, 9 lines on p. 174), the former attributing it to 'the daily practice of hard and even excessive drinking' learned in his militia days; and 9 lost lines on p. 93 cut out Gibbon's trenchant criticisms of Mme Pavilliard's stingy housekeeping, the poor food and grubby table-cloth. Some of Gibbon's interesting general observations are also sacri-ficed: 20 lines on pp. 118–19 dealing with the origins of polytheism, 10 lines on p. 109 on the proverbial hatred of stepmothers in antiquity; and the end of Chapter VI (p. 154) is cut down to exclude Gibbon's frank comment on the fact that however sincerely we mourn our parents, we would not really want them back.

Delicacy was presumably what led Lord Sheffield to change 'loss of my literary maidenhead' (p. 117) to 'petty circumstances and period of my first publication', which is not in Gibbon, and to substitute 'cultivation' for 'manure' on p. 174; and perhaps 'the French disease' (p. 173) had possible innuendos which his coinage 'the Gallic phrenzy' did not. But why 'taste', coupled with Virgil's irreligion, as a reason for the 'lame and impotent conclusion' of *Aeneid* VI (p. 149)? It is quite clear in draft C that Gibbon wrote 'haste'.

It is unnecessary to multiply examples when there is no intention of belittling Lord Sheffield's total achievement, on which D. M. Low remarks in concluding his life of Gibbon: 'He took liberties which would be heinous in a modern editor. But gratitude far outweighs any other feeling about his work.' Yet for all their lack of revision by Gibbon himself, the Memoirs are so remarkable a reflection of a unique personality that their readers can only be the losers if anything Gibbon wrote is glossed over or withheld. Here we have one of the world's great historians in the making, as we follow Gibbon reviewing his past in relation to his achievement in *The Decline and Fall* and repeatedly drawing attention to the formative influences on his life's work.

His ill-health in early childhood, which interrupted all attempts at formal schooling, fostered his 'early and invincible love of reading', in the care of his aunt Catherine Porten; the free run of his grandfather's library encouraged his lively curiosity, so that he writes, 'This year 1748, the twelfth of my age, I shall note as the most propitious to the growth of my intellectual stature.' By the age of fifteen his 'indiscriminate appetite subsided by degrees in the *historic* line', and the 'undigested chaos' of his voracious enthusiasm for world history had been disciplined by 'an early and rational application to the order of time and place'. (Gibbon's grasp of relative chronology and of geographic factors is one of his great strengths as a historian.) Only Oxford failed dismally to come up to his eager expectations. The 'decent easy men' who were his college tutors did nothing for a precocious scholar, either to correct 'the same blind and boyish taste for the pursuit of exotic history' or to improve on his inadequate grounding in Latin. His fourteen months at Magdalen were later to be judged as 'the most idle and unprofitable of my whole life'.

His precipitate removal by his father to Protestant Lausanne, in order to counter his conversion into the Catholic Church, was the real turning point of his life. In the pastor Daniel Pavilliard he had a wise and sympathetic teacher who trusted to his intellectual honesty to reason his way back to the Protestant way of thinking, and, once he had mastered the French language, the best works of the Age of Enlightenment were open to him at an impressionable age. European scholarship at the time was practically a French monopoly; *The Decline and Fall* could never have been written without the French ecclesiastical scholars and antiquarians who supply so many of its footnotes, while its guiding principles were those of the sceptic empiricist Bayle and the political thinker Montesquieu. The *Dictionnaire historique et critique* taught Gibbon to weigh the validity of facts to be used as historical evidence, not allowing them to be perverted by the prejudices of religion or human vanity. Montesquieu's *Considérations sur les causes de la grandeur des Romains et de leur décadence* traced the collapse of the Empire to its immoderate growth and consequent corruption of the 'general spirit' of the Republic. This term he defined and expanded in his major work, *L'Esprit des lois*: a nation or a society has a general spirit to which its laws should ideally conform. That is, he judged institutions by reference to the social systems within which they functioned, and to the economic, historical and geographical factors creating patterns of society. It is as Montesquieu's disciple that Gibbon treated all religions as social phenomena, and refused to judge Christianity as superior to other religions in which he was equally interested; the notorious Chapters XV and XVI are directed against institutionalized Christianity as an alien and divisive element in Roman society which contributed to Rome's downfall. At the same time Gibbon learned from his French model Pascal how to use his 'grave and temperate irony' as the most effective way of discomfiting an opponent; he says he re-read the *Lettres provinciales* nearly every year. Very rightly then, thirty years later he wrote, 'Such as I am in genius or learning or in manners, I owe my creation to Lausanne.'

The 'four years, ten months and fifteen days' of his absence from England also gave Gibbon the opportunity to return to the basic grammar of Latin and to make a proper start in Greek. M. Pavilliard was a stimulating tutor and encouraged the boy to forge ahead at his own pace. Gibbon systematically devoured the major Latin classics and several of the Greek authors, though his ability to read Greek never matched his fluency in Latin. He singled out 'the last eight months of the year 1755 as the period of the most extraordinary diligence and rapid progress'; and by the time he left Lausanne he knew that his classical model as a historian would always be Tacitus, and was able to correspond in Latin on textual problems with professors in Zurich and Paris.

He also began to enjoy Lausanne society and the French theatre, made a friend for life in young Georges Deyverdun, and fell in love with Suzanne Curchod. This romance came to nothing, as is generally well known, but Gibbon is often unfairly criticized for his apparently passive acceptance of his father's veto. He really had no choice; his recall to England in April 1758 was intended to coincide with his twenty-first birthday and his father's request that he should agree to breaking the entail on the encumbered estate in return for an annuity of £300, to be paid in England. The Curchods could provide no dowry and expected their daughter to live in Switzerland. Gibbon did not really care for the cramped bourgeois style of the Swiss, and he was later to write of matrimony as something he had no taste for and never contemplated again, which means, I think, that he came to see that a well-ordered independent life was essential for him as a historian. The real choice lay between the life of a scholar and that of a husband. The fact that he and Suzanne, after she became Mme Necker, could maintain an affectionate friendship is proof both of their intelligence and of their genuine feeling for each other. We know from their correspondence that she found it painful to give him up; and after more than thirty years Gibbon could write of the 'delicate subject' of his early love as an experience he was glad to have had. His definition of true romantic love (p. 104) as something different from gallantry or simple sexual desire is both frank and touching.

Gibbon's first published work, the *Essai sur l'étude de la littérature*, was written in French, 'the familiar language of my conversation and studies in which it was easier for me to write than in my mother-tongue'; it defended the study of classical literature against its current dismissal as irrelevant by the *philosophes* in their contempt of the *érudits*. It was published during Gibbon's militia service, two and a half years spent amongst 'rustic officers' neither scholars nor gentlemen, when reading could only be in time snatched from manoeuvres. Yet with hindsight Gibbon is optimistic about what he gained – 'a break from the habits of a sedentary life', meeting with new faces and new friends, a clearer grasp of military tactics and the workings of the civil and military system of his country: in short, 'my principal obligation to the militia was the making me an Englishman and a soldier'.

There is an entry in Gibbon's Journal for 8 May 1762, written some months before he was able to leave the militia, which deserves quotation for its self-analysis:

This was my birthday, on which I entered into the 26th year of my age. This gave me occasion to look a little into myself, and consider impartially my good and bad qualities. It appeared to me, upon this enquiry, that my character was virtuous, incapable of a base action and formed for generous ones; but that it was proud, violent, and disagreeable in society. These qualities I must endeavour to cultivate, extirpate, or restrain, according to their different tendency. Wit I have none. My imagination is rather strong than pleasing. My memory both capacious and retentive. The shining qualities of my understanding are extensiveness and penetration; but I want both quickness and exactness. As to my situation in life, tho' I may sometimes repine at it, it perhaps is the best adapted to my character. I can command all the conveniences of life, and I can command too that independence (that first earthly blessing) which is hardly to be met with in a higher or lower fortune. When I talk of my situation, I must exclude that temporary one of being in the Militia. Tho' I go thro' it with spirit and application, it is both unfit for and unworthy of me.

The £300 annuity was the least that could keep a gentleman in any style at this time, but more than once in the Memoirs Gibbon repeats the point made here – that it gave him independence, leisure and perseverance to work at his history, which as a richer or a poorer man he might never have written: 'Few works of merit and importance have been executed in a garret or a palace.' Admittedly he was better off after his father died, and was glad of a minor post in the Board of Trade which gave him another £750 a year from July 1779; the loss of it after the post was discontinued was one reason for his return to settle in Lausanne, where his expenses were lower than in London. The publication of *The Decline and Fall* made him a comparatively rich man, but he never really developed a rich man's tastes.

Freedom from the militia meant the Grand Tour at last, with £1,200 promised by his father for his travelling expenses; but first came the preparatory work Gibbon set himself in the libraries of Paris and Lausanne. He worked on 'the topography of Rome, the ancient geography of Italy and the science of medals', while reading all the best sources available to equip himself as a true 'philosophic traveller', one who was observant and eager to learn, well-informed, unprejudiced – and possessed of a stamina few of us could achieve. Gibbon liked to think that his first view of Italy and Rome determined his choice of subject, and the grandeur and decay of the monuments certainly stimulated his romantic imagination; but the inspiration which came to him in the famous moment on the Capitol would seem to be more a crystallization of thoughts which he had been formulating over the years.

His planned travels were cut short when he had to come home to cope with his father's deteriorating health and mismanagement of his finances, and the next five years were those of which Gibbon wrote – with detachment, not bitterness – that they were 'the portion of my life which I passed with the least enjoyment, and which I remember with the least satisfaction'. After his father's death in 1770 it took another two years to let and sell the Gibbon properties and save what he could of his inheritance. Meanwhile he could not settle down to any major project: 'the decline and fall of Rome I still contemplated at an awful distance.' He is frank about his frustrations and did his best to surmount them, publishing a few learned articles, building up his library, reading extensively for his history, and enjoying prolonged visits from Georges Deyverdun, whose help he sought on the German sources for a proposed *History of the Liberty of the Swiss*. This was soon abandoned, but fortunately Gibbon sent the first chapters to David Hume, whose sound advice was that he should stop writing in French. Gibbon was thirty-five when he was finally rid of his family problems and freed from his prolonged dependency.

In modern terms his childhood had been deprived, even traumatic: the five brothers and a sister – wistfully recalled – born after him all dying in infancy; a mother whose social life gave her little time for him and who died before he was nine, when his father's inconsolable transports of grief were something he never forgot. His wretched health meant frequent changes of tutors of varying competence, and of schools where he was conscious of his 'timid reserve' and could not join in the rough-and-tumble of normal boyhood. Then came the ill-prepared entry to Oxford at too early an age and the abrupt removal to unknown Lausanne. Though in later life he could feel 'never less lonely than when by myself' he had known acute loneliness when amongst people he found uncongenial – at Westminster School, at Magdalen College, during the first weeks at Lausanne 'as an exile and a prisoner', when his French was minimal and his meagre pocket-money prevented his mixing with English residents, and on his first return to England, of which he wrote, 'While coaches were rattling through Bond Street I have passed many a solitary evening in my lodging with my books.' What we must admire is his resilience, his optimism, his determination to find some advantage in his situation. It is a rare character which can emerge as he did from such a childhood and adolescence unscarred by bitterness or resentment.

Gibbon started to write his first volume as soon as he settled into his house in Bentinck Street in 1772, and at the same time he joined several London clubs. At the Literary Club he met the leading writers of the day, including Dr Johnson, though the two men never took to each other. The following year he became a Member of Parliament, and he supported the North government through the war with America. He was a conscientious attender at the House of Commons and, though he never made a speech, he heard some of the great orators of the day – Burke, Fox, Pitt, Sheridan – who may well have been an influence on the prose style he developed. At the same time he could say that 'The eight sessions that I sat in Parliament were a school of civil prudence, the first and most essential virtue of a historian.' But by the time the North government fell and he lost his 'convenient salary', he had decided to continue *The Decline and Fall* beyond the collapse of the Western Empire which he had covered in the first three volumes. 'The tumult of London and the attendance on Parliament were grown more irksome', and he was glad to retire to Lausanne, where 'a moderate fortune would secure the blessings of ease, leisure and independence'.

For the period the Memoirs cover, remarkably little can be added from the Letters, Journals and other sources. One attractive detail we owe to a note by Lord Sheffield in his edition of the *Miscellaneous Works*:

M. Pavilliard has described to me the astonishment with which he gazed on Mr Gibbon standing before him: a thin little figure, with a large head, disputing and urging, with the greatest ability, all the best arguments that had ever been used in favour of popery. Mr Gibbon many years ago became very fat and corpulent, but he had uncommonly small bones, and was very slightly made.

This must have been told to Sheffield (then still John Holroyd) when he was staying at Lausanne and met Gibbon on his second visit before the Italian tour. And there was an episode which shows the seventeen-year-old Gibbon in a rare state of panic. In January 1755 he went to a faro party and lost 110 guineas to an Englishman named Gee. He had no means of paying, got Gee to sell him a horse, a watch and other necessities, to be paid for with the rest of the debt, and set off (in a Swiss winter), intending to make for London and somehow obtain the cash to settle his debt of honour. M. Pavilliard caught up with him in Geneva, and brought him back. Letters were written appealing for help to Catherine Porten, which she showed to Gibbon's father, and M. Pavilliard also wrote; somehow the debt was substantially reduced, but whether Mr Gibbon settled the final £50 we do not know. Nor do we know why the Memoirs say nothing about the affair (see Low, pp. 54–7).

The Memoirs stop in 1791. Some details of Gibbon's last three years can be supplied from the Letters, which are always lively reading, from the affectionate, sometimes irreverent comments on 'The Gib' by Maria Josepha Holroyd, and from the writings on the Pays de Vaud by Meredith

Read and the de Séverys. We know that Gibbon became set in his ways and something of a dandy, a bon viveur and mildly flirtatious with the ladies; he was no more than five feet tall, extremely fat and red-haired (the lock of hair preserved inside the cover of the bound volume of MSS is still a bright brown). The much-quoted 'scribble, scribble' remark appears in more than one version, but was probably made by the Duke of Gloucester when he was presented with the second volume of *The Decline and Fall*: 'Another damned thick, square book! Always scribble, scribble, scribble! Eh! Mr Gibbon?' (See variants in Low, p. 315.) All this is perilously near caricature. But we must not go to the Memoirs expecting to find a laughable little man, when the Gibbon who emerges is a giant in intellectual capacity and honest self-appraisal. His frank comments on his juvenilia ('The discovery of my own weakness was the first symptom of taste', p. 83) are matched by his detached analysis of the public criticisms made of his early volumes (p. 163). He gives us the secret of his developed style (p. 161) and his admirable habit of mentally reviewing what he knows on a subject during 'a solitary walk' before serious reading of a new book (p. 114). When he concludes that there is nothing to be gained from submitting work in progress to friends (p. 158), for 'The author himself is the best judge of his own performance: none has so deeply meditated on the subject, none is so sincerely interested in the event,' I do not think it would have occurred to him that to some this might appear arrogant; he knows that his capacities match his intentions, and is being truthful about himself.

One of the memorable features of Gibbon's writing of history is the way its steady flow of eloquent periods is never allowed to meander into prolonged generalizations, but is kept down to earth by the vivid detailed descriptions of chosen scenes. In somewhat the same way the Memoirs offer sudden brief glimpses into Gibbon's life which are unforgettable. I can always see the little boy shouting the names of his father's political opponents in revenge for a whipping (p. 61); driving with his mother to the school at Kingston, the only clear recollection he gives of her (p. 64); 'surrounded with a heap of folios' to the surprise of his father's friends, or at Stourhead, 'immersed in the passage of the Goths over the Danube when the summons of the dinner-bell reluctantly dragged me from my intellectual feast' (p. 72). There are many welcome details of life at Buriton: the farm horses harnessed to the coach for visiting on moonlit nights, the tediously long meals, Gibbon's father at the races or galloping on his fleet hunter, while his son takes a book on his walks and his Greek Testament to read in church. Nothing could better convey Gibbon's first dismay on arrival at the Pavilliard house than the fact that his poky little room lacked 'a companionable fire' and 'must be warmed by the dull invisible heat of a stove'. His awareness of the continuity of history, which came to him so vividly on 15 October 1764, reaches us through the scene of the Franciscan friars singing vespers in the church built on the site of a pagan temple (pp. 16 and 143). This, Gibbon says, was the moment of conception of his life's work. No less memorable is the scene of his deliverance on 27 June 1797: the summer-house and acacia walk in the garden at La Grotte, the silent night, and the moon reflected in the still waters of the lake (p. 169).

Through the Memoirs Gibbon is also able to express what some of his critics have denied him: the warmth of his feelings. He was a naturally affectionate man, genuinely fond of his stepmother, and devoted to the Aunt Catherine who brought him up; he is patient with his father, who had been all that he was not – attractive and popular, volatile and ineffective – and always writes of him with filial affection. Georges Deyverdun was the first to provide the friendship into which Gibbon channelled his generous affection; John Holroyd was another – it was the unexpected death of Lady Sheffield which made him start at once on the long and hazardous journey to England to be with his friend. He was devoted to the de Sévery family and to all the Holroyds, and enjoyed the same affection from them. He also felt his intellectual enthusiasms strongly; this is obvious from every account of his early reading and from what he says about his conversion to Catholicism at the age of sixteen. It was hardly a conversion in the true religious sense. He had long enjoyed 'religious disputation' with his puzzled aunt and, with no one in his Oxford college who thought of directing 'the ardour of a curious mind', his solitary reading (not contact with any 'popish missionary') convinced him that if the miracles attested by the early Church Fathers were accepted as proof of the 'visible interposition of the Deity', miracles of a later date were no less evidence of the continuity of the Catholic Church (pp. 85–6). It is typical of Gibbon to call these miracles 'marvellous tales', for it was his romantic imagination which was captivated: 'Youth is sincere and impetuous; and a momentary glow of enthusiasm had raised me above all temporal considerations.' Looking back on the episode from the standpoint of one who, like Henri Bayle, had been designed by Nature 'to think as he pleased and to speak as he thought', Gibbon writes in almost the same terms as he does of his romantic love: 'For my own part I am proud of an honest sacrifice of interest to conscience; I can never blush if my tender mind was entangled.'

In summing up his life at the age of fifty-four, Gibbon wrote that 'The love of study, a passion which derives fresh vigour from enjoyment, supplies each day, each hour, with a perpetual source of independent and rational pleasure'; and this was an enduring passion which was part of his love of life. His engaging zest for information on every available subject is apparent in the Catalogue of his library, which is full of surprises: along with the editions of classical texts and historical works are titles such as the *Bhagavatgita* and *The Natural History of Norway*, together with accounts of travels in Russia, Tartary and the Far East, histories of the Colony of Massachusetts, of Greenland, of Portugal, of Sumatra, dissertations on freemasonry, precious stones, astronomy, chemistry, fishes, and Frederick II on falconry. With such enthusiasm went the resilience and cheerful optimism which carried him through life and made him confident of another good twenty years if the operation on his hydrocele – too long postponed – were successful. These qualities inform *The Decline and Fall* in combination with the immense learning and clear vision which marshal its facts into a coherent whole; without Gibbon's warm feeling for his subject it would lack the great imaginative descriptive passages and the vivid moments of insight, and sink to a plain narrative of events. And for all its title and the fact that it covers 'the greatest, perhaps the most awful scene in history', *The Decline and Fall* is not a depressing book, thanks to Gibbon's belief in the Enlightenment and his humanist optimism in the future of the world he knew. When, for instance, in Chapter LXI he passed judgement on the wastage of the two hundred years of the Crusades in Europe, he could see them as a turning point, 'undermining the Gothic edifice' of feudalism, and indirectly bringing benefit and greater freedom 'to the most numerous and useful part of the community. The conflagration which destroyed the tall and barren trees of the forest gave air and scope to the vegetation of the smaller and nutritive plants of the world.'

Gibbon's concept of freedom was of course politically that of his eighteenth-century background: rational freedom for the enlightened upper classes who would provide the benevolent control which the masses needed for their wellbeing. He had no sympathy with 'wild theories of equal and boundless freedom' which he saw leading to the atrocities of the French Revolution. Yet he consistently opposed slavery, when Lord Sheffield, as Member for Bristol, supported it, and he counted it his great good fortune that he had been born 'in a free and enlightened country'. His attack on the network of the Christian Church was directed more against the superstition, asceticism and fanaticism which he saw as destructive of human liberty than against its wealth and temporal power, though he retained 'a deep and lasting impression' of 'the profuse ostentation of riches in the poorest corner of Europe' when he saw the Abbey of Einsiedeln (p. 101). But his most trenchant words are aimed at a system of education which fettered young imaginations, denying them what they most need: 'Freedom is the first wish of our heart; freedom is the first blessing of our nature ...' But 'A school is the cavern of fear and sorrow (p. 73).'

Such terms may seem exaggerated, and Gibbon himself largely escaped the system against which they are directed. At Dr Wooddeson's school he learned only enough Latin syntax to enable him to struggle through Phaedrus and Cornelius Nepos; at Westminster he 'painfully climbed into the third form, never reaching the fourth, where Greek was taught'; with his tutor at Bath he gained 'an imperfect and transient enjoyment of the Latin poets' from some Odes of Horace and passages from Virgil; from Oxford he recalled nothing but 'a dry and literal interpretation' of a few plays of Terence. His true introduction to the classics started with translations, first eagerly read for their romance, so that Pope's Homer and Dryden's Virgil took their place alongside the *Arabian Nights*, and then for their contribution to world history and geography. He even expressed a dislike for languages, and argued with his aunt that he could get at 'the thoughts of the original' better through translation – a 'silly sophism' of youth, as he afterwards admitted (p. 71).

It was later, with the help of the tactful M. Pavilliard, that he made a thorough, systematic study of the classic Latin texts, and he was eighteen before he began on Greek – with neither the same enthusiasm nor success. (Nearly all the Greek authors catalogued in his library have a Latin facing text, and the twenty-four small volumes in his travelling library, now in Christ Church, Oxford, are all in Latin.) His own written Latin became fluent, but remained faulty, as he knew himself: 'the private or voluntary student who possesses the sense and spirit of the Classics may offend by a false quantity the scrupulous ear of a well-flogged critic' (p. 69). He makes use of non-classical words such as the purist would eschew, he is not always verbally accurate in his quotations, and is capable of misquoting quantitive classical verse apparently without noticing that he is destroying the scansion. Language in all its refinements was never his interest, and, in spite of his ear for the rhythms of English prose, he shows no deep feeling for verse; perhaps because he was unmusical. But no one has exceeded his capacity for absorbing a subject and retaining it in a memory as well indexed as it was capacious, and no historian has achieved a better combination of assembled material and imaginative insight.

Gibbon was proud of his unorthodox early education. He knew that it had served him well as a historian, and that the dead languages had come to life for him through his youthful enthusiasm for the ancient world. It seems less unorthodox to us today, now that children are not subjected to an early start on Latin and Greek grammar, and a classical education has to compete for a place amongst alternative disciplines. But if a spark of interest in Greece and Rome once kindled in the young can light their path towards a readier grasp of the languages which are the basis of western civilization, then educationists may take heart from the knowledge that Gibbon is on their side.

Betty Radice
Highgate 1983

SELECT BIBLIOGRAPHY

THE MEMOIRS

Edward Gibbon, *Memoirs of My Life and Writings*, ed. John Lord Sheffield, 2 vols., London, 1827

The Autobiographies of Edward Gibbon, ed. John Murray, London, 1896, 1897

Memoirs of the Life of Edward Gibbon, ed. G. Birkbeck Hill, London, 1900

Edward Gibbon, *Autobiography*, Everyman edition, London, 1911

Edward Gibbon, *Memoirs of My Life*, ed. Georges A. Bonnard, London, 1966

GIBBON'S OTHER WORKS

The History of the Decline and Fall of the Roman Empire:
    1st edn, 6 vols., London, 1776–88
    ed. H. H. Milman, 12 vols., London, 1838–9
    ed. J. B. Bury, 7 vols., London, 1909–14
    Everyman edition, 6 vols., London, 1910, 1978

Gibbon's Journal to January 28th, 1763, ed. D. M. Low, London, 1929

Le Journal de Gibbon à Lausanne, ed. G. A. Bonnard, Lausanne, 1945

Gibbon's Journey from Geneva to Rome, ed. G. A. Bonnard, London, 1961

The Letters of Edward Gibbon, ed. J. E. Norton, 3 vols., London, 1956

The Miscellaneous Works of Edward Gibbon, ed. John Lord Sheffield, 2 vols., 1796; 5 vols., London, 1814 (Vol. I, Memoirs and Letters; II, Letters; III, Historical and Critical; IV, Classical and Critical; V, Miscellaneous)

BOOKS ON GIBBON

J. H. Adeane, *The Girlhood of Maria Josepha Holroyd*, London, 1896

Gavin de Beer, *Gibbon and his World*, London, 1968

Patricia B. Braddock, *Young Edward Gibbon, Gentleman of Letters*, Baltimore and London, 1982

David P. Jordan, *Gibbon and his Roman Empire*, Chicago, 1971

Select Bibliography

Geoffrey Keynes, *The Library of Edward Gibbon: A Catalogue of his Works*, London, 1940

D. M. Low, *Edward Gibbon*, London, 1937

J. E. Norton, *A Bibliography of the Works of Edward Gibbon*, Oxford, 1940

General Meredith Read, *Historic Studies in Vaud, Berne and Savoy*, London, 1897

M. and Mme de Sévery, *La Vie de société dans le Pays de Vaud à la fin du 18me siècle*, Lausanne and Paris, 1912

J. W. Swain, *Edward Gibbon: The Historian*, London, 1966

MAIN DATES IN GIBBON'S LIFE

1737	8 May. Born at Putney.
1746	December. Mother dies.
1752	April. Enters Magdalen College, Oxford.
1753	Converted to Catholicism; removed from Oxford and sent to Lausanne.
1753–8	Educated by Daniel Pavilliard.
1754	Returns to Protestantism.
1755	September–October. Tour in Switzerland.
1757	Meets and loves Suzanne Curchod.
1758	April. Returns to England; accepts annuity and breaks entail.
1759	23 February. Writes letter of renunciation to Suzanne.
1760	May–December 1762. Active service in Hampshire Militia.
1761•	June. Publishes his *Essai sur l'étude de la littérature*.
1763	January–May. First visit to Paris. May–April 1764. Second stay in Lausanne.
1764	April–April 1765. Grand Tour of Italy. 2 October. Reaches Rome.
1765	June. Recalled home to England.
1765–72	Divides time between Buriton and London.
1768	Starts and abandons *History of the Liberty of the Swiss*.
1770	January. Publishes *Critical Observations on the Sixth Book of the Aeneid*. November. Father dies.

1772   October. Settles in 7 Bentinck Street.

1773   February. Starts writing *Decline and Fall*.

1774   Joins the Literary Club.

1774–80   M.P. for Liskeard.

1776   February. Publishes Volume I of *Decline and Fall*.
                American Declaration of Independence; Gibbon supports
                Lord North.

1777   May–November. Second visit to Paris.
                17 October. General Burgoyne surrenders to Americans;
                Gibbon critical of North government.

1778   January–February. Gibbon votes with Fox in Parliament.
                February. France allied with America and at war with
                England.

1779   Publishes his *Vindication*.
                July. Appointed to Board of Trade.
                October. Writes *Mémoire justificatif*.

1780   Position threatened by Burke's Reform Bill.
                September. Not re-nominated for Liskeard.

1781–3   M.P. for Lymington

1781   March. Publishes Volumes II and III of *Decline and Fall*.

1782   March. North government falls.
                July. Board of Trade abolished.

1783   Writes Volume IV of *Decline and Fall*.
                September. Leaves London to settle in Lausanne with
                Deyverdun.

1784–7   Completes Volumes V and VI at La Grotte. (Volume VI
                finished on 27 June 1787.)

1788   In London; Volumes IV, V and VI published 8 May. Returns
                to Lausanne.

1789   Deyverdun dies; Gibbon stays on at La Grotte.

1788–93   Writes six drafts for Memoirs; last entry 2 March 1791.

1793   April. Lady Sheffield dies.
            May. Leaves Lausanne; spends summer at Sheffield Place.

1794   16 January. Dies in London.

1796   Lord Sheffield publishes his version of the Memoirs.

EDVARDUS GIBBON

CRITICUS ACRI INGENIO ET MULTIPLICI DOCTRINA ORNATUS
IDEMQUE HISTORICORUM QUI FORTUNAM
IMPERII ROMANI
VEL LABENTIS ET INCLINATI VEL EVERSI ET FUNDITUS DELETI
LITTERIS MANDAVERINT
OMNIUM FACILE PRINCEPS
CUJUS IN MORIBUS ERAT MODERATIO ANIMI
CUM LIBERALI QUADAM SPECIE CONJUNCTA
IN SERMONE
MULTAE GRAVITATI COMITAS SUAVITER ADSPERSA
IN SCRIPTIS
COPIOSUM SPLENDIDUM
CONCINNUM ORBE VERBORUM
ET SUMMO ARTIFICIO DISTINCTUM
ORATIONIS GENUS
RECONDITAE EXQUISITAEQUE SENTENTIAE
ET IN MOMENTIS RERUM POLITICARUMQUE OBSERVANDIS
ACUTA ET PERSPICAX PRUDENTIA
VIXIT ANNOS LVI MENS. VII DIES XXVIII
DECESSIT XVII CAL. FEB. ANNO SACRO
MDCCLXXXXIV
ET IN HOC MAUSOLEO SEPULTUS EST
EX VOLUNTATE JOHANNIS DOMINI SHEFFIELD
QUI AMICO BENE MERENTI ET CONVICTORI HUMANISSIMO
H. TAB. P.C.

Dr Samuel Parr

EDWARD GIBBON

A CRITIC ENDOWED WITH KEEN INTELLIGENCE AND
MANIFOLD LEARNING
AND OF ALL THE HISTORIANS WHO HAVE RECORDED IN
WRITING THE FORTUNES OF THE ROMAN EMPIRE
EITHER AS IT WAVERED AND DECLINED
OR WAS OVERTHROWN AND COMPLETELY DESTROYED
EASILY THE FOREMOST
HIS CHARACTER COMBINED MODERATION OF SPIRIT
WITH A CERTAIN FREEDOM OF ADDRESS
HIS CONVERSATION
DISPLAYED HIGH SERIOUSNESS PLEASANTLY SEASONED
WITH WIT
HIS LITERARY STYLE
WAS COPIOUS AND BRILLIANT
DISTINGUISHED BY ELEGANT HARMONY
AND SUPREME ARTISTRY IN ITS ROUNDED PERIODS
AND BY PROFOUND AND EXQUISITE EPIGRAMS
WHILE IN HIS OBSERVATIONS ON THE TURNING POINTS OF
HISTORY AND POLITICS
HIS INSIGHT WAS ACUTE AND PENETRATING
HE LIVED FIFTY-SIX YEARS SEVEN MONTHS AND
TWENTY-EIGHT DAYS
AND DIED ON THE SIXTEENTH OF JANUARY
IN THE YEAR OF OUR LORD 1794
AND IS BURIED IN THIS VAULT
BY THE WISH OF JOHN LORD SHEFFIELD
WHO HAD THIS TABLET SET UP AS A TRIBUTE
TO HIS ESTIMABLE FRIEND AND HIGHLY CULTIVATED
COMPANION

MEMOIRS
OF MY LIFE

father p.108

INTRODUCTION[1]

In the fifty-second year of my age, after the completion of a toilsome and successful work, I now propose to employ some moments of my leisure in reviewing the simple transactions of a private and literary life. Truth, naked unblushing truth, the first virtue of more serious history, must be the sole recommendation of this personal narrative: the style shall be simple and familiar; but style is the image of character, and the habits of correct writing may produce, without labour or design, the appearance of art and study. My own amusement is my motive and will be my reward; and, if these sheets are communicated to some discreet and indulgent friends, they will be secreted from the public eye till the author shall be removed beyond the reach of criticism or ridicule. The reasons and examples which may furnish some apology will be reserved for the last chapter of these Memoirs, when the order of time will lead me to account for this vain undertaking.

A sincere and simple narrative of my own life may amuse some of my leisure hours, but it will expose me, and perhaps with justice, to the imputation of vanity. Yet I may judge from the experience both of past and of the present times, that the public is always curious to *know* the men who have left behind them any image of their minds: the most scanty accounts are compiled with diligence and perused with eagerness; and the student of every class may derive a lesson or an example from the lives most similar to his own. The author of an important and success-ful work may hope without presumption that he is not totally indifferent to his numerous readers: my name may hereafter be placed among the thousand articles of a Biographia Britannica: and I must be conscious that no one is so well qualified as myself to describe the series of my thoughts and actions.

The authority of my masters, of the grave Thuanus and the philosophic Hume, might be sufficient to justify my design: but it would not be difficult to produce a long list of ancients and moderns who in various forms have exhibited their own portraits. Such portraits are often the most interesting, and sometimes the only interesting parts of their writings; and, if they be sincere, we seldom complain of the minuteness or prolixity of these personal memorials. The lives of the younger Pliny, of Petrarch and of Erasmus are expressed in the epistles which they themselves have given to the world; the essays of Montaigne and Sir William Temple bring us home to the houses and bosoms of the authors; we smile without contempt at the headstrong passions of Benvenuto Cellini, and the gay follies of Colley Cibber. The confessions of St Austin and Rousseau disclose the secrets of the human heart; the commentaries of the learned Huet have survived his Evangelical demonstration; and the memoirs of Goldoni are more truly dramatic than his Italian comedies. The Heretic and the Churchman are strongly marked in the characters and fortunes of Whiston and Bishop Newton; and even the dullness of Michael de Marolles and Anthony Wood acquires some value from the faithful representation of men and manners. That I am the equal or superior of some of these biographers the efforts of modesty or affection cannot force me to dissemble.

Chapter I[1]

Family History

A lively desire of knowing and recording our ancestors so generally prevails that it must depend on the influence of some common principle in the minds of men. Our imagination is always active to enlarge the narrow circle in which Nature has confined us. Fifty or a hundred years may be allotted to an individual; but we stretch forwards beyond death with such hopes as Religion and Philosophy will suggest, and we fill up the silent vacancy that precedes our birth by associating ourselves to the authors of our existence. We seem to have lived in the persons of our forefathers: it is the labour and reward of vanity to extend the term of this ideal longevity; and few there are who can sincerely despise in others an advantage of which they are secretly ambitious to partake. The knowledge of our own family from a remote period will be always esteemed as an abstract pre-eminence since it can never be promiscuously enjoyed, but the longest series of peasants and mechanics would not afford much gratification to the pride of their descendant. We wish to discover our ancestors, but we wish to discover them possessed of ample fortunes, adorned with honourable titles, and holding an eminent rank in the class of hereditary nobles, which has been maintained for the wisest and most beneficial purposes, in almost every climate of the globe, and in almost every form of political society. If any of these have been conspicuous above their equals by personal merit and glorious achievements, the generous feelings of the heart will sympathize in an alliance with such characters; nor does the man exist who would not peruse with warmer curiosity the life of a hero from whom his name and blood were lineally derived. The Satirist may laugh, the Philosopher may preach; but reason herself will respect the prejudices and habits which have been consecrated by the experience of mankind.

Our calmer judgement will rather tend to moderate than to suppress the pride of an ancient and worthy race: but in the estimate of honour we should learn to value the gifts of Nature above those of fortune; to esteem in our ancestors the qualities that best promote the interest of society, and to pronounce the descendant of a king less truly noble than the offspring of a man of genius whose writings will instruct or delight the latest posterity. The family of Confucius is in my opinion the most illustrious in the world. After a painful ascent of eight or ten centuries, our barons and princes of Europe are lost in the darkness of the middle age: but in the vast equality of the Empire of China, the posterity of Confucius has maintained above two thousand two hundred years its peaceful honours and perpetual succession; and the chief of the family is still revered by the sovereign and the people as the living image of the wisest of mankind. The nobility of the Spencers has been illustrated and enriched by the trophies of Marlborough; but I exhort them to consider the *Faery Queen* as the most precious jewel of their coronet:

> Nor less praise-worthy are the ladies three
> The honour of that noble familie
> Of which I meanest boast myself to be.[2]

Our immortal Fielding was of a younger branch of the Earls of Denbigh who draw their origin from the Counts of Habsburg,[3] the lineal descendants of Eltrico, in the seventh century Duke of Alsace. Far different have been the fortunes of the English and German divisions of the family of Habsburg. The former, the knights and sheriffs of Leicestershire, have slowly risen to the dignity of a peerage: the latter, the Emperors of Germany, and Kings of Spain, have threatened the liberty of the old and invaded the treasures of the new world. The successors of Charles the Fifth may disdain their brethren of England: but the romance of *Tom Jones*, that exquisite picture of human manners, will outlive the palace of the Escurial and the imperial eagle of the house of Austria.

A philosopher may reasonably despise the pride of ancestry; and if the philosopher himself be a plebeian, his own pride will be gratified by the indulgence of such contempt. It is an obvious truth that parts and virtue cannot be transmitted with the inheritance of estates and titles; and that even the claim of our legal descent must rest on a basis not perhaps sufficiently firm, the unspotted chastity of *all* our female progenitors. Yet in every age and country the common sense or common prejudice of mankind has agreed to respect the son of a respectable father, and each successive generation is supposed to add a new link to the chain of hereditary splendour. Wherever the distinction of birth is allowed to form a superior order in the state, education and example should always and will often produce among them a dignity of sentiment, and propriety of conduct which is guarded from dishonour by their own and the public esteem. If we read of some illustrious line, so ancient that it has no beginning, so worthy that it ought to have no end, we sympathize in its various fortunes; nor can we blame the generous enthusiasm, or even the harmless vanity of those who are associated to the honours of its name. In the study of past events our curiosity is stimulated by the immediate or indirect reference to ourselves; within its own precincts a local history is always popular; and the connection of a family is more dear and intimate than that of a kingdom, a province or a city. For my own part, could I draw my pedigree from a general, a statesman, or a celebrated author, I should study their lives or their writings with the diligence of filial love, and I suspect that from this casual relation some emotions of pleasure, shall I say of vanity, might arise in my breast. Yet I will add that I should take more delight in their personal merit than in the memory of their titles or possessions; that I should be more affected by literary than by martial fame; and that I would rather descend from Cicero than from Marius, from Chaucer than from one of the first Companions of the Garter. The family of Confucius is in my opinion the noblest upon earth. Seventy *authentic* generations have elapsed from that philosopher to the present chief of his posterity; who reckons one hundred and thirty-five degrees from the Emperor Hoang-ti, the father, as it is believed, of an illustrious line which has now flourished in China four thousand four hundred and twenty-five years. I have exposed my private feelings, as I shall always do, without scruple or reserve. Let every reader, whether noble or plebeian, examine his own conscience on the same subject.

That these sentiments are just or at least natural I am the more inclined to believe, since I do not feel myself interested in the cause, for I can derive from *my* ancestors neither glory nor shame.

My family is originally derived from the county of Kent, whose inhabitants have maintained from the earliest antiquity a provincial character of civility, courage and freedom. The southern district of the country, which borders on Sussex and the sea, was formerly overspread with the great forest Anderida, and even now retains the denomination of the *Weald* or Woodland. In this district, and in the hundred and parish of Rolvenden, the Gibbons were possessed of lands in the year one thousand three hundred and twenty-six; and the elder branch of the family, without much increase or diminution of property, still adheres to its native soil. Fourteen years after the first appearance of his name

John Gibbon is recorded as the *Marmorarius* or Architect of King Edward the Third; the strong and stately castle of Queenborough which guarded the entrance of the Medway was a monument of his skill; and the grant of an hereditary toll on the passage from Sandwich to Stonar in the Isle of Thanet is the reward of no vulgar artist. In the visitations of the heralds the Gibbons are frequently mentioned: they held the rank of Esquire in an age when that title was less promiscuously assumed; one of them under the reign of Queen Elizabeth was captain of the militia of Kent; and a free school in the neighbouring town of Benenden proclaims the charity and opulence of its founder. But time or their own obscurity has cast a veil of oblivion over the virtues and vices of my Kentish ancestors: their character or station confined them to the labours and pleasures of a rural life; nor is it in my power to follow the advice of the poet in an enquiry after a name:

> Go! search it there, where to be born, and die
> Of rich and poor makes all the history.[4]

So recent is the institution of our parish registers.

In the beginning of the seventeenth century a younger branch of the Gibbons of Rolvenden migrated from the country to the city, and from this branch I do not blush to descend. The Law requires some abilities; the Church imposes some restraints; and before our army and navy, our civil establishments and Indian Empire had opened so many paths of fortune, the mercantile profession was more frequently chosen by youths of a liberal race and education who aspired to create their own independence. Our most respectable families have not disdained the counting-house or even the shop: their names are enrolled in the livery and companies of London: and in England as well as in the Italian commonwealths, heralds have been compelled to declare that gentility is not degraded by the exercise of trade.

The armorial ensigns which in the times of chivalry adorned the crest and shield of the soldier are now become an empty decoration, which every man who has money to build a carriage may paint according to his fancy on the panels. My family arms are the same which were borne by the Gibbons of Kent in an age when the College of Heralds religiously guarded the distinctions of blood and name; *a Lion rampant gardant, between three scallop-shells argent on a field azure.* I should not however have been tempted to blazon my coat of arms, the most useless of all coats, were it not connected with a whimsical anecdote. About the reign of James the First the three harmless scallop-shells were changed by

Edmund Gibbon Esquire into three *Ogresses*[5] or female cannibals, with the design of stigmatizing three ladies, his kinswomen who had provoked him by an unjust law-suit. But this singular mode of revenge, for which he obtained the sanction of Sir William Segar, king at arms, soon expired with its author; and on his own monument in the Temple church, the monsters vanish, and the three scallop-shells resume their proper and hereditary place.

Our alliances by marriage, it is not disgraceful to mention. Blue-mantle Poursuivant, who will soon be introduced to the reader's acquaintance, enumerates the Phillips de la Weld in Tenterden, the Whetnals of East-Peckham, the Edgars of Suffolk, the Cromers, the Bercleys of Beauston, the Hextalls, the Ellenbriggs, the Calverleys, the Whetnalls of Cheshire – modestly checking his pen lest he should seem to indulge the pride of pedigree: *nam genus et proavos*, etc.[6] As such pride would be ridiculous, it would be scarcely less ridiculous to disclaim it; and I shall simply observe that the Gibbons have been immediately or remotely connected with several worthy families of the old gentry of England. The Memoirs of the Count de Grammont, a favourite book of every man and woman of taste, immortalize the Whetnalls or Whitnells of Peckham; 'la blanche Whitnell et le triste Peckham'. But the insipid charms of the lady, and the dreary solitude of the mansion were sometimes enlivened by Hamilton and love; and had not *our* alliance preceded *her* marriage I should be less confident of my descent from the Whetnalls of Peckham. The Cromers in the fifteenth century were twice Sheriffs of Kent and twice Lord Mayors of London. But the chief honour of my ancestry is James Fiens, Baron Say and Seale and Lord High Treasurer of England in the reign of Henry the Sixth; from whom by the Phillips, the Whetnalls and the Cromers I am lineally descended in the eleventh degree. His dismission and imprisonment in the Tower were insufficient to appease the popular clamour; and the Treasurer with his son-in-law Cromer was beheaded (1450), after a mock trial by the Kentish insurgents.

The black list of his offences, as it is exhibited in Shakespeare, displays the ignorance and envy of a plebeian tyrant. Besides the vague reproaches of selling Maine and Normandy to the Dauphin, the Treasurer is specially accused of luxury for riding on a foot-cloth, and of treason for speaking French, the language of our enemies.

Thou hast most traiterously corrupted the youth of the Realm [says Jack Cade to the unfortunate Lord], in erecting a grammar school: and whereas before, our fore-fathers had no other books than the score and the tally, thou hast caused printing to be used; and, contrary to the King, his crown, and dignity, thou hast built a paper-mill. It will be proved to thy face, that thou hast men about thee, who usually talk of a noun, and a verb, and such abominable words as no Christian ear can endure to hear.[7]

Our dramatic poet is generally more attentive to character than to history; and I much fear that the art of printing was not introduced into England till several years after Lord Say's death: but of some of these meritorious crimes I should hope to find my ancestor guilty; and a man of letters may be proud of his descent from a patron and martyr of learning.

In the beginning of the last century, Robert Gibbon Esquire of Rolvenden in Kent, who died in 1618, had a son of the same name of Robert, who settled in London in trade and became a member of the Cloth-workers Company. His wife was a daughter of the Edgars, who flourished above four hundred years in the county of Suffolk, and produced an eminent and wealthy Serjeant-at-law, Sir Gregory Edgar, in the reign of Henry the Seventh. Of the sons of Robert Gibbon, who died in 1643,[8] Matthew did not aspire above the station of a linen-draper in Leadenhall street in the parish of St Andrews, but John has given the public some curious memorials of his existence, his character and his family. He was born on the third of November in the year 1629; his education was liberal at a grammar-school, and afterwards in Jesus College at Cambridge, and he celebrates the retired content which he enjoyed at Allesborough in Worcestershire, in the house of Thomas Lord Coventry where John Gibbon was employed as domestic tutor, the same office which Mr Hobbes exercised in the Devonshire family. But the spirit of my kinsman soon emerged into more active life: he visited foreign countries as a soldier and a traveller, acquired the knowledge of the French and Spanish languages, passed some time in the isle of Jersey, crossed the Atlantic, and resided upwards of a twelvemonth (1659) in the rising colony of Virginia. In this remote province his taste or rather passion for heraldry found a singular gratification at a war dance of the native Indians. As they moved in measured steps, brandishing their tomahawks, his curious eye contemplated their little shields of bark and their naked bodies, which were painted with the colours and symbols of his favourite science. 'At which I exceedingly wondered; and concluded that heraldry was ingrafted *naturally* into the sense of human race. If so, it deserves a greater esteem than now-a-days is put upon it.'

His return to England after the Restoration was soon followed by his marriage, his settlement in an house in St Catherine's Cloister, near the Tower, which devolved to my grandfather, and his introduction into the Heralds' College (in 1671) by the style and title of Blue-mantle Poursuivant at Arms. In this office he enjoyed near fifty years the rare felicity of uniting in the same pursuit his duty and inclination: his name is remembered in the College, and many of his letters are still preserved. Several of the most respectable characters of the age, Sir William Dugdale, Mr Ashmole, Dr John Betts, and Dr Nehemiah Grew, were his friends; and in the society of such men, John Gibbon may be recorded without disgrace as the member of an Astrological Club. The study of hereditary honours is favourable to the Royal prerogative; and my kinsman, like most of his family, was a high Tory in Church and State. In the latter end of the reign of Charles the Second, his pen was exercised in the cause of the Duke of York: the Republican faction he most cordially detested; and as each animal is conscious of its proper arms, the herald's revenge was emblazoned on a most diabolical escutcheon. But the triumph of the Whig Government checked the preferment of Blue-mantle; and he was even suspended from his office till his tongue could learn to pronounce the oath of abjuration. His life was prolonged to the age of ninety; and in the expectation of the inevitable though uncertain hour, he wished to preserve the blessings of health, competence and virtue. In the year 1682 he published at London his *Introductio ad Latinam Blasoniam*,[9] an original attempt which Camden had desiderated, to define in the Roman idiom the terms and attributes of a Gothic institution. His manner is quaint and affected; his order is confused; but he displays some wit, more reading, and still more enthusiasm; and if an enthusiast be often absurd, he is never languid. An English text is perpetually interspersed with Latin sentences in prose and verse; but in his own poetry he claims an exemption from the laws of prosody. Amidst a profusion of genealogical knowledge my kinsman could not be forgetful of his own name; and to him I am indebted for almost the whole of my information concerning the Gibbon family. From this small work, a duodecimo of one hundred and sixty five pages, the author expected immortal fame; and at the conclusion of his labour, he sings in a strain of self-exultation:

> Usque huc corrigitur Romana Blasonia per me,
>   Verborumque dehinc barbara forma cadat.
> Hic liber in meritum si forsitan incidet usum
>   Testis rite meae sedulitatis erit.
> Quicquid agat Zoilus, ventura fatebitur aetas
>   Artis quod fueram non Clypearis inops.[10]

Such are the hopes of authors! In the failure of those hopes, John Gibbon has not been the first of his profession, and very possibly may not be the last of his name.

His brother, Matthew Gibbon the linen draper of Leadenhall Street, had one daughter and two sons, my grandfather Edward who was born in the year 1666, and Thomas, afterwards Dean of Carlisle. According to the mercantile creed that the best book is a profitable ledger, the writings of John the Herald would be much less precious than those of his nephew Edward; but an author professes at least to write for the public benefit; and the slow balance of trade can only be pleasing to those persons to whom it is advantageous. The successful industry of my grandfather raised him above the level of his immediate ancestors; he appears to have launched into various and extensive dealings; even his opinions were subordinate to his interest, and I find him in Flanders clothing King William's troops; while he would have contracted with more pleasure, though not perhaps at a cheaper rate, for the service of King James.

During his residence abroad, his concerns at home were managed by his mother Hester, an active and notable[11] woman. Her second husband was a widower of the name of Acton;[12] they united the children of their first nuptials. After his marriage with the daughter of Richard Acton, goldsmith in Leadenhall Street, he gave his own sister to Sir Whitmore Acton of Aldenham; and I am thus connected by a triple alliance with that ancient and loyal family of Shropshire baronets. It consisted about that time of seven brothers, all of gigantic stature; one of whom, a pigmy of six feet two inches, confessed himself the last and least of the seven; adding in the true spirit of party, that such men were not born since the Revolution. Under the Tory administration of the four last years of Queen Anne (1710–1714), Mr Edward Gibbon was appointed one of the Commissioners of the Customs; he sat at that board with Prior, but the merchant was better qualified for his station than the poet; since Lord Bolingbroke has been heard to declare that he never conversed with a man who more clearly understood the commerce and finances of England. In the year 1716 he was elected one of the directors of the South Sea Company; and his books exhibited the proof that before his acceptance of this fatal office, he had acquired an independent fortune of sixty thousand pounds.

But his fortune was overwhelmed in the shipwreck of the year twenty, and the labours of thirty years were blasted in a single day. Of the use or abuse of the South Sea scheme, of the guilt or innocence of my grandfather and his brother-directors, I am neither a competent nor a disinterested judge. Yet the equity of modern times must condemn the violent and arbitrary proceedings which would have disgraced the cause of justice, and would render injustice still more odious. No sooner had the nation awakened from its golden dream than a popular and even a parliamentary clamour demanded their victims: but it was acknowledged on all sides that the South Sea directors, however guilty, could not be touched by any known laws of the land. The speech of Lord Molesworth, the author of *The State of Denmark*, may show the temper or rather the intemperance of the House of Commons. 'Extraordinary crimes [exclaimed that ardent Whig] call aloud for extraordinary remedies. The Roman lawgivers had not foreseen the possible existence of a parricide. But as soon as the first monster appeared he was sewn in a sack and cast headlong into the river; and I shall be content to inflict the same treatment on the authors of our present ruin.' His motion was not literally adopted; but a bill of pains and penalties was introduced, a retroactive statute to punish the offences which did not exist at the time they were committed. Such a pernicious violation of liberty and law can only be excused by the most imperious necessity: nor could it be defended on this occasion by the plea of impending danger or useful example.

The Legislature restrained the persons of the directors, imposed an exorbitant security for their appearance, and marked their characters with a previous note of ignominy: they were compelled to deliver upon oath the strict value of their estates, and were disabled from making any transfer or alienation of any part of their property. Against a bill of pains and penalties it is the common right of every subject to be heard by his counsel at the bar. They prayed to be heard; their prayer was refused; and their oppressors, who required no evidence, would listen to no defence. It had been at first proposed that one eighth of their respective estates should be allowed for the future support of the directors: but it was speciously urged, that in the various shades of opulence and guilt, such an equal proportion would be too light for many, and for some might possibly be too heavy. The character and conduct of each man were separately weighed; but instead of the calm solemnity of a judicial enquiry, the fortune and honour of three and thirty Englishmen were made the topic of hasty conversation, the sport of a lawless majority; and the basest member of the committee, by a malicious word or a silent vote, might indulge his general spleen or personal animosity. Injury was aggravated by insult; and insult was embittered by pleasantry. Allowances of twenty pounds or one shilling were facetiously moved. A vague report that a director had formerly been concerned in *another* project by which some unknown persons had lost their money, was admitted as a proof of his actual guilt. One man was ruined because he had dropped a foolish speech, that his horses should feed upon gold; another because he was grown so proud that one day at the Treasury he had refused a civil answer to persons much above him. All were condemned, absent and unheard, in arbitrary fines and forfeitures which swept away the greatest part of their substance.

Such bold oppression can scarcely be shielded by the omnipotence of Parliament; and yet it may be seriously questioned whether the judges of the South Sea directors were the true and legal representatives of their country. The first Parliament of George the First had been chosen (1715) for three years: the term had elapsed; their trust was expired; and the four additional years (1718–1722) during which they continued to sit were derived not from the people, but from themselves; from the strong measure of the Septennial Bill, which can only be paralleled by *il serrar di Consiglio* of the Venetian history. Yet candour will own that to the same Parliament every Englishman is deeply indebted: the Septennial Act,[13] so vicious in its origin, has been sanctioned by time, experience and the national consent: its first operation secured the House of Hanover on the throne, and its permanent influence maintains the peace and stability of government. As often as a repeal has been moved in the House of Commons, I have given in its defence a clear and conscientious vote.

My grandfather could not expect to be treated with more lenity than his companions. His Tory principles and connections rendered him obnoxious to the ruling powers; his name is reported in a suspicious secret; and his well-known abilities could not plead the excuse of ignorance or error. In the first proceedings against the South Sea directors, Mr Gibbon is one of the few who were taken into custody; and in the final sentence the measure of his fine proclaims him eminently guilty. The total estimate which he delivered on oath to the House of Commons amounted to one hundred and six thousand five hundred and forty three pounds, five shillings and six pence, exclusive of antecedent settlements. Two different allowances of fifteen and of ten thousand pounds were moved for Mr Gibbon: but on the question being put it was carried without a division for the smaller sum; and as a philosopher, I *should* mention without a sigh the irreparable loss of above ninety six thousand pounds of which, in a single moment and by an arbitrary vote I have been ultimately deprived.

The provision reserved for his wife could not be very considerable; but the valuable gift which he afterwards received from his friend and companion Mr Francis Acton was understood in the family to be the restitution of an honourable trust. Against irresistible rapine the use of fraud is almost legitimate: in the dexterous anticipation of a conveyance some fragments of property might escape; debts of honour will not be annulled by any positive law; and the frequent imposition of oaths had enlarged and fortified the Jacobite conscience. On these ruins, with the skill and credit of which Parliament had not been able to despoil him, my grandfather, at a mature age, erected the edifice of a new fortune; the labours of sixteen years were amply rewarded, and I have reason to believe that the second temple was not much inferior to the first. A large stock of money was vested in the funds and in trade: and his warehouses at Cadiz were replenished with naval stores for which he had contracted to supply the Court of Madrid. But he had realized a very considerable property in Sussex, Hampshire, Buckinghamshire, and the New River Company; and had acquired a spacious house with gardens and lands at Putney in Surrey, where he resided in decent hospitality. His portraits represent a stern and sensible countenance; his children trembled in his presence; tradition informs me that the independent visitors who might have smiled at his anger were awed by his frown; and as he was the richest, or wisest or oldest of his neighbours, he soon became the oracle and the tyrant of a petty kingdom. His own wrongs had not reconciled him to the House of Hanover; his wishes might be expressed in some harmless toasts, but he was disqualified from all public trust; and in the daily devotions of the family the name of the king for whom they prayed was prudently omitted. My grandfather died at Putney in December, 1736, at the age of seventy, leaving Edward, his only son, and two daughters, Hester and Catherine.

My father, Edward Gibbon, was born in October 1707: at the age of thirteen he could scarcely feel that he was disinherited by Act of Parliament; and as he advanced towards manhood new prospects of fortune opened on his view. A parent is most attentive to supply in his children the deficiencies of which he is conscious in himself: my grandfather's knowledge was derived from a strong understanding and the experience of the ways of men; but my father enjoyed the benefits of a liberal education, as a scholar and a gentleman. At Westminster School, and afterwards at Emmanuel College in Cambridge, he passed through a regular course of academical discipline; and the care of his learning and morals was entrusted to his private tutor, the celebrated Mr William Law. But the mind of a saint is above or below the present world; and while the pupil proceeded on his travels, the tutor remained at Putney, the much-honoured friend and spiritual director of the whole family. My father resided some time at Paris to acquire the fashionable exercises; and, as his temper was warm and social, he indulged in those pleasures for which the strictness of his former education had given him a keener relish. He afterwards visited several provinces of France; but his excursions were neither long nor remote, and the slender knowledge which he had gained of the French language was gradually obliterated. His passage through Besançon is marked by a singular consequence in the chain of human events. In a dangerous illness Mr Gibbon was attended at his own request by one of his kinsmen of the name of Acton, the younger brother of a younger brother, who had applied himself to the study of physic. During the slow recovery of his patient, the physician himself was attacked by the malady of love: he married his mistress, renounced his country and religion, settled at Besançon, and became the father of three sons, the eldest of whom, General Acton, is conspicuous in Europe as the principal minister of the King of the Two Sicilies. By an uncle whom another stroke of fortune had transplanted to Leghorn, he was educated in the naval service of the Emperor; and his valour and conduct in the command of the Tuscan frigates protected the retreat of the Spaniards from Algiers.

On my father's return to England he was chosen, at the general election of 1734, to serve in Parliament for the borough of Petersfield, a burgage tenure[14] of which my grandfather possessed a weighty share, till he alienated I know not why, such important property. Prejudice and society connected his son with the Tories, or as they were pleased to style themselves, the country gentlemen: with them he gave many a vote, with them he drank many a bottle. Without acquiring the fame of an orator or statesman he eagerly joined in the great opposition, which, after a seven years' chase, hunted down Sir Robert Walpole; and in the pursuit of an unpopular minister, he gratified a private revenge against the oppressor of his family in the South Sea persecution.

The union to which I owe my birth was a marriage of inclination and esteem. Mr James Porten, a merchant of London, resided with his family at Putney in a house adjoining to the bridge and churchyard, where I have passed many happy hours of my childhood. Of his son Stanier and of a daughter Catherine, who preserved her maiden name, I shall hereafter speak; another daughter married Mr Darrel of Richmond, and her two sons are opulent and worthy; the youngest and handsomest of the three sisters was Judith, my mother. In the society of Putney the two families lived in friendly and frequent intercourse: the familiar habits of the young people improved into a tender attachment; and their mutual affection, according to the difference of the sexes, was ardently professed and modestly acknowledged. These sentiments were justified by a more perfect knowledge of each other: my father's constancy was neither chilled by absence nor dissolved by pleasure; and after his return from his travels and his election into parliament, he seriously resolved to unite himself for ever with the object of his choice.

> Notitiam primosque gradus vicinia fecit:
> Tempore crevit amor, taedae quoque jure coïssent;
> Sed vetuere patres. Quod non potuere vetare
> Ex aequo captis ardebant mentibus ambo[15]

Such is the beginning of a love tale at Babylon or at Putney.

On the present occasion, however, the opposition of the two fathers was not equally strenuous or sincere. The slender fortunes and dubious credit of Mr Porten would have been pleased with such an alliance; but he was provoked by a sense of honour to imitate the reluctance of his wealthy and ambitious neighbour. The usual consequences ensued: harsh threats and tender protestations, frowns and sighs; the seclusion of the lady, the despair of the lover; clandestine correspondence and stolen interviews. At the distance of forty years my aunt Catherine Porten could relate with pleasure the innocent artifices which she practised to second or screen her beloved sister; and I have found among my father's papers many letters of both parties that breathe a spirit of constancy and love. All their acquaintance, the whole neighbourhood of Putney was favourable to their wishes; my paternal grandfather yielded a tardy and ungracious consent; and as soon as the marriage ceremony had been performed, the young couple was received into his house on the hard terms of implicit obedience and a precarious maintenance. Yet such were the charms and talents of my mother, with such soft dexterity did she follow and lead the morose humour of the old tyrant, that in a few months she became his favourite. Could he have embraced the first child of which she was pregnant at the time of his decease, it is probable that a will executed in anger would have been cancelled by affection; and that he would have moderated the shares of his two daughters, whom in resentment to his son he had enriched beyond the measure of female inheritance.

Of my two wealthy aunts on the father's side, Hester persevered in a life of celibacy, while Catherine became the wife of Mr Edward Elliston, a Captain in the service of the East India Company, whom my grandfather styles his nephew in his will. Both Mr and Mrs Elliston were dead before the date of my birth, or at least of my memory; and their only daughter and heiress will be mentioned in her proper place. These two ladies are described by Mr Law under the names of Flavia and Miranda, the Pagan and the Christian sister. The sins of Flavia, which excluded her from the hope of salvation, may not appear to our carnal apprehension of so black a dye. Her temper was gay and lively: she followed the fashion in her dress, and indulged her taste for company and public amusements: but her expense was regulated by economy: she practised the decencies of religion, nor is she accused of neglecting the essential duties of a wife or a mother.

The sanctity of her sister, the original or the copy of Miranda, was indeed of a higher cast. By austere penance Mrs[16] Hester Gibbon laboured to atone for the faults of her youth, for the profane vanities into which she had been led or driven by authority and example. But no sooner was she mistress of her own actions and plentiful fortune, than the pious virgin abandoned for ever the house of a brother from whom she was alienated by the interest of this world and of the next. With her spiritual guide, and a widow lady of the name of Hutchinson, she retired to a small habitation at Cliffe in Northamptonshire, where she lived almost half a century, surviving many years the loss of her two friends. It is not my design to enumerate or extenuate the Christian virtues of Miranda as they are described by Mr Law. Her charity even in its excess commands our respect. Her fortune (says the historian) is divided between herself 'and several *other* poor people; and she has only her part of relief from it.' The sick and lame, young children and aged persons, were the first objects of her benevolence, but she seldom refused to give alms to a common beggar: 'and instead [I resume Mr Law's words] of driving him away as a cheat, because she does not know him, she relieves because he *is* a stranger, and unknown to her. Excepting her victuals she never spent ten pounds a year upon herself. If you was to see her you would wonder what poor body it was, that was so surprisingly neat and clean. She eats and drinks only for the sake of living; and with so regular an abstinence, that every meal is an exercise of self denial, and she humbles her body every time that she is forced to feed it.' Her only study was the Bible, with some legends and books of piety, which she read with implicit faith: she prayed five times each day; and, as singing, according to the *Serious Call*,[17] is an indispensable part of devotion, she rehearsed the psalms and hymns of thanksgiving, which she now, perhaps, may chant in a full chorus of saints and angels. Such is the portrait and such was the life of that holy virgin who by gods was Miranda called, and by men Mrs Hester Gibbon. Of the pains and pleasures of a spiritual life *I* am ill-qualified to speak; yet I am inclined to believe that her lot, even on earth has not been unhappy. Her penance was voluntary, and, in her own eyes, meritorious; her time was filled by regular occupations; and instead of the insignificance of an old maid, she was surrounded by dependents, poor and abject as they were, who implored her bounty and imbibed her lessons. In the course of these Memoirs I shall not forget to introduce my personal acquaintance with the saint.

At an advanced age, about the year 1761, Mr Law died in the house, I may not say in the arms, of his beloved Miranda. In our family he has left the reputation of a worthy and pious man, who believed all that he professed and practised all that he enjoined. The character of a nonjuror[18] which he maintained to the last is a sufficient evidence of his principles in Church and State, and the sacrifice of interest to conscience will be always respectable. His theological writings, which our domestic connection has tempted me to peruse, preserve an imperfect sort of life, and I can pronounce with more confidence and knowledge on the merits of the author. His last compositions are darkly tinctured with the incomprehensible visions of Jacob Behmen, and his discourse on the absolute unlawfulness of stage-entertainments is sometimes quoted for a ridiculous intemperance of sentiment and language. 'The actors and spectators must all be damned: the play-house is the porch of Hell, the place of the Devil's abode, where he holds his filthy court of evil spirits: a play is the Devil's triumph; a sacrifice performed to his glory, as much as in the Heathen temples of Bacchus or Venus etc. etc.' But these sallies of religious phrenzy must not extinguish the praise which is due to Mr William Law as a wit and a scholar. His argument on topics of less absurdity is specious and acute, his manner is lively, his style forcible and clear; and had not his vigorous mind been clouded by enthusiasm, he might be ranked with the most agreeable and ingenious writers of the times. While the Bangorian controversy[19] was a fashionable theme he entered the lists on the subject of Christ's kingdom, and the authority of the priesthood. Against the plain account of the sacrament of the Lord's Supper he resumed the combat with Bishop Hoadly, the object of Whig idolatry and Tory abhorrence, and at every weapon of attack and defence the nonjuror, on the ground which is common to both, approves himself at least equal to the prelate. On the appearance of the *Fable of the Bees*,[20] he drew his pen against the licentious doctrine that private vices are public benefits, and morality as well as religion must join in his applause.

Mr Law's master-work, the *Serious Call*, is still read as a popular and powerful book of devotion. His precepts are rigid, but they are founded on the Gospel; his satire is sharp, but it is drawn from the knowledge of human life; and many of his portraits are not unworthy of the pen of La Bruyère. If he finds a spark of piety in his reader's mind he will soon kindle it to a flame; and a philosopher must allow that he exposes with equal severity and truth the strange contradiction between the faith and practice of the Christian world. Hell-fire and eternal damnation are darted from every page of the book: and it is indeed somewhat whimsical that the fanatics who most vehemently inculcate the love of God should be those who despoil him of every amiable attribute.

Chapter II[1]

Early Years · Westminster School
(1737–52)

I was born at Putney in Surrey, the twenty seventh of April, O.S., the eighth of May, N.S.,[2] in the year one thousand seven hundred and thirty-seven, within a twelvemonth of my father's marriage with Judith Porten his first wife. From my birth I have enjoyed the right of primogeniture; but I was succeeded by five brothers and one sister, all of whom were snatched away in their infancy. They died so young and I was myself so young at the time of their deaths, that I could not then feel, nor can I now estimate their loss, the importance of which could only have been ascertained by future contingencies. The shares of fortune to which younger children are reduced by our English laws would have been sufficient however to oppress my inheritance; and the compensation of their friendship must have depended on the uncertain event of character and conduct, on the affinity or opposition of our reciprocal sentiments. My five brothers, whose names may be found in the Parish register of Putney, I shall not pretend to lament: but from my childhood to the present hour I have deeply and sincerely regretted my sister; whose life was somewhat prolonged, and whom I remember to have seen an amiable infant. The relation of a brother and a sister, especially if they do not marry, appears to me of a very singular nature. It is a familiar and tender friendship with a female, much about our own age; an affection, perhaps softened by the secret influence of sex, but pure from any mixture of sensual desire, the sole species of Platonic love that can be indulged with truth and without danger.

About four months before the birth of their eldest son my parents were delivered from a state of servitude and my father inherited a considerable estate, which was magnified in his own eyes by flattery and hope. The prospect of Spanish gold from our naval contract with the Court of Madrid was suddenly overclouded about three years after my grandfather's decease. The public faith had been pledged for the security of the English merchants: their effects were seized (in 1740), on the first hostilities between the two nations. After the return of peace (in 1748 and 1763) the contractors or their representatives demanded the restitution of their property with a large claim of damages and interest.[3] But the Catholic kings absolve themselves from the engagements of their predecessors: the helpless strangers were referred by the ministers to the judges, and from the judges to the ministers, and this antiquated debt has melted away in oblivion and despair. Such a stroke could not have been averted by any foresight or care: but the arts of industry were not devolved from the father to the son, and several undertakings which had been profitable in the hands of the merchant became barren or adverse in those of the gentleman.

At the general election of 1741 Mr Gibbon and Mr Delmé stood an expensive and successful contest against Mr Dummer and Mr Henley, afterwards Lord Chancellor and Earl of Northington. The Whig candidates had a majority of the resident voters; but the corporation was firm in the Tory interest. A sudden creation of one hundred and seventy new freemen turned the scale; and a supply was readily obtained of respectable volunteers who flocked from all parts of England to support the cause of their political friends. The new Parliament opened with the victory of an opposition which was fortified by strong clamour and strange coalitions. From the event of the first divisions, Sir Robert Walpole perceived that he could no longer lead a majority in the House of Commons, and prudently resigned after a reign of one and twenty years the sceptre of the State (1742). But the fall of an unpopular Minister was not succeeded, according to general expectation, by a millennium of happiness and virtue: some courtiers lost their places, some patriots lost their characters, Lord Orford's offences vanished with his power, and, after a short vibration, the Pelham government was fixed on the old basis of the Whig aristocracy. In the year 1745 the throne and the constitution were attacked by a rebellion[4] which does not reflect much honour on the national spirit; since the English friends of the Pretender wanted courage to join his standard, and his enemies (the bulk of the people) allowed him to advance into the heart of the kingdom. Without daring, perhaps without desiring to aid the rebels, my father invariably adhered to the Tory opposition: in the most critical season he accepted for the service of the party the office of alderman in the city of London; but the duties were so repugnant to his inclination and habits, that he resigned his gown at the end of a few months. The second parliament in which he sat was prematurely dissolved (1747); and as he was unable or unwilling to maintain a second contest for Southampton, the life of the senator expired in that dissolution.

At home my father possessed the inestimable treasure of an amiable and affectionate wife, the constant object during a twelve years' marriage of his tenderness and esteem. My mother's portraits convey some idea of her beauty; the elegance of her manners has been attested by surviving friends; and my aunt Porten could descant for hours on the talents and virtues of her amiable sister. A domestic life would have been the choice, and the felicity of my mother, but she vainly attempted to check with a silken rein the passions of an independent husband. The world was open before him: his spirit was lively, his appearance splendid, his aspect cheerful, his address polite; he gracefully moved in the highest circles of society, and I have heard him boast that he was the only member of opposition admitted into the Old Club at White's where the first names of the country were often rejected. Yet such was the pleasing flexibility of his temper that he could accommodate himself with ease and almost with indifference to every class: to a meeting of lords or farmers, of citizens or foxhunters; and without being admired as a wit, Mr Gibbon was everywhere beloved as a companion and esteemed as a man. But in the pursuit of pleasure, his happiness, alas! and his fortune were gradually injured. Economy was superseded by fashion; his income proved inadequate to his expense. His house at Putney, in the neighbourhood of London, acquired the dangerous fame of hospitable entertainment; against the more dangerous temptation of play he was not invulnerable; and large sums were silently precipitated into that bottomless pit. Few minds have sufficient resources to support the weight of idleness, and had he continued to walk in the path of mercantile industry my father might have been a happier and his son would be a richer man.

Of these public and private scenes and of the first years of my own life, I must be indebted not to memory but to information. Our fancy may create and describe a perfect Adam born in the mature vigour of his corporeal and intellectual faculties:

> As new-waked from soundest sleep,
> Soft on the flowery herb I found me laid,
> In balmy sweat, which with his beams the Sun
> Soon dried, and on the reeking moisture fed.
> Straight towards Heaven my wandering eyes I turned
> And gazed a while the ample sky, till, raised
> By quick instinctive motion, up I sprung,
> As thitherward endeavouring, and upright

Stood on my feet. About me round I saw
Hill, dale, and shady woods, and sunny plains,
And liquid lapse of murmuring streams; by these,
Creatures that lived and moved, and walked or flew,
Birds on the branches warbling; all things smiled;
With fragrance and with joy my heart o'erflowed.
Myself I then perused, and limb by limb
Surveyed, and sometimes went, and sometimes ran
With supple joints, as lively vigour led;
But who I was, or where, or from what cause,
Knew not. To speak I tried, and forthwith spake;
My tongue obeyed, and readily could name
Whate'er I saw.[5]

It is thus that the poet has animated his statue: the theologian must infuse a miraculous gift of science and language, the philosopher might allow more time for the gradual exercise of his new senses, but all would agree that the consciousness and memory of Adam might proceed in a regular series from the moment of his birth. Far different is the origin and progress of human nature, and I may confidently apply to myself the common history of the whole species. Decency and ignorance cast a veil over the mystery of generation, but I may relate that after floating nine months in a liquid element I was painfully transported into the vital air. Of a new-born infant it cannot be predicated 'he thinks, therefore he *is*';[6] it can only be affirmed 'he suffers, therefore he feels'. But in this imperfect state of existence I was still unconscious of myself and of the universe, my eyes were open without the power of vision, and, according to M. de Buffon, the rational soul, that secret and incomprehensible energy, did not manifest its presence till after the fortieth day. During the first year I was below the greatest part of the brute creation, and must inevitably have perished had I been abandoned to my own care. Three years at least had elapsed before I acquired our peculiar privileges, the facility of erect motion, and the intelligent use of articulate and discriminating sounds. Slow is the growth of the body; that of the mind is still slower: at the age of seven years I had not attained to one half of the strength and proportions of manhood; and could the mental powers be measured with the same accuracy, their deficiency would appear far more considerable. The exercise of the understanding combines the past with the present: but the youthful fibres are so tender, the cells are so minute, that the first impressions are obliterated by new images; and I strive without much success to recollect the persons and objects which might appear at the time most forcibly to affect me. The local scenery of my education is however before my eyes: my father's contest for Southampton when I must have been between three and four years old, and my childish revenge in shouting, after being whipped, the names of his opponents is the first event that I seem to remember: but even that belief may be illusive, and I may only repeat the hearsay of a riper season. In the entire period of ten or twelve years from our birth, our pains and pleasures, our actions and designs are remotely connected with our present mode of existence; and according to a just computation we should begin to reckon our life from the age of puberty.

The death of a new-born child before that of its parents may seem an unnatural but it is strictly a probable event: since of any given number, the greater part are extinguished before their ninth year, before they possess the faculties of the mind or body. Without accusing the profuse waste or imperfect workmanship of Nature, I shall only observe that this unfavourable chance was multiplied against my infant existence. So feeble was my constitution, so precarious my life, that, in the baptism of each of my brothers, my father's prudence successively repeated my Christian name of Edward, that in case of the departure of the eldest son, this patronymic appellation might be still perpetuated in the family.[7]

– Uno avulso non deficit alter.[8]

To preserve and to rear so frail a being, the most tender assiduity was scarcely sufficient, and my mother's attention was somewhat diverted by her frequent pregnancies, by an exclusive passion for her husband, and by the dissipation of the world in which his taste and authority obliged her to mingle. But the maternal office was supplied by my aunt, Mrs Catherine Porten, at whose name I feel a tear of gratitude trickling down my cheek. A life of celibacy transferred her vacant affection to her sister's first child: my weakness excited her pity: her attachment was fortified by labour and success, and if there are any, as I trust there are some who rejoice that I live, to that dear and excellent woman they must hold themselves indebted. Many anxious and solitary days did she consume in the patient trial of every mode of relief and amusement. Many wakeful nights did she sit by my bedside in trembling expectation that each hour would be my last. My poor aunt has often told me with tears in her eyes how I was nearly starved by a nurse that had lost her milk; how long she herself was apprehensive lest my crazy frame, which is now of common shape, should remain for ever crooked and deformed.

From one dangerous malady, the small-pox, I was indeed rescued by the practice of inoculation which had been recently introduced into England, and was still opposed by medical, religious, and even political prejudice. But it is only against the small-pox that a preservative has been found. I was successively afflicted by lethargies and fevers; by opposite tendencies to a consumptive and a dropsical habit; by a contraction of my nerves, a fistula in my eye, and the bite of a dog most vehemently suspected of madness; and in the list of my sufferings from my birth to the age of puberty few physical ills would be omitted. From Sir Hans Sloane and Dr Mead, to Ward and the Chevalier Taylor, every practitioner was called to my aid: the fees of doctors were swelled by the bills of apothecaries and surgeons; there was a time when I swallowed more physic than food, and my body is still marked with the indelible scars of lancets, issues and caustics. Of the various and frequent disorders of my childhood my own recollection is dark; nor do I wish to expatiate on so disgusting a topic. I will not follow the vain example of Cardinal Quirini, who has filled half a volume of his memoirs with medical consultations on his particular case; nor shall I imitate the naked frankness of Montaigne, who exposes all the symptoms of his malady, and the operation of each dose of physic on his nerves and bowels. It may not however be useless to observe that in this early period, the care of my mind was too frequently neglected for that of my health: compassion always suggested an excuse for the indulgence of the master, or the idleness of the pupil; and the chain of my education was broken as often as I was recalled from the school of learning to the bed of sickness.

As soon as the use of speech had prepared my infant reason for the admission of knowledge, I was taught the arts of reading, writing and vulgar arithmetic. So remote is the date, so vague is the memory of their origin in myself, that were not the error corrected by analogy, I should be tempted to conceive them as innate. In the improved state of society in which I have the good fortune to exist, these attainments are so generally diffused that they no longer constitute the liberal distinctions of scholars and gentlemen. The operations of writing and reading must seem on an abstract view to require the labour of genius; to transform articulate sounds into visible signs by the swift and almost spontaneous motion of the hand; to render visible signs into articulate sounds by the voluntary and rapid utterance of the voice. Yet experience has proved that these operations of such apparent difficulty, when they are taught to all may be learned by all, and that the meanest capacity in the most tender age is not inadequate to the task. Between the sister arts there exists however a material difference: the one is connected with mental intelligence, the other with manual dexterity. The excellence of reading, if the vocal organ be not defective, the propriety of the cadence, the tones, and the pauses is always in just proportion to the knowledge, taste and feelings of the reader. But an illiterate scribe may delineate a correct and elegant copy of penmanship: while the sense and style of the philosopher or poet are most awkwardly scrawled in such ill-formed and irregular characters, that the authors themselves, after a short interval, will be incapable of deciphering them. My own writing is of a middle cast, legible rather than fair: but I may observe that age and long practice which are often productive of negligence have rather improved than corrupted my hand. The science of numbers, the third element of our primitive education, may be esteemed the best scale to measure the degrees of the human understanding: a child or a peasant performs with ease and assurance the four first rules of arithmetic; the profound mysteries of algebra are reserved for the disciples of Newton and Bernouilli. In my childhood I was praised for the readiness with which I could multiply and divide by memory alone two sums of several figures: such praise encouraged my growing talent; and had I persevered in this line of application, I might have acquired some fame in mathematical studies.

After this previous institution at home or at a day-school at Putney, I was delivered at the age of seven (April 1744) into the hands of Mr John Kirkby, who exercised about eighteen months the office of my domestic tutor. His own words, which I shall here transcribe, inspire in his favour a sentiment of pity and esteem:

During my abode in my native county of Cumberland, in quality of an indigent curate, I used now and then, in a summer, when the pleasantness of the season invited, to take a solitary walk to the sea-shore, which lies about two miles from the town where I lived. Here I would amuse myself, one while in viewing at large the agreeable prospect which surrounded me, and another while (confining my sight to nearer objects) in admiring the vast variety of beautiful shells, thrown upon the beach, some of the choicest of which I always picked up to divert my little ones upon my return. One time among the rest, taking such a journey in my head, I sat down upon the declivity of the beach, with my face to the sea, which was now come up within a few yards of my feet; when immediately the sad thoughts of the wretched condition of my family, and the unsuccessfulness of all endeavours to amend it, came crowding into my mind, which drove me into a deep melancholy and ever and anon forced tears from my eyes.[9]

Distress at last forced him to leave the country. His learning and virtue introduced him to my father, and at Putney he might have found at least a temporary shelter, had not an act of indiscretion again driven him into the world. One day, reading prayers in the parish church, he most unluckily forgot the name of King George. His patron, a loyal subject, dismissed him with some reluctance and a decent reward; and *how* the poor man ended his days I have never been able to learn.

Mr John Kirkby is the author of two small volumes, the *Life of Automathes* (London 1745), and an *English and Latin Grammar* (London 1746), which as a testimony of gratitude he dedicated (November 5 1745) to my father. The books are before me; from them the pupil may judge the preceptor and, upon the whole, the judgement will not be unfavourable. The grammar is executed with accuracy and skill, and I know not whether any better existed at the time in our language; but the *Life of Automathes* aspires to the honours of a philosophical fiction. It is the story of a youth, the son of a shipwrecked exile, who lives alone on a desert island from infancy to the age of manhood. A hind is his nurse; he inherits a cottage with many useful and curious instruments; some ideas remain of the education of his two first years, some arts are borrowed from the beavers of a neighbouring lake, some truths are revealed in supernatural visions. With these helps and his own industry Automathes becomes a self-taught though speechless philosopher, who had investigated with success his own mind, the natural world, the abstract sciences, and the great principles of morality and religion. The author is not entitled to the merit of invention, since he has blended the English story of Robinson Crusoe with the Arabian romance of Hai Ebn Yokhdan, which he might read in the Latin version of Pocock.[10] In the *Automathes* I cannot praise either the depth of thought or elegance of style, but the book is not devoid of entertainment or instruction; and among several interesting passages I would select the discovery of fire, which produces by accidental mischief the discovery of conscience. A man who had thought so much on the subjects of language and education was surely no ordinary preceptor. My childish years and his hasty departure prevented me from enjoying the full benefit of his lessons; but they enlarged my knowledge of arithmetic and left a clear impression of the English and Latin rudiments.

In my ninth year (January 1746), in a lucid interval of comparative health, my father adopted the convenient and customary mode of English education, and I was sent to Kingston-upon-Thames, to a school of about seventy boys which was kept by Dr Woodson and his assistants. Every time I have since passed over Putney Common I have always noticed the spot where my mother, as we drove along in the coach, admonished me that I was now going into the world, and must learn to think and act for myself. The expression may appear ludicrous; yet there is not in the course of life a more remarkable change than the removal of a child from the luxury and freedom of a wealthy house to the frugal diet and strict subordination of a school, from the tenderness of parents and the obsequiousness of servants to the rude familiarity of his equals, the insolent tyranny of his seniors, and the rod, perhaps, of a cruel and capricious pedagogue. Such hardships may steel the mind and body against the injuries of fortune, but my timid reserve was astonished by the crowd and tumult of the school; the want of strength and activity disqualified me for the sports of the play-field; nor have I forgot how often in the year forty-six I was reviled and buffeted for the sins of my Tory ancestors.

By the common methods of discipline, at the expense of many tears and some blood, I purchased the knowledge of the Latin syntax: and not long since I was possessed of the dirty volumes of Phaedrus and Cornelius Nepos, which I painfully construed and darkly understood. The choice of these authors is not injudicious. The *Lives* of Cornelius Nepos, the friend of Atticus and Cicero, are composed in the style of the purest age: his simplicity is elegant, his brevity copious: he exhibits a series of men and manners; and with such illustrations, as every pedant is not indeed qualified to give, this classic biographer may initiate a young student in the history of Greece and Rome. The use of fables or apologues has been approved in every age from ancient India to modern Europe: they convey in familiar images the truths of morality and prudence; and the most childish understanding (I advert to the scruples of Rousseau) will not suppose either that beasts *do* speak, or that men *may* lie. A fable represents the genuine characters of animals, and a skilful master might extract from Pliny and Buffon some pleasing lessons of natural history, a science well adapted to the taste and capacity of children. The Latinity of Phaedrus is not exempt from an alloy of the Silver age; but his manner is concise, terse and sententious: the Thracian slave discreetly breathes the spirit of a freeman; and when the text is sound, the style is perspicuous. But his fables, after a long oblivion, were first published by Peter Pithou from a corrupt manuscript. The labours of fifty editors confess the defects of the copy, as well as the value of the original; and a schoolboy may have been whipped for misapprehending a passage which Bentley could not restore, and which Burman could not explain.

My studies were too frequently interrupted by sickness; and after a real or nominal residence at Kingston school of near two years, I was finally recalled (December 1747)[11] by my mother's death, which was occasioned,

in her thirty-eighth year, by the consequences of her last labour. As I
had seldom enjoyed the smiles of maternal tenderness she was rather
the object of my respect than of my love. Some natural tears were soon
wiped; I was too young to feel the importance of my loss; and the image
of her person and conversation is faintly imprinted in my memory. The
affectionate heart of my aunt Catherine Porten bewailed a sister and a
friend, but my poor father was inconsolable; and the transport of grief
seemed to threaten his life or his reason. I can never forget the scene
of our first interview, some weeks after the fatal event; the awful silence,
the room hung with black, the mid-day tapers, his sighs and tears; his
praises of my mother, a saint in heaven, his solemn adjuration that I
would cherish her memory, and imitate her virtues; and the fervour with
which he kissed and blessed me as the sole surviving pledge of their loves.
The storm of passion insensibly subsided into calmer melancholy: but
he persevered in the use of mourning much beyond the term which has
been fixed by decency and custom. Three years after my mother's death,
his situation is described by Mr Mallet who then resided at Putney, and
with whose family my father had formed a very intimate connection.
In a pleasing little composition entitled *The Wedding-day*, Cupid and
Hymen undertake the office of inviting some chosen friends to celebrate
the ninth anniversary (October 2 1750) of the poet's nuptials. Cupid flies
eastward to London.

> His brother too, with sober cheer,
> For the same end did westward steer:
> But first a pensive love forlorn,
> Who three long weeping years has borne
> His torch revers'd, and all around,
> Where once it flam'd with cypress bound,
> Sent off, to call a neighbouring friend,
> On whom the mournful train attend:
> And bid him, this one day at least,
> For such a pair, at such a feast,
> Strip off the sable vest, and wear
> His once-gay look and happier air.

At a convivial meeting of his friends, Mr Gibbon might affect or enjoy
a gleam of cheerfulness: but his plan of happiness was for ever destroyed,
and after the loss of his companion, he was left alone in a world of which
the business and pleasure were to him irksome or insipid. After some
unsuccessful trials he renounced the tumult of London and the hospitality
of Putney, and buried himself in the rural or rather rustic solitude of

Buriton, from which during several years he seldom emerged. It must not however be dissembled that the sorrowful widower was urged to this resolution by the growing perplexity of his affairs. His fortune was impaired: his debts had multiplied, and as long as his son was a minor, he could not disengage his estate from the legal fetters of an entail. Had my mother lived, he must soon have retired into the country, with more comfort indeed, but without the credit of a pious and disinterested motive. Shall I presume to add, that a secret inconstancy, which always adhered to his disposition, might impel him at once to sink the man of fashion in the character and occupations of a Hampshire farmer?

As far back as I can remember, the house near Putney bridge and churchyard of my maternal grandfather appears in the light of my proper and native home. It was there that I was allowed to spend the greatest part of my time, in sickness or in health, during my school vacations and my parents' residence in London, and finally after my mother's death. Three months after that event, in the spring of 1748, the commercial ruin of her father, Mr James Porten, was accomplished and declared. He suddenly absconded; but as his effects were not sold, nor the house evacuated till the Christmas following, I enjoyed during the whole year the society of my aunt without much consciousness of her impending fate. I feel a melancholy pleasure in commemorating my obligations to that excellent woman, Mrs Catherine Porten, the true mother of my mind as well as of my health. Her natural good sense was improved by the perusal of the best books in the English language; and if her reason was sometimes clouded by prejudice, her sentiments were never disguised by hypocrisy or affectation. Her indulgent tenderness, the frankness of her temper, and my innate rising curiosity soon removed all distance between us: like friends of an equal age we freely conversed on every topic, familiar or abstruse: and it was her delight and reward to observe the first shoots of my young ideas. Pain and languor were often soothed by the voice of instruction and amusement; and to her kind lessons I ascribe my early and invincible love of reading, which I would not exchange for the treasures of India.

I should perhaps be astonished were it possible to ascertain the date at which a favourite tale[12] was engraved by frequent repetition in my memory; the Cavern of the Winds, the Palace of Felicity, and the fatal moment at the end of three months or centuries, when Prince Adolphus is overtaken by Time, who had worn out so many pair of wings in the pursuit. Before I left Kingston school, I was well acquainted with Pope's Homer, and the Arabian Nights Entertainments, two books which will always please by the moving picture of human manners and specious miracles.[13] The verses of Pope accustomed my ear to the sound of poetic harmony: in the death of Hector and the shipwreck of Ulysses I tasted the new emotions of terror and pity, and seriously disputed with my aunt on the vices and virtues of the heroes of the Trojan War. From Pope's Homer to Dryden's Virgil was an easy transition; but I know not how, from some fault in the author, the translator or the reader, the pious Aeneas did not so forcibly seize on my imagination, and I derived more pleasure from Ovid's *Metamorphoses*, especially in the fall of Phaethon, and the speeches of Ajax and Ulysses. My grandfather's flight unlocked the door of a tolerable library, and I turned over many English pages of poetry and romance, of history and travels. Where a title attracted my eye, without fear or awe I snatched the volume from the shelf, and Mrs Porten, who indulged herself in moral and religious speculation, was more prone to encourage than to check a curiosity above the strength of a boy. This year 1748, the twelfth of my age,[14] I shall note as the most propitious to the growth of my intellectual stature.

After such satisfaction as could be given to his creditors, the relics of my grandfather's fortune afforded a bare annuity for his own maintenance; and his daughter, my worthy aunt, who had already passed her fortieth year, was left naked and destitute. Her more wealthy relations were not *absolutely* without bowels, but her noble spirit scorned a life of obligation and dependence; and after revolving several schemes, she preferred the humble industry of keeping a boarding-house for Westminster School, where she laboriously earned a competence for her old age. This singular opportunity of blending the advantages of private and public education decided my father. After the Christmas holidays, in January 1749, I accompanied Mrs Porten to her new house in College Street, and was immediately entered in the school, of which Dr John Nicoll was at that time headmaster. At first I was alone; but my aunt's resolution was praised, her character was esteemed; her friends were numerous and active; in the course of some years she became the mother of forty or fifty boys, for the most part of family and fortune; and as her primitive habitation was too narrow, she built and occupied a spacious mansion in Dean's Yard.

I shall always be ready to join in the common opinion that our public schools, which have produced so many eminent characters, are the best adapted to the genius and constitution of the English people. A boy of spirit may acquire a previous and practical experience of the world, and his playfellows may be the future friends of his heart or his interest. In a free intercourse with his equals the habits of truth, fortitude and prudence will insensibly be matured; birth and riches are measured by the standard of personal merit; and the mimic scene of a rebellion has displayed in their true colours the ministers and patriots of the rising generation. Our seminaries of learning do not exactly correspond with the precept of a Spartan king[15] 'that the child should be instructed in the arts which will be useful to the man', since a finished scholar may emerge from the head of Westminster or Eton in total ignorance of the business and conversation of English gentlemen in the latter end of the eighteenth century. But these schools may assume the merit of teaching all that they pretend to teach, the Latin and Greek languages; they deposit in the hands of a disciple the keys of two valuable chests; nor can he complain if they are afterwards lost or neglected by his own fault. The necessity of leading in equal ranks so many unequal powers of capacity and application will prolong to eight or ten years the juvenile studies which might be dispatched in half that time by the skilful master of a single pupil. Yet even the repetition of exercise and discipline contributes to fix in a vacant mind the verbal science of grammar and prosody; and the private or voluntary student who possesses the sense and spirit of the classics may offend by a false quantity the scrupulous ear of a well-flogged critic. For myself I must be content with a very small share of the civil and literary fruits of a public school. In the space of two years (1749, 1750), interrupted by danger and debility, I painfully climbed into the third form: and my riper age was left to acquire the beauties of the Latin and the rudiments of the Greek tongue. Instead of audaciously mingling in the sports, the quarrels, and the connections of our little world, I was still cherished at home under the maternal wing of my aunt; and my removal from Westminster long preceded the approach of manhood. In our domestic society I formed however an intimate acquaintance with a young nobleman of my own age,[16] and vainly flattered myself that our sentiments would prove as lasting as they seemed to be mutual. On my return from abroad his coldness repelled such faint advances as my pride allowed me to make, and in our different walks of life, we gradually became strangers to each other. Yet his private character, for Lord H. has never affected a public name, leaves me no room to accuse the propriety and merit of my early choice.

The violence and variety of my complaints, which had excused my frequent absence from Westminster School, at length engaged Mrs Porten, with the advice of physicians, to conduct me to Bath; at the end of the Michaelmas vacation (1750) she quitted me with reluctance, and I remained several months under the care of a trusty maid-servant. A strange nervous affection which alternately contracted my legs, and produced without any visible symptoms the most excruciating pain, was ineffectually opposed by the various methods of bathing and pumping. From Bath I was transported to Winchester, to the house of a physician, and after the failure of his medical skill we had again recourse to the virtues of the Bath waters. During the intervals of these fits I moved with my father to Buriton and Putney, and a short unsuccessful trial was attempted to renew my attendance at Westminster School. But my infirmities could not be reconciled with the hours and discipline of a public seminary; and instead of a domestic tutor, who might have watched the favourable moments, and gently advanced the progress of my learning, my father was too easily content with such occasional teachers as the different places of my residence could supply. I was never forced and seldom was I persuaded to admit these lessons: yet I read with a clergyman at Bath some odes of Horace and several episodes of Virgil, which gave me an imperfect and transient enjoyment of the Latin poets.

It might now be apprehended that I should continue for life an illiterate cripple; but as I approached my sixteenth year, Nature displayed in my favour her mysterious energies. My constitution was fortified and fixed: and my disorders, instead of growing with my growth and strengthening with my strength, most wonderfully vanished. I have never possessed or abused the insolence of health; but since that time few persons have been more exempt from real or imaginary ills; and till I am admonished by the gout, the reader shall no more be troubled with the history of any bodily complaints. My unexpected recovery again encouraged the hope of my education, and I was placed at Esher in Surrey, in the house of the Reverend Mr Philip Francis, in a pleasant spot which promised to unite the various benefits of air, exercise and study (January 1752). Mr Francis was recommended, I believe by the Mallets, as a scholar and a wit: his two tragedies have been coldly received, but his version of Demosthenes, which I have not seen, supposes some knowledge of Greek literature, and he had executed with success and applause the arduous task of a complete translation of Horace in English verse. Besides a young gentleman whose name I do not remember, our family consisted only of myself and his son, who has since been conspicuous in the supreme council of India, from whence he is returned to England with an ample fortune. It was stipulated that his father should always confine himself to a small number; and with so able a preceptor, in this private academy, the time which I had lost might have been speedily retrieved. But the experience of a few weeks was sufficient to discover that Mr Francis's spirit was too lively for his profession; and while he indulged himself in the pleasures of London, his pupils were left idle at Esher in the custody of a Dutch usher, of low manners and contemptible learning. From such careless or unworthy hands I was indignantly rescued; but my father's perplexity rather than his prudence was urged to embrace a singular and desperate measure. Without preparation or delay he carried me to Oxford; and I was matriculated in the University, as a Gentleman Commoner of Magdalen College, before I accomplished the fifteenth year of my age (April 3 1752).

The curiosity which had been implanted in my infant mind was still alive and active: but my reason was not sufficiently informed to understand the value, or to lament the loss of three precious years from my entrance at Westminster to my admission at Oxford. Instead of repining at my long and frequent confinement to the chamber or the couch, I secretly rejoiced in those infirmities which delivered me from the exercises of the school and the society of my equals. As often as I was tolerably exempt from danger and pain, reading, free desultory reading, was the employment and comfort of my solitary hours; at Westminster my aunt sought only to amuse and indulge me; in my stations at Bath and Winchester, at Buriton and Putney, a false compassion respected my sufferings, and I was allowed without control or advice to gratify the wanderings of an unripe taste. My indiscriminate appetite subsided by degrees in the *historic* line: and, since philosophy has exploded all innate ideas and natural propensities, I must ascribe this choice to the assiduous perusal of the *Universal History* as the octavo volumes successively appeared. This unequal work, and a treatise of Hearne, the *Doctor Historicus*, referred and introduced me to the Greek and Roman historians, to as many at least as were accessible to an English reader. All that I could find were greedily devoured, from Littlebury's lame Herodotus, and Spelman's valuable Xenophon, to the pompous folios of Gordon's Tacitus, and a ragged Procopius of the beginning of the last century.

The cheap acquisition of so much knowledge confirmed my dislike to the study of languages, and I argued with Mrs Porten that, were I master of Greek and Latin, I must interpret to myself in English the thoughts of the original, and that such extemporary versions must be inferior to the elaborate translations of professed scholars: a silly sophism, which could not easily be confuted by a person ignorant of any other language than her own. From the ancient I leaped to the modern world: many crude lumps of Speed, Rapin, Mézeray, Davila, Machiavel, Father Paul,

Bower etc. passed through me like so many novels, and I swallowed with the same voracious appetite the descriptions of India and China, of Mexico and Peru. Our family collection was decently furnished; the circulating libraries of London and Bath afforded rich treasures; I borrowed many books, and some I contrived to purchase from my scanty allowance. My father's friends who visited the boy were astonished at finding him surrounded with a heap of folios, of whose titles *they* were ignorant and on whose contents *he* could pertinently discourse.

My first introduction to the historic scenes, which have since engaged so many years of my life, must be ascribed to an accident. In the summer of 1751 I accompanied my father on a visit to Mr Hoare's in Wiltshire: but I was less delighted with the beauties of Stourhead than with discovering in the library a common book, the continuation of Echard's *Roman History*, which is indeed executed with more skill and taste than the previous work. To me the reigns of the successors of Constantine were absolutely new; and I was immersed in the passage of the Goths over the Danube when the summons of the dinner-bell reluctantly dragged me from my intellectual feast. This transient glance served rather to irritate than to appease my curiosity, and no sooner was I returned to Bath than I procured the second and third volumes of Howell's *History of the World*, which exhibit the Byzantine period on a larger scale. Mahomet and his Saracens soon fixed my attention: and some instinct of criticism directed me to the genuine sources. Simon Ockley, an original in every sense, first opened my eyes, and I was led from one book to another till I had ranged round the circle of Oriental history. Before I was sixteen I had exhausted all that could be learned in English of the Arabs and Persians, the Tartars and Turks, and the same ardour urged me to guess at the French of d'Herbelot, and to construe the barbarous Latin of Pocock's *Abulpharagius*. Such vague and multifarious reading could not teach me to think, to write or to act; and the only principle that darted a ray of light into the indigested chaos was an early and rational application to the order of time and place. The maps of Cellarius and Wells imprinted in my mind the picture of ancient geography: from Strauchius I imbibed the elements of chronology: the tables of Helvicus and Anderson, the annals of Usher and Prideaux distinguished the connection of events, and I engraved the multitude of names and dates in a clear and indelible series. But in the discussion of the first ages I overleaped the bounds of modesty and use. In my childish balance I presumed to weigh the systems of Scaliger and Petavius, of Marsham and Newton, which I could seldom study in the originals; the dynasties of Assyria and Egypt were my top and cricket-ball; and my sleep has been disturbed by the difficulty of reconciling the Septuagint with the Hebrew computation. I arrived at Oxford with a stock of erudition that might have puzzled a doctor, and a degree of ignorance of which a schoolboy would have been ashamed.

At the conclusion of this first period of my life, I am tempted to enter a protest against the trite and lavish praise of the happiness of our boyish years, which is echoed with so much affectation in the world. That happiness I have never known; that time I have never regretted, and were my poor aunt still alive she would bear testimony to the early and constant uniformity of my sentiments. It will indeed be replied that *I* am not a competent judge: that pleasure is incompatible with pain, that joy is excluded from sickness; and that the felicity of a schoolboy consists in the perpetual motion of thoughtless and playful agility, in which I was never qualified to excel. My name, it is most true, could never be enrolled among the sprightly race, the idle progeny of Eton or Westminster, who delight to cleave the water with pliant arm, to urge the flying ball, and to chase the speed of the rolling circle.[17] But I would ask the warmest and most active hero of the play-field, whether he can seriously compare his childish with his manly enjoyments; whether he does not feel, as the most precious attribute of his existence, the vigorous maturity of sensual and spiritual powers, which Nature has reserved for the age of puberty. A state of happiness arising only from the want of foresight and reflection shall never provoke my envy; such degenerate taste would tend to sink us in the scale of beings from a man to a child, a dog, and an oyster, till we had reached the confines of brute matter, which cannot suffer, because it cannot feel. The poet may gaily describe the short hours of recreation; but he forgets the daily tedious labours of the school, which is approached each morning with anxious and reluctant steps. Degrees of misery are proportioned to the mind rather than to the object: *parva leves capiunt animos*;[18] and few men, in the trials of life, have experienced a more painful sensation than the poor schoolboy, with an imperfect task, who trembles on the eve of the black Monday.

A school is the cavern of fear and sorrow: the mobility of the captive youths is chained to a book and a desk; an inflexible master commands their attention, which every moment is impatient to escape. They labour, like the soldiers of Persia, under the scourge;[19] and their education is nearly finished before they can apprehend the sense or utility of the harsh lessons which they are forced to repeat. Such blind and absolute dependence may be necessary, but can never be delightful. Freedom is the first wish of our heart; freedom is the first blessing of our nature; and, unless we bind ourselves with the voluntary chains of interest or passion, we advance in freedom as we advance in years.

Chapter III

Oxford
(1752–3)

A traveller who visits Oxford or Cambridge is surprised and edified by
the apparent order and tranquillity that prevail in the seats of the English
muses. In the most celebrated universities of Holland, Germany and Italy,
the students, who swarm from different countries, are loosely dispersed
in private lodgings at the houses of the burghers; they dress according
to their fancy and fortune; and in the intemperate quarrels of youth and
wine, their *swords*, though less frequently than of old, are sometimes
stained with each other's blood. The use of arms is banished from our
English universities: the uniform habit of the academics, the square cap,
and black gown, is adapted to the civil and even clerical profession; and
from the doctor in divinity to the undergraduate, the degrees of learning
and age are externally distinguished. Instead of being scattered in a town,
the students of Oxford and Cambridge are united in Colleges: their maintenance is provided at their own expense, or that of the founders; and
the stated hours of the hall and chapel represent the discipline of a regular,
and, as it were, a religious community. The eyes of the traveller are
attracted by the size or beauty of the public edifices; and the principal
colleges appear to be so many palaces which a liberal nation has erected
and endowed for the habitation of science. My own introduction to the
University of Oxford forms a new era in my life, and at the distance of
forty years I still remember my first emotions of surprise and satisfaction.
In my fifteenth year I felt myself suddenly raised from a boy to a man;
the persons whom I respected as my superiors in age and academical
rank entertained me with every mark of attention and civility; and my
vanity was flattered by the velvet cap and silk gown which discriminate
a gentleman commoner from a plebeian student. A decent allowance,
more money than a schoolboy had ever seen, was at my own disposal,
and I might command among the tradesmen of Oxford an indefinite and
dangerous latitude of credit. A key was delivered into my hands which

gave me the free use of a numerous and learned library; my apartment consisted of three elegant and well furnished rooms in the new building,[1] a stately pile, of Magdalen College; and the adjacent walks, had they been frequented by Plato's disciples, might have been compared to the Attic shade on the banks of the Ilissus. Such was the fair prospect of my entrance (April 3 1752) into the University of Oxford.

A venerable prelate, whose taste and erudition must reflect honour on the society in which they were formed, has drawn a very interesting picture of his academical life:

I was educated (says Bishop Lowth) in the UNIVERSITY OF OXFORD. I enjoyed all the advantages both public and private, which that famous seat of learning so largely affords. I spent many years in that illustrious society, in a well-regulated course of useful discipline and studies, and in the agreeable and improving commerce of gentlemen and of scholars; in a society where emulation without envy, ambition without jealousy, contention without animosity incited industry and awakened genius; where a liberal pursuit of knowledge, and a genuine freedom of thought was raised, encouraged, and pushed forward by example, by commendation, and by authority. I breathed the same atmosphere that the HOOKERS, the CHILLINGWORTHS, and the LOCKES had breathed before: whose benevolence and humanity were as extensive as their vast genius and comprehensive knowledge, who always treated their adversaries with civility and respect, who made candour, moderation, and liberal judgement as much the rule and law as the subject of their discourse. And do you reproach me with my education in this place, and with my relation to this most respectable body; which I shall always esteem my greatest advantage, and my highest honour?

I transcribe with pleasure this eloquent passage, without examining what benefits or what rewards were derived by Hooker or Chillingworth or Locke from their academical institution, without enquiring whether in this angry controversy the spirit of Lowth himself is purified from the intolerant zeal, which Warburton had ascribed to the genius of the place. The expression of gratitude is a virtue and a pleasure: a liberal mind will delight to cherish and celebrate the memory of its parents, and the teachers of science are the parents of the mind. I applaud the filial piety which it is impossible for me to imitate: since I must not confess an imaginary debt to assume the merit of a just or generous retribution.

To the University of Oxford *I* acknowledge no obligation, and she will as cheerfully renounce me for a son, as I am willing to disclaim her for a mother. I spent fourteen months at Magdalen College: they proved the fourteen months the most idle and unprofitable of my whole life. The reader will pronounce between the school and the scholar: but I cannot affect to believe that Nature had disqualified me for all literary pursuits. The specious and ready excuse of my tender age, imperfect preparation, and hasty departure may doubtless be alleged, nor do I wish to defraud such excuses of their proper weight. Yet in my sixteenth year I was not devoid of capacity or application; even my childish reading had displayed an early though blind propensity for books; and the shallow flood might have been taught to flow in a deep channel and a clear stream. In the discipline of a well-constituted academy, under the guidance of skillful and vigilant professors, I should gradually have risen from translations to originals, from the Latin to the Greek classics, from dead languages to living science: my hours would have been occupied by useful and agreeable studies: the wanderings of fancy would have been restrained, and I should have escaped the temptations of idleness which finally precipitated my departure from Oxford.

Perhaps, in a separate annotation I may coolly examine the fabulous and real antiquities of our sister universities, a question which has kindled such fierce and foolish disputes among their fanatic sons. In the meanwhile, it will be acknowledged that these venerable bodies are sufficiently old to partake of all the prejudices and infirmities of age. The schools of Oxford and Cambridge were founded in a dark age of false and barbarous science; and they are still tainted with the vices of their origin. Their primitive discipline was adapted to the education of priests and monks; and the government still remains in the hands of the clergy, an order of men whose manners are remote from the present world, and whose eyes are dazzled by the light of philosophy. The legal incorporation of these societies by the charters of popes and kings had given them a monopoly of the public instruction; and the spirit of monopolists is narrow, lazy and oppressive. Their work is more costly and less productive than that of independent artists; and the new improvements so eagerly grasped by the competition of freedom are admitted with slow and sullen reluctance in those proud corporations, above the fear of a rival, and below the confession of an error. We may scarcely hope that any reformation will be a voluntary act, and so deeply are they rooted in law and prejudice that even the omnipotence of Parliament would shrink from an enquiry into the state and abuses of the two universities.

The use of academical degrees, as old as the thirteenth century, is visibly borrowed from the mechanic corporations in which an apprentice, after serving his time, obtains a testimonial of his skill, and a licence to practise his trade and mystery. It is not my design to depreciate those honours which could never gratify or disappoint my ambition: and I should applaud the institution, if the degrees of bachelor or licentiate were bestowed as the reward of manly and successful study: if the name and rank of doctor or master were strictly reserved for the professors of science who have approved their title to the public esteem. The mysterious faculty of theology must not be scanned by a profane eye, the cloak of reason sits awkwardly on our fashionable divines, and in the ecclesiastical studies of the fathers and councils their modesty will yield to the Catholic universities. Our English civilians and canonists[2] have never been famous: their real business is confined to a small circle; and the double juris-prudence of Rome is overwhelmed by the enormous profession of common lawyers, who, in the pursuit of honours and riches disdain the mock majesty of our *budge* doctors.[3] We are justly proud of the skill and learning of our physicians: their skill is acquired in the practice of the hospitals; they seek their learning in London, in Scotland, or on the continent; and few patients would trust their pulse to a medical student, if he had passed the fourteen years of his noviciate at Oxford or Cambridge, whose degrees however, are exclusively admitted in the Royal College. The *Arts* are supposed to include the liberal knowledge of philosophy and literature: but I am informed that some tattered shreds of the old logic and meta-physics compose the exercises for a bachelor and master's degree; and that modern improvements, instead of introducing a more rational trial, have only served to relax the forms which are now the object of general contempt.

In all the universities of Europe except our own, the languages and sciences are distributed among a numerous list of effective professors: the students, according to their taste, their calling, and their diligence apply themselves to the proper masters, and in the annual repetition of public and private lectures, these masters are assiduously employed. Our curiosity may enquire what number of professors has been instituted at Oxford (for I shall now confine myself to my own university), by whom are they appointed, and what may be the probable chances of merit or incapacity? How many are stationed to the three faculties, and how many are left for the liberal arts? What is the form, and what the substance of their lessons? But all these questions are silenced by one short and singular answer, 'That, in the university of Oxford, the greater part of the public professors have for these many years, given up altogether even the pretence of teaching.' Incredible as the fact may appear, I must rest my belief on the positive and impartial evidence of a philosopher who had himself resided at Oxford. Dr Adam Smith[4] assigns as the cause of their indolence that, instead of being paid by voluntary contributions which would urge them to increase the number, and to deserve the gratitude of their pupils, the Oxford professors are secure in the enjoyment of a fixed stipend, without the necessity of labour or the apprehension of control.

It has indeed been observed, nor is the observation absurd, that except in experimental sciences, which demand a costly apparatus and a dexterous hand, the many valuable treatises that have been published on every subject of learning may now supersede the ancient mode of oral instruction. Were this principle true in its utmost latitude, I should only infer that the offices and salaries which are become useless ought without delay to be abolished. But there still remains a material difference between a book and a professor: the hour of the lecture enforces attendance; attention is fixed by the presence, the voice, and the occasional questions of the teacher; the most idle will carry something away; and the more diligent will compare the instructions which they have heard in the school, with the volumes which they peruse in their chamber. The advice of a skilful professor will adapt a course of reading to every mind and every situation; his learning will remove difficulties, and solve objections: his authority will discover, admonish, and at last chastise the negligence of his disciples; and his vigilant enquiries will ascertain the steps of their literary progress. Whatsoever science he professes, he may illustrate in a series of discourses, composed in the leisure of his closet, pronounced on public occasions, and finally delivered to the press. I observe with pleasure that in the university of Oxford, Dr Lowth, with equal eloquence and erudition, has executed this task in his incomparable *Praelections* on the poetry of the Hebrews.

The College of St Mary Magdalen (it is vulgarly pronounced Maudlin) was founded in the fifteenth century by a Bishop of Winchester; and now consists of a president, forty fellows, and a number of inferior students.[5] It is esteemed one of the largest and most wealthy of our academical corporations, which may be compared to the Benedictine abbeys of Catholic countries: and I have loosely heard that the estates belonging to Magdalen College, which are leased by those indulgent landlords at small quit-rents and occasional fines, might be raised, in the hands of private avarice, to an annual revenue of near thirty thousand pounds. Our colleges are supposed to be schools of science as well as of education: nor is it unreasonable to expect that a body of literary men, addicted to a life of celibacy, exempt from the care of their own subsistence, and amply provided with books, should devote their leisure to the prosecution of study, and that some effects of their studies should be manifested to the world. The shelves of their library groan under the weight of the Benedictine folios, of the editions of the fathers and the collections of the Middle Ages, which have issued from the single Abbey of St Germain des Prés[6] at Paris. A composition of genius must be the offspring of one mind: but such works of industry as may be divided among many hands, and must be continued during many years, are the peculiar province of a laborious community. If I enquire into the manufactures of the monks at Magdalen, if I extend the enquiry to the other colleges of Oxford and Cambridge, a silent blush, or a scornful frown will be the only reply. The fellows or monks of my time were decent easy men who supinely enjoyed the gifts of the founder. Their days were filled by a series of uniform employments: the chapel and the hall, the coffee house and the common room, till they retired, weary and well-satisfied, to a long slumber. From the toil of reading or thinking or writing they had absolved their conscience, and the first shoots of learning and ingenuity withered on the ground without yielding any fruit to the owners or the public. The only student was a young fellow[7] (a future Bishop), who was deeply immersed in the follies of the Hutchinsonian system; the only author was a half-starved chaplain, Ballard was his name, who begged subscriptions for some Memoirs concerning the learned ladies of Great Britain.

As a gentleman commoner I was admitted to the society of the fellows, and fondly expected that some questions of literature would be the amusing and instructive topics of their discourse. Their conversation stagnated in a round of college business, Tory politics, personal stories and private scandal; their dull and deep potations excused the brisk intemperance of youth; and their constitutional toasts were not expressive of the most lively loyalty for the House of Hanover. A general election was now approaching: the great Oxfordshire contest already blazed with all the malevolence of party-zeal. Magdalen College was devoutly attached to the old interest; and the names of Wenman and Dashwood were more frequently pronounced than those of Cicero and Chrysostom. The example of the senior fellows could not inspire the undergraduates with a liberal spirit or studious emulation; and I cannot describe, as I never knew, the discipline of the college. Some duties may possibly have been imposed on the poor scholars, whose ambition aspired to the peaceful honours of a fellowship (*ascribi quietis ordinibus ... deorum*[8]): but no independent members were admitted, below the rank of a gentleman commoner; and our velvet cap was the cap of liberty. A tradition prevailed that some of our predecessors had spoken Latin declamations in the hall, but of this ancient custom no vestige remained; the obvious methods of public exercises and examinations were totally unknown; and I have never heard that either the president or the society interfered in the private economy of the tutors and their pupils.

The silence of the Oxford professors, which deprives the youth of public instruction, is imperfectly supplied by the tutors, as they are styled, of the several colleges. Instead of confining themselves to a single science, which had satisfied the ambition of Burman or Bernouilli, they teach or promise to teach either history or mathematics, or ancient literature or moral philosophy; and as it is possible that they may be defective in all, it is highly probable that of some they will be ignorant. They are paid indeed by private contributions; but their appointment depends on the head of the house: their diligence is voluntary, and will consequently be languid, while the pupils themselves and their parents are not indulged in the liberty of choice or change. The first tutor into whose hands I was resigned, appears to have been one of the best of the tribe. Dr Waldegrave was a learned and pious man, of a mild disposition, strict morals and abstemious life, who seldom mingled in the politics or the jollity of the college. But his knowledge of the world was confined to the university; his learning was of the last, rather than the present age, his temper was indolent; his faculties, which were not of the first rate, had been relaxed by the climate; and he was satisfied, like his fellows, with the slight and superficial discharge of an important trust. As soon as my tutor had sounded the insufficiency of his disciple in school-learning he proposed that we should read every morning from ten to eleven the comedies of Terence. The sum of my improvement in the university of Oxford is confined to three or four Latin plays; and even the study of an elegant classic which might have been illustrated by a comparison of ancient and modern theatres was reduced to a dry and literal interpretation of the author's text. During the first weeks I constantly attended these lessons in my tutor's room; but as they appeared equally devoid of profit and pleasure, I was once tempted to try the experiment of a formal apology. The apology was accepted with a smile: I repeated the offence with less ceremony, the excuse was admitted with the same indulgence; the slightest motive of laziness or indisposition, the most trifling avocation at home or abroad was allowed as a worthy impediment, nor did my tutor appear conscious of my absence or neglect. Had the hour of lecture been constantly filled, a single hour was a small portion of my academic leisure. No plan of study was recommended for my use; no exercises were prescribed for his inspection; and at the most precious season of youth whole days and weeks were suffered to elapse without labour or amusement, without advice or account. I should have listened to the voice of reason and of my tutor: his mild behaviour had gained my confidence; I preferred his society to that of the younger students; and in our evening walks to the top of Headington Hill we freely conversed on a variety of subjects.

Since the days of Pocock and Hyde, Oriental learning has always been the pride of Oxford, and I once expressed an inclination to study Arabic. His prudence discouraged this childish fancy: but he neglected the fair occasion of directing the ardour of a curious mind. During my absence in the summer vacation, Dr Waldegrave accepted a college living at Washington in Sussex, and on my return I no longer found him at Oxford. From that time I have lost sight of my first tutor; but at the end of thirty years (1781) he was still alive; and the practice of exercise and temperance had entitled him to a healthy old age.

The long recess between the Trinity and Michaelmas terms empties the colleges of Oxford as well as the courts of Westminster. I spent at my father's house at Buriton in Hampshire the two months of August and September, which, in the year 1752, were curtailed, to my great surprise, of eleven days, by the alteration of the style.[9] It is whimsical enough that as soon as I left Magdalen College my taste for books began to revive, but it was the same blind and boyish taste for the pursuit of exotic history. Unprovided with original learning, unformed in the habits of thinking, unskilled in the arts of composition, I resolved – to write a book. The title of this first Essay, *The Age of Sesostris*, was perhaps suggested by Voltaire's *Age of Louis XIV* which was new and popular, but my sole object was to investigate the probable date of the life and reign of the Conqueror of Asia. I was then enamoured of Sir John Marsham's *Canon Chronicus*, an elaborate work of whose merits and defects I was not yet qualified to judge. According to his specious, though narrow plan, I settled my hero about the time of Solomon, in the tenth century before the Christian era. It was therefore incumbent on me, unless I would adopt Sir Isaac Newton's shorter chronology,[10] to remove a formidable objection; and my solution, for a youth of fifteen, is not devoid of ingenuity. In his version of the sacred books, Manetho the high priest has identified Sethosis or Sesostris with the elder brother of Danaus who landed in Greece, according to the Parian marble, fifteen hundred and ten years before Christ. But in my supposition, the high priest is guilty of a voluntary error; flattery is the prolific parent of falsehood, and falsehood, I will now add, is not incompatible with the sacerdotal character. Manetho's history of Egypt is dedicated to Ptolemy Philadelphus, who derived a fabulous or illegitimate pedigree from the Macedonian kings of the race of Hercules: Danaus is the ancestor of Hercules; and after the failure of the elder branch, his descendants the Ptolemies are the sole representatives of the royal family, and may claim by inheritance the kingdom which they hold by conquest. Such were my juvenile discoveries; at a riper age I no longer presume to connect the Greek, the Jewish and the Egyptian antiquities which are lost in a distant cloud; nor is this the only instance, in which the belief and knowledge of the child are superseded by the more rational ignorance of the man. During my stay at Buriton my infant labour was diligently prosecuted without much interruption from company or country diversions, and I already heard the music of public applause. The discovery of my own weakness was the first symptom of taste. On my return to Oxford, *The Age of Sesostris* was wisely relinquished; but the imperfect sheets remained twenty years at the bottom of a drawer, till in a general clearance of papers (November 1772) they were committed to the flames.

After the departure of Dr Waldegrave, I was transferred with the rest of his livestock to a senior fellow, whose literary and moral character did not command the respect of the college. Dr Winchester well remembered that he had a salary to receive, and only forgot that he had a duty to perform. Instead of guiding the studies and watching over the behaviour of his disciple, I was never summoned to attend even the ceremony of a lecture; and except one voluntary visit to his rooms, during the eight months of his titular office, the tutor and pupil lived in the same college as strangers to each other. The want of experience, of advice and of occupation soon betrayed me into some improprieties of conduct, ill-chosen company, late hours and inconsiderate expense. My growing debts might be secret; but my frequent absence was visible and scandalous; and a tour to Bath, a visit into Buckinghamshire, and four excursions to London in the same winter, were costly and dangerous frolics. They were indeed without a meaning, as without an excuse. The irksomeness of a cloistered life repeatedly tempted me to wander; but my chief pleasure was that of travelling, and I was too young and bashful to enjoy like a manly Oxonian in town, the taverns and bagnios of Covent Garden. In all these excursions I eloped from Oxford; I returned to college; in a few days I eloped again, as if I had been an independent stranger in a hired lodging, without once hearing the voice of admonition, without once feeling the hand of control. Yet my time was lost, my expenses were multiplied, my behaviour abroad was unknown; folly as well as vice should have awakened the attention of my superiors, and my tender years would have justified a more than ordinary degree of restraint and discipline.

It might at least be expected that an ecclesiastical school should inculcate the orthodox principles of religion. But our venerable mother had contrived to unite the opposite extremes of bigotry and indifference: an heretic or unbeliever was a monster in her eyes; but she was always, or often, or sometimes, remiss in the spiritual education of her own children. According to the statutes of the university, every student, before he is matriculated, must subscribe his assent to the thirty-nine articles of the Church of England, which are signed by more than read, and read by more than believe them. My insufficient age excused me however from the immediate performance of this legal ceremony; and the Vice-Chancellor directed me to return, so soon as I should have accomplished my fifteenth year, recommending me in the meanwhile to the instruction of my college. My college forgot to instruct; I forgot to return, and was myself forgotten by the first magistrate of the university. Without a single lecture, either public or private, either Christian or protestant, without any academical subscription, without any episcopal confirmation, I was left, by the dim light of my catechism, to grope my way to the chapel and communion-table, where I was admitted, without a question how far, or by what means, I might be qualified to receive the sacrament. Such almost incredible neglect was productive of the worst mischiefs. From my childhood I had been fond of religious disputation: my poor aunt has been often puzzled by my objections to the mysteries which she strove to believe; nor had the elastic spring been totally broken by the weight of the atmosphere of Oxford. The blind activity of idleness urged me to advance without armour into the dangerous mazes of controversy, and at the age of sixteen I bewildered myself in the errors of the Church of Rome.

The progress of my conversion may tend to illustrate, at least, the history of my own mind. It was not long since Dr Middleton's *Free Enquiry* had sounded an alarm in the theological world: much ink and much gall had been spilt in the defence of the primitive miracles; and the two dullest of their champions[11] were crowned with academic honours by the university of Oxford. The name of Middleton was unpopular; and his proscription very naturally tempted me to peruse his writings and those of his antagonists. His bold criticism, which approaches the precipice of infidelity, produced on my mind a singular effect; and had I persevered in the communion of Rome I should now apply to my own fortune the prediction of the Sibyl,

Via prima salutis
Quod minimum reris, Graia pandetur ab urbe.[12]

The elegance of style and freedom of argument were repelled by a shield
of prejudice. I still revered the characters, or rather the names of the saints
and fathers whom Dr Middleton exposes, nor could he destroy my implicit
belief that the gift of miraculous powers was continued in the Church
during the first four or five centuries of Christianity. But I was unable
to resist the weight of historical evidence, that within the same period,
most of the leading doctrines of popery were already introduced in theory
and practice: nor was my conclusion absurd, that miracles are the test
of truth, and that the Church must be orthodox and pure, which was
so often approved by the visible interposition of the Deity. The marvellous
tales, which are so boldly attested by the Basils and Chrysostoms, the
Austins and Jeroms, compelled me to embrace the superior merits of
celibacy, the institution of the monastic life, the use of the sign of the
Cross, of holy oil, and even of images, the invocation of saints, the worship
of relics, the rudiments of purgatory in prayers for the dead, and the
tremendous mystery of the sacrifice of the body and blood of Christ, which
insensibly swelled into the prodigy of Transubstantiation.

In these dispositions, and already more than half a convert, I formed
an unlucky intimacy with a young gentleman of our college whose name
I shall spare. With a character less resolute Mr —[13] had imbibed the same
religious opinions, and some popish books, I know not through what
channel, were conveyed into his possession. I read, I applauded, I believed:
the English translations of two famous works of Bossuet, Bishop of Meaux,
the *Exposition of the Catholic Doctrine*, and the *History of the Protestant
Variations*, achieved my conversion, and I surely fell by a noble hand.
I have since examined the originals with a more discerning eye, and shall
not hesitate to pronounce that Bossuet is indeed a master of all weapons
of controversy. In the *Exposition*, a specious apology, the orator assumes,
with consummate art, the tone of candour and simplicity: and the ten-
horned Monster[14] is transformed, at his magic touch, into the milk-white
hind, who must be loved as soon as she is seen.[15] In the *History*, a bold
and well-aimed attack, he displays with a happy mixture of narrative
and argument, the faults and follies, the changes and contradictions of
our first reformers; whose variations (as he dexterously contends) are the
mark of heretical error, while the perpetual unity of the Catholic Church
is the sign and test of infallible truth. To my actual feelings it seems
incredible that I could ever believe that I believed in Transubstantiation!

But my conqueror oppressed me with the sacramental words *Hoc est corpus meum*, and dashed against each other the figurative half-meanings of the Protestant sects: every objection was resolved into omnipotence; and after repeating at St Mary's the Athanasian creed, I humbly acquiesced in the mystery of the real presence.

> To take up half on trust, and half to try,
> Name it not faith, but bungling bigotry,
> Both knave and fool the merchant we may call,
> To pay great sums and to compound the small,
> For who would break with Heaven, and would not
>   break for all?[16]

No sooner had I settled my new religion than I resolved to profess myself a Catholic. Youth is sincere and impetuous; and a momentary glow of enthusiasm had raised me above all temporal considerations.

By the keen protestants, who would gladly retaliate the example of persecution, a clamour is raised of the increase of popery: and they are always loud to declaim against the toleration of priests and Jesuits who pervert so many of His Majesty's subjects from their religion and allegiance. On the present occasion the fall of one, or more, of her sons, directed this clamour against the university: and it was confidently affirmed that popish missionaries were suffered, under various disguises, to introduce themselves into the colleges of Oxford. But the love of truth and justice enjoins me to declare that as far as relates to myself, this assertion is false, and that I never conversed with a priest or even with a papist, till my resolution from books was absolutely fixed. In my last excursion to London, I addressed myself to a Roman Catholic bookseller in Russell Street, Covent Garden, who recommended me to a priest of whose name and order I am at present ignorant.[17] In our first interview he soon discovered that persuasion was needless; after sounding the motives and merits of my conversion, he consented to admit me into the pale of the Church: and at his feet on the eighth of June, 1753, I solemnly, though privately abjured the errors of heresy. The seduction of an English youth of family and fortune was an act of as much danger as glory; but he bravely overlooked the danger of which I was not then sufficiently informed. 'Where a person is reconciled to the See of Rome, or procures others to be reconciled, the offence (says Blackstone[18]) amounts to high treason.' And if the humanity of the age would prevent the execution of this sanguinary statute, there were other laws, of a less odious cast, which condemned the priest to perpetual imprisonment, and transferred the proselyte's estate to his nearest relation.

An elaborate controversial epistle, approved by my director and addressed to my father, announced and justified the step which I had taken. My father was neither a bigot nor a philosopher; but his affection deplored the loss of an only son; and his good sense was astonished at my strange departure from the religion of my country. In the first sally of passion he divulged a secret, which prudence might have suppressed; and the gates of Magdalen College were for ever shut against my return. Many years afterwards, when the name of Gibbon was become as notorious as that of Middleton, it was industriously whispered at Oxford that the historian had formerly 'turned papist':[19] my character stood exposed to the reproach of inconstancy; and this invidious topic would have been handled without mercy by my opponents, could they have separated my cause from that of the University. For my own part I am proud of an honest sacrifice of interest to conscience; I can never blush if my tender mind was entangled in the sophistry that seduced the acute and manly understandings of CHILLINGWORTH and BAYLE, who afterwards emerged from superstition to scepticism.

While Charles the First governed England, and was himself governed by a Catholic queen, it cannot be denied that the missionaries of Rome laboured with impunity and success in the Court, the country, and even the universities. One of his sheep,

> Whom the grim wolf, with privy paw
> Daily devours apace, and nothing said,[20]

is Mr William Chillingworth, Master of Arts, and fellow of Trinity College, who, at the ripe age of twenty-eight years, was persuaded to elope from Oxford to the English seminary of Douay in Flanders. Some disputes with Fisher, a subtle Jesuit, might first awaken him from the prejudices of education, but he yielded to his own victorious argument 'That there must be somewhere an infallible judge, and that the Church of Rome is the only Christian society, which either does or can pretend to that character.' After a short trial of a few months Mr Chillingworth was again tormented by religious scruples; he returned home, resumed his studies, unravelled his mistakes, and delivered his mind from the yoke of authority and superstition. His new creed was built on the principle that the Bible is our sole judge, and private reason our sole interpreter: and he ably maintains this principle in the *Religion of a Protestant*, a book (1634) which, after startling the doctors of Oxford, is still esteemed the most solid defence of the Reformation. The learning, the virtue, the recent merits of the author entitled him to fair preferment, but the slave had now broken his fetters, and the more he weighed, the less was he disposed to subscribe the thirty-nine articles of the Church of England. In a private letter he declares, with all the energy of language, that he could not subscribe them, without subscribing his own damnation, and that if ever he should depart from this immoveable resolution, he would allow his friends to think him a madman or an atheist. As the letter is without a date, we cannot ascertain the number of weeks or months that elapsed between this passionate abhorrence, and the Salisbury Register which is still extant. '*Ego Gulielmus Chillingworth ... omnibus hisce articulis et singulis in iisdem contentis, volens et ex animo subscribo, et consensum meum iisdem praebeo. 20 die Julii 1638.*'[21] But alas! the chancellor and prebendary of Sarum soon deviated from his own subscription; as he more deeply scrutinized the article of the Trinity, neither Scripture nor the primitive fathers could long uphold his orthodox belief, 'and he could not but confess, that the doctrine of Arius is either a truth, or at least no damnable heresy'. From this middle region of the air, the descent of his reason would naturally rest on the firmer ground of the Socinians: and if we may credit a doubtful story and the popular opinion, his anxious enquiries at last subsided in philosophic indifference. So conspicuous however were the candour of his nature and the innocence of his heart, that this apparent levity did not affect the reputation of Chillingworth. His frequent changes proceeded from too nice an inquisition into truth. His doubts grew out of himself, he assisted them with all the strength of his reason: he was then too hard for himself; but finding as little quiet and repose in those victories, he quickly recovered by a new appeal to his own judgement; so that in all his sallies and retreats, he was, in fact, his own convert.

Bayle was the son of a Calvinist minister in a remote province of France at the foot of the Pyrenees.[22] For the benefit of education, the Protestants were tempted to risk their children in the Catholic universities; and in the twenty-second year of his age young Bayle was seduced by the arts and arguments of the Jesuits of Toulouse. He remained about seventeen months (19th March 1669 – 19th August 1670) in their hands, a voluntary captive; and a letter to his parents, which the new convert composed or subscribed (15th April 1670) is darkly tinged with the spirit of popery. But Nature had designed him to think as he pleased and to speak as he thought: his piety was offended by the excessive worship of creatures; and the study of physics convinced him of the impossibility of Transubstantiation, which is abundantly refuted by the testimony of our senses. His return to the communion of a falling sect was a bold and disinterested step that exposed him to the rigour of the laws, and a speedy flight to Geneva protected him from the resentment of his spiritual tyrants, unconscious as they were of the full value of the prize which they had lost. Had Bayle adhered to the Catholic Church, had he embraced the ecclesiastical profession, the genius and favour of such a proselyte might have aspired to wealth and honours in his native country; but the hypocrite would have found less happiness in the comforts of a benefice or the dignity of a mitre than he enjoyed at Rotterdam, in a private state of exile, indigence and freedom. Without a country, or a patron or a prejudice, he claimed the liberty and subsisted by the labours of his pen: the inequality of his voluminous works is explained and excused by his alternately writing for himself, for the booksellers, and for posterity; and if a severe critic would reduce him to a single folio, that relic, like the books of the Sibyl, would become still more valuable.

A calm and lofty spectator of the religious tempest, the philosopher of Rotterdam condemned with equal firmness the persecution of Louis XIV and the republican maxims of the Calvinists, their vain prophecies, and the intolerant bigotry which sometimes vexed his solitary retreat. In reviewing the controversies of the times, he turned against each other the arguments of the disputants: successively wielding the arms of the Catholics and Protestants, he proves that neither the way of authority, nor the way of examination can afford the multitude any test of religious truth; and dexterously concludes that custom and education must be the sole grounds of popular belief. The ancient paradox of Plutarch, that atheism is less pernicious than superstition,[23] acquires a tenfold vigour when it is adorned with the colours of his wit, and pointed with the acuteness of his logic. His critical Dictionary is a vast repository of facts and opinions; and he balances the *false* religions in his sceptical scales, till the opposite quantities (if I may use the language of algebra) annihilate each other. The wonderful power, which he so boldly exercised, of assembling doubts and objections had tempted him jocosely to assume the title of the νεφεληγερέτα Ζεύς, the cloud-compelling Jove; and in a conversation with the ingenious Abbé (afterwards Cardinal) de Polignac, he freely disclosed his universal Pyrrhonism. 'I am most truly [said Bayle] a protestant; for I protest indifferently against all systems, and all sects.'[24]

The academical resentment which I may possibly have provoked will prudently spare this plain narrative of my studies, or rather of my idleness, and of the unfortunate event which shortened the term of my residence at Oxford. But it may be suggested that my father was unlucky in the choice of a society, and the chance of a tutor. It will perhaps be asserted that in the lapse of forty years many improvements have taken place in the college and the university. I am not unwilling to believe that some tutors might have been found more active than Dr Waldegrave, and less contemptible than Dr Winchester. About the same time and in the same walk, a Bentham was still treading in the footsteps of a Burton, whose maxims he had adopted and whose life he has published. The biographer indeed preferred the school-logic to the new philosophy, Burgersdicius to Locke; and the hero appears in his own writings a stiff and conceited pedant. Yet even these men, according to the measure of their capacity, might be diligent and useful; and it is recorded of Burton that he taught his pupils what he knew, some Latin, some Greek, some ethics and metaphysics, referring them to proper masters for the languages and sciences of which he was ignorant. At a more recent period, many students have been attracted by the merit and reputation of Sir William Scott, then a tutor in University College, and now conspicuous in the profession of the Civil law. My personal acquaintance with that gentleman has inspired me with a just esteem for his abilities and knowledge; and I am assured that his lectures on history would compose, were they given to the public, a most valuable treatise. Under the auspices of the present Archbishop of York, Dr Markham, himself an eminent scholar, a more regular discipline has been introduced, as I am told, at Christ Church: a course of classical and philosophical studies is proposed and even pursued in that numerous seminary: learning has been made a duty, a pleasure and even a fashion; and several young gentlemen do honour to the college in which they have been educated. According to the will of the donor the profit of the second part of Lord Clarendon's History has been applied to the establishment of a riding school, that the polite exercises might be taught, I know not with what success, in the University.[25] The Vinerian professorship is of far more serious importance; the laws of his country are the first science of an Englishman of rank and fortune, who is called to be a magistrate, and may hope to be a legislator. This judicious institution was coldly entertained by the graver doctors, who complained, I have heard the complaint, that it would take the young people from their books; but Mr Viner's benefaction is not unprofitable, since it has at least produced the excellent commentaries of Sir William Blackstone.

The manners and opinions of our universities must follow at a distance the progressive motion of the age; and some prejudices, which reason could not subdue, have been slowly obliterated by time. The last generation of Jacobites is extinct; 'the right Divine of Kings to govern wrong' is now exploded even at Oxford; and the remains of Tory principles are rather salutary than hurtful, at a time when the constitution has nothing to fear from the prerogative of the Crown, and can only be injured by popular innovation. But the inveterate evils which are derived from their birth and character must still cleave to our ecclesiastical corporations; the fashion of the present day is not propitious, in England, to discipline and economy; and even the exceptionable mode of foreign education has been lately preferred by the highest and most respectable authority in the kingdom.[26] I shall only add that Cambridge appears to have been less deeply infected than her sister with the vices of the cloister: her loyalty to the house of Hanover is of a more early date; and the name and philosophy of her immortal Newton were first honoured in his native academy.

Chapter IV[1]

Lausanne
(1753–8)

No sooner was my reason subdued than I resolved to approve my faith
by my works and to enter without delay into the pale of the Church of
Rome ... In the sacrifice of this world to the next, I might affect the glory
of a confessor: but I must freely acknowledge that the sincere change
of my speculative opinions was not inflamed by any lively sense of
devotion or enthusiasm; and that in the giddiness of my age I had not
seriously weighed the temporal consequences of this rash step. The intelligence which I imparted to my father in an elaborate controversial epistle
struck him with astonishment and grief: he was neither a bigot nor a
philosopher; but his affection deplored the loss of an only son, and his
good sense could not understand or excuse my strange departure from
the religion of my country. After carrying me to Putney to the house of
his friend Mr Mallet, by whose philosophy I was rather scandalized than
reclaimed, it was necessary to form a new plan of education, and to devise
some method, which if possible might effect the cure of my spiritual
malady. The gates of Oxford were shut against my return; in every part
of England I might be accessible to the seductions of my new friends,
and after much debate it was determined from the advice and personal
experience of Mr Eliot (now Lord Eliot) to fix me during some years at
Lausanne in Switzerland. M. Frey, a Swiss gentleman of Basil, undertook
the conduct of the journey; we left London the 19th of June, crossed the
sea from Dover to Calais, travelled post through several provinces of
France by the direct road of St Quentin, Rheims, Langres and Besançon,
and arrived the 30th of June at Lausanne, where I was immediately settled
under the roof and tuition of M. Pavilliard, a Calvinist minister.

The first marks of my father's displeasure rather astonished than
afflicted me: when he threatened to banish and disown and disinherit
a rebellious son, I cherished a secret hope that he would not be able or
willing to effect his menaces, and the pride of conscience encouraged me

to sustain the honourable and important part which I was now acting. My spirits were raised and kept alive by the rapid motion of the journey, the new and various scenes of the continent, and the civility of M. Frey, a man of sense who was not ignorant of books or the world. But after he had resigned me into Pavilliard's hands and I was fixed in my new habitation, I had leisure to contemplate the strange and melancholy prospect. My first complaint arose from my ignorance of the language. In my childhood I had once studied the French grammar, and I could imperfectly understand the easy prose of a familiar subject. But when I was thus suddenly cast on a foreign land I found myself deprived of the use of speech and of hearing; and during some weeks, incapable not only of enjoying the pleasures of conversation, but even of asking or answering a question in the common intercourse of life. To a homebred Englishman every object, every custom was offensive, but the native of any country might have been disgusted with the general aspect of his lodging and entertainment. The minister's wife, Madame Pavilliard, governed our domestic economy: I now speak of her without resentment, but in sober truth she was ugly, dirty, proud, ill-tempered and covetous. Our hours, of twelve for dinner, of seven for supper were arbitrary, though inconvenient customs; the appetite of a young man might have over-looked the badness of the materials and cookery, but his appetite was far from being satisfied with the scantiness of our daily meals, and more than one sense was offended by the appearance of the table, which during eight successive days was regularly covered with the same linen. I had now exchanged my elegant apartment in Magdalen College for a narrow, gloomy street, the most unfrequented of an unhandsome town; for an old inconvenient house, and for a small chamber ill-contrived and ill-furnished, which on the approach of winter, instead of a companionable fire must be warmed by the dull invisible heat of a stove. From a man I was again degraded to the dependence of a school-boy: M. Pavilliard managed my expenses which had been reduced to a diminutive scale: I received a small monthly allowance for my pocket money; and helpless and awkward as I have ever been, I no longer enjoyed the indispensable comfort of a servant. My condition seemed as destitute of hope as it was devoid of pleasure. I was separated for an indefinite, which appeared an infinite term from my native country; and I had lost all connection with my Catholic friends. I have since reflected with surprise, that as the Romish clergy of every part of Europe maintain a close correspondence with each other, they never attempted, by letters or messages, to rescue me from the hands of the heretics, or at least to confirm my zeal and constancy in the profession of the faith.[2] Such was my first introduction to Lausanne, a place where I spent near five years with pleasure and profit, which I afterwards revisited without compulsion, and which I have finally selected as the most grateful retreat for the decline of my life.

But it is the peculiar felicity of youth that the most unpleasing objects and events seldom make a deep or lasting impression. At the flexible age of sixteen I soon learned to endure and gradually to adopt the new forms of arbitrary manners: the real hardships of my situation, the house, the table and the mistress were alleviated by time; and to this coarse and scanty fare I am perhaps indebted for the establishment of my constitution. Had I been sent abroad in a more splendid style, such as the fortune and bounty of my father might have supplied, I might have returned home with the same stock of language and science as our countrymen usually import from the continent. An exile and a prisoner as I was, their example betrayed me into some irregularities of wine, of play and of idle excursions;[3] but I soon felt the impossibility of associating with them on equal terms, and after the departure of my first acquaintance I held a cold and civil correspondence with their successors. This seclusion from English society was attended with the most solid benefits. In the Pays de Vaud the French language is used with less imperfection than in most of the distant provinces of France; in Pavilliard's family, necessity compelled me to listen and to speak; and if I was at first disheartened by the apparent slowness, in a few months I was astonished by the rapidity of my progress. My pronunciation was formed by the constant repetition of the same sounds; the variety of words and idioms, the rules of grammar and distinctions of genders were impressed in my memory; ease and freedom were obtained by practice, correctness and elegance by labour; and before I was recalled home, French, in which I spontaneously thought, was more familiar than English to my ear, my tongue and my pen.

The first effect of this opening knowledge was the revival of my love of reading, which had been chilled at Oxford, and I soon turned over without much choice almost all the French books in my tutor's library. Even these amusements were productive of real advantage: my taste and judgement were now somewhat riper; I was introduced to a new mode of style and literature; by the comparison of manners and opinions my views were enlarged, my prejudices were corrected, and a copious voluntary abstract of the *Histoire de l'Eglise et de l'Empire* by le Sueur may be placed in a middle line between my childish and my manly studies. As soon as I was able to converse with the natives, I began to feel some satisfaction in their company; my awkward timidity was polished and emboldened, and I frequented for the first time assemblies of men and women. The acquaintance of the Pavilliards prepared me by degrees for more elegant society; I was received with kindness and indulgence in the best families of Lausanne, and it was in one of these that I formed an intimate lasting connection with M. Deyverdun, a young man of an amiable temper and excellent understanding. In the arts of fencing and dancing small indeed was my proficiency, and some expensive months were idly wasted in the riding-school. My unfitness to bodily exercise reconciled me to a sedentary life, and the horse, the favourite of my countrymen, never contributed to the pleasures of my youth.

My obligations to the lessons of M. Pavilliard, gratitude will not suffer me to forget: but truth compels me to own that my best preceptor was not himself eminent for genius or learning. Even the real measure of his talents was underrated in the public opinion: the soft credulity of his temper exposed him to frequent imposition; and his want of eloquence and memory in the pulpit disqualified him for the most popular duty of his office. But he was endowed with a clear head and a warm heart; his innate benevolence had assuaged the spirit of the Church; he was rational because he was moderate. In the course of his studies he had acquired a just though superficial knowledge of most branches of literature, by long practice he was skilled in the arts of teaching; and he laboured with assiduous patience to know the character, gain the affection, and open the mind of his English pupil. As soon as we began to understand each other, he gently led me into the path of instruction. I consented with pleasure that a portion of the morning hours should be consecrated to a plan of modern history and geography, and to the critical perusal of the French and Latin classics, and at each step I felt myself invigorated by the habits of application and method. The principles of philosophy were associated with the examples of taste, and by a singular chance the book as well as the man which contributed the most effectually to my education has a stronger claim on my gratitude than on my admiration. M. de Crousaz, the adversary of Bayle and Pope, is not distinguished by lively fancy or profound reflection, and even in his own country, at the end of a few years his name and writings are almost obliterated. But his philosophy had been formed in the school of Locke, his divinity in that of Limborch and Le Clerc; in a long and laborious life several generations of pupils were taught to think and even to write. His lessons rescued the Academy of Lausanne from Calvinistic prejudice, and he had the rare merit of diffusing a more liberal spirit among the clergy and people of the Pays de Vaud. His system of logic, which in the last editions has swelled to six tedious and prolix volumes, may be praised as a clear and methodical abridgement of the art of reasoning, from our simple ideas to the most complex operations of the human understanding. This system I studied, and meditated and abstracted, till I have obtained the free command of a universal instrument which I soon presumed to exercise on my Catholic opinions.

Pavilliard was not unmindful that his first task, his most important duty, was to reclaim me from the errors of popery: the intermixture of sects has rendered the Swiss clergy acute and learned on the topics of controversy; and I have some of his letters in which he celebrates the dexterity of his attack, and my gradual concessions after a firm and well-managed defence. I was willing and I am now willing to allow him a handsome share of the honour of my conversion; yet I must observe that it was principally effected by my private reflections, and I still remember my solitary transport at the discovery of a philosophical argument against the doctrine of Transubstantiation: that the text of Scripture which seems to inculcate the real presence is attested only by a single sense, our sight; while the real presence itself is disproved by three of our senses, the sight, the touch and the taste. The various articles of the Romish creed disappeared like a dream, and after a full conviction, on Christmas Day, 1754, I received the sacrament in the church of Lausanne. It was here that I suspended my religious enquiries, acquiescing with implicit belief in the tenets and mysteries which are adopted by the general consent of Catholics and Protestants.

Such from my arrival at Lausanne during the first eighteen or twenty months (July 1753–March 1755) were my useful studies, the foundation of all my future improvements. But in the life of every man of letters, there is an era, a level from whence he soars with his own wings to his proper height, and the most important part of his education is that which he bestows on himself. My worthy tutor had the good sense and modesty to discern how far he could be useful; as soon as he felt that I advanced beyond his speed and measure he wisely left me to my genius; and the hours of lesson were soon lost in the voluntary labour of the whole morning, and sometimes of the whole day. The desire of prolonging my time gradually confirmed the salutary habit of early rising to which I have always adhered with some regard to seasons and situations: but it is happy for my eyes and my health, that my temperate ardour has never been seduced to trespass on the hours of the night. During the last three years of my residence at Lausanne I may assume the merit of serious and solid application, but I am tempted to distinguish the last eight months of the year 1755 as the period of the most extraordinary diligence and rapid progress. In my French and Latin translations I adopted an excellent method, which from my own success I would recommend to the imitation of students. I chose some classic writer, such as Cicero and Vertot, the most approved for purity and elegance of style. I translated, for instance, an epistle of Cicero into French, and after throwing it aside till the words and phrases were obliterated from my memory, I re-translated my French into such Latin as I could find, and then compared each sentence of my imperfect version with the ease, the grace, the propriety of the Roman orator. A similar experiment was made on some pages of the *Revolutions* of Vertot; I turned them into Latin, returned them after a sufficient interval into my own French, and again scrutinized the resemblance or dissimilitude of the copy and the original. By degrees I was less ashamed, by degrees I was more satisfied with myself, and I persevered in the practice of these double translations, which filled several books, till I had acquired the knowledge of both idioms, and the command at least of a correct style.

This useful exercise of writing was accompanied and succeeded by the more pleasing occupation of reading the best authors. Dr Middleton's history, which I then appreciated above its true value, naturally directed me to the writings of Cicero. The most perfect editions, that of Olivet which may adorn the shelves of the rich, that of Ernesti which should lie on the table of the learned, were not in my power. For the familiar epistles I used the text and English commentary of Bishop Ross; but my general edition was that of Verburgius, published at Amsterdam in two large volumes in folio, with an indifferent choice of various notes. I read with application and pleasure *all* the epistles, *all* the orations, and the important treatises of rhetoric and philosophy, and as I read, I applauded the observation of Quintilian[4] that every student may judge of his own proficiency by the satisfaction which he receives from the Roman Orator. Cicero in Latin and Xenophon in Greek are indeed the two ancients whom I would first propose to a liberal scholar, not only for the merit of their style and sentiments, but for the admirable lessons which may be applied almost to every situation of public and private life. Cicero's epistles may in particular afford the models of every form of correspondence, from the careless effusions of tenderness and friendship to the well-guarded declaration of discreet and dignified resentment.

After finishing this great author, a library of eloquence and reason, I formed a more extensive plan of reviewing the Latin classics under the four divisions of 1, Historians; 2, Poets; 3, Orators; and 4, Philosophers, in a chronological series from the days of Plautus and Sallust to the decline of the language and empire of Rome: and this plan in the last twenty-seven months of my residence at Lausanne (January 1756–April 1758), I *nearly* accomplished. Nor was this review, however rapid, either hasty or superficial. I indulged myself in a second, and even a third perusal of Terence, Virgil, Horace, Tacitus etc., and studied to imbibe the sense and spirit most congenial to my own. I never suffered a difficult or corrupt passage to escape till I had viewed it in every light of which it was susceptible; though often disappointed, I always consulted the most learned of ingenious commentators, Torrentius and Dacier on Horace, Catrou and Servius on Virgil, Lipsius on Tacitus, Meziriac on Ovid, etc.; and in the ardour of my enquiries I embraced a large circle of historical and critical erudition. My abstracts of each book were made in the French language; my observations often branched into particular essays, and I can still read without contempt a dissertation of eight folio pages on eight lines (287–294) of the fourth Georgic of Virgil.[5] M. Deyverdun, my friend whose name will be frequently repeated, had joined with equal zeal though not with equal perseverance in the same undertaking. To him every thought, every composition was instantly communicated; with him I enjoyed the benefits of a free conversation on the topics of our common studies.

But it is scarcely possible for a mind endowed with any active curiosity to be long conversant with the Latin classics without aspiring to know the Greek originals whom they celebrate as their masters, and of whom they so warmly recommend the study and imitation.

Vos exemplaria Graeca
Nocturna versate manu, versate diurna.[6]

It was now that I regretted the early years which had been wasted in sickness or idleness, or more idle reading, that I condemned the perverse method of our schoolmasters who, by first teaching the mother language, might descend with so much ease and perspicuity to the origin and etymology of a derivative idiom. In the nineteenth year of my age I determined to supply this defect, and the lessons of Pavilliard again contributed to smooth the entrance of the way, the Greek alphabet, the grammar and the pronunciation according to the French accent. As he possessed only such a stock as was requisite for an ecclesiastic, our first book was St John's Gospel, and we should probably have construed the whole of the New Testament had I not represented the absurdity of adhering to the corrupt dialect of the Hellenist Jews. At my earnest request we presumed to open the Iliad; and I had the pleasure of beholding, though darkly and through a glass,[7] the true image of Homer, whom I had long since admired in an English dress. After my tutor, conscious of his inability, had left me to myself I worked my way through about half the Iliad, and afterwards interpreted alone a large portion of Xenophon and Herodotus. But my ardour, destitute of aid and emulation, was gradually cooled, and from the barren task of searching words in a lexicon, I withdrew to the free and familiar conversation of Virgil and Tacitus. Yet in my residence at Lausanne I had laid a solid foundation, which enabled me in a more propitious season to prosecute the study of Grecian literature.

From a blind idea of the usefulness of such abstract science, my father had been desirous and even pressing that I should devote some time to the mathematics, nor could I refuse to comply with so reasonable a wish. During two winters I attended the private lectures of M. de Traytorrens, who explained the elements of algebra and geometry as far as the conic sections of the Marquis de l'Hôpital, and appeared satisfied with my diligence and improvement. But as my childish propensity for numbers and calculations was totally extinct, I was content to receive the passive impression of my professor's lectures, without any active exercise of my own powers. As soon as I understood the principles, I relinquished for ever the pursuit of the mathematics; nor can I lament that I desisted before my mind was hardened by the habit of rigid demonstration so destructive of the finer feelings of moral evidence which must however determine the actions and opinions of our lives.

I listened with more pleasure to the proposal of studying the law of nature and nations, which was taught in the Academy of Lausanne by M. Vicat, a professor of some learning and reputation. But instead of attending his public or private course, I preferred in my closet the lessons of his masters and my own reason. Without being disgusted by the pedantry of Grotius or the prolixity of Pufendorf, I studied in their writings the duties of a man, the rights of a citizen, the theory of justice (it is alas! a theory) and the laws of peace and war which have had some influence on the practice of modern Europe. My fatigues were alleviated by the good sense of their commentator Barbeyrac. Locke's *Treatise of Government* instructed me in the knowledge of Whig principles, which are rather founded in reason than experience; but my delight was in the frequent perusal of Montesquieu, whose energy of style and boldness of hypothesis were powerful to awaken and stimulate the genius of the age. The logic of de Crousaz had prepared me to engage with his master Locke and his antagonist Bayle, of whom the former may be used as a bridle and the latter as a spur to the curiosity of a young philosopher. According to the nature of their respective works, the schools of argument and objection, I carefully went through the *Essay on Human Understanding*, and occasionally consulted the most interesting articles of the *Philosophic Dictionary*.[8] In the infancy of my reason I turned over as an idle amusement the most serious and important treatises; in its maturity the most trifling performance could exercise my taste or judgement; and more than once I have been led by a novel into a deep and instructive train of thinking.

But I cannot forbear to mention three particular books, since they may have remotely contributed to form the historian of the Roman Empire. 1. From the *Provincial Letters* of Pascal, which almost every year I have perused with new pleasure, I learned to manage the weapon of grave and temperate irony even on subjects of ecclesiastical solemnity. 2. *The Life of Julian* by the Abbé de la Blèterie, first introduced me to the man and the times; and I should be glad to recover my first essay on the truth of the miracle which stopped the rebuilding of the temple of Jerusalem. 3. In Giannone's *Civil History of Naples*, I observed with a critical eye the progress and abuse of sacerdotal power, and the revolutions of Italy in the darker ages. This various reading, which I now conducted with skill and discretion, was digested according to the precept and model of Mr Locke into a large commonplace book, a practice however which I do not strenuously recommend. The action of the pen will doubtless imprint an idea on the mind as well as on the paper: but I much question whether the benefits of this laborious method are adequate to the waste of time; and I must agree with Dr Johnson (*Idler* No. 74) 'that what is twice read is commonly better remembered than what is transcribed'.

During two years, if I forget some boyish excursions of a day or a week, I was fixed at Lausanne; but at the end of the third summer, my father consented that I should make the tour of Switzerland with Pavilliard, and our short absence of one month (September 21–October 20 1755) was a reward and relaxation of my assiduous studies. The fashion of climbing the mountains, and viewing the *glaciers* had not yet been introduced by foreign travellers who seek the sublime beauties of nature. But the political face of the country is not less diversified by the forms and spirit of so many various republics, from the jealous government of the *few* to the licentious freedom of the *many*. I contemplated with pleasure the new prospects of men and manners; though my conversation with the natives would have been more free and instructive had I possessed the German as well as the French language. We passed through most of the principal towns of Switzerland, Neufchâtel, Bienne, Soleurre, Arau, Baden, Zurich, Basil and Bern: in every place we visited the churches, arsenals, libraries and all the most eminent persons; and after my return,

I digested my notes in fourteen or fifteen sheets of a French journal,[9] which I dispatched to my father as a proof that my time and his money had not been misspent. Had I found this journal among his papers, I might be tempted to select some passages, but I will not transcribe the printed accounts; and it may be sufficient to notice a remarkable spot, which left a deep and lasting impression on my memory. From Zurich we proceeded on a pilgrimage not of devotion but of curiosity to the Benedictine Abbey of Einsidlen, more commonly styled Our Lady of the Hermits. I was astonished by the profuse ostentation of riches in the poorest corner of Europe: amidst a savage scene of woods and mountains, a palace appears to have been erected by magic; and it *was* erected by the potent magic of religion. A crowd of palmers and votaries was prostrate before the altar; the title and worship of the Mother of God provoked my indignation; and the lively naked image of superstition suggested to me, as in the same place it had done to Zuinglius, the most pressing argument for the reformation of the Church. About two years after this tour, I passed at Geneva a useful and agreeable month, but this excursion and some short visits in the Pays de Vaud did not materially interrupt my studious and sedentary life at Lausanne.

My thirst of improvement and the languid state of science[10] at Lausanne soon prompted me to solicit a literary correspondence with several men of learning whom I had not an opportunity of personally consulting:

1. In the perusal of Livy (xxx, 44) I had been stopped by a sentence in a speech of Hannibal, which cannot be reconciled by any torture with his character or argument. The commentators dissemble or confess their perplexity: it occurred to me that the change of a single letter, by substituting *Otio* instead of *Odio*, might restore a clear and consistent sense;[11] but I wished to weigh my emendation in scales less partial than my own. I addressed myself to M. Crévier, the successor of Rollin and a Professor in the University of Paris, who had published a large and valuable edition of Livy. His answer was speedy and polite; he praised my ingenuity and adopted my conjecture, which I must still applaud as easy and happy.

2. I maintained a Latin correspondence, at first anonymous and afterwards in my own name, with Professor Breitinger of Zurich, the learned editor of a Septuagint Bible. In our frequent letters we discussed many questions of antiquity, many passages of the Latin Classics. I proposed my interpretations and amendments; his censures, for he did not spare my boldness of conjecture, were sharp and strong; and I was encouraged by the consciousness of my strength, when I could stand in free debate against a critic of such eminence and erudition.

3. I corresponded on similar topics with the celebrated Professor Matthew Gesner of the University of Göttingen, and he accepted as courteously as the two former, the invitation of an unknown youth. But his abilities might possibly be decayed; his elaborate letters were feeble and prolix; and when I asked his proper direction, the vain old man covered half a sheet of paper with the foolish enumeration of his titles and offices.

4. These professors of Paris, Zurich and Göttingen were strangers whom I presumed to address on the credit of their name, but M. Allamand, minister at Bex, was my personal friend, with whom I maintained a more free and interesting correspondence. He was a master of language, of science, and above all of dispute; and his acute and flexible logic could support with equal address and perhaps with equal indifference the adverse sides of every possible question. His spirit was active but his pen had been indolent. M. Allamand had exposed himself to much scandal and reproach by an anonymous letter (1745) to the protestants of France, in which he labours to persuade them that *public* worship is the exclusive right and duty of the State, and that their numerous assemblies of dissenters and rebels are not authorized by the law or the Gospel. His style is animated, his arguments are specious; and if the papist may seem to lurk under the mask of a protestant, the philosopher is concealed under the disguise of a papist. After some trials in France and Holland which were defeated by his fortune or his character, a genius that might have enlightened or deluded the world was buried in a country living, unknown to fame and discontented with mankind. *Est sacrificulus in pago et rusticos decipit.*[12] As often as private or ecclesiastical business called him to Lausanne I enjoyed the pleasure and benefit of his conversation, and we were mutually flattered by our attention to each other. Our correspondence in his absence chiefly turned on Locke's metaphysics which he attacked and I defended, the origin of ideas, the principles of evidence, and the doctrine of liberty.

And found no end, in wandering mazes lost.[13]

By fencing with so skilful a master, I acquired some dexterity in the use of my philosophic weapons, but I was still the slave of education and prejudice; he had some measures to keep; and I much suspect that he never showed me the true colours of his secret scepticism.

Before I was recalled from Switzerland I had the satisfaction of seeing the most extraordinary man of the age, a poet, a historian, a philosopher, who has filled thirty quartos of prose and verse with his various productions, often excellent and always entertaining: need I add the name of Voltaire? After forfeiting by his own misconduct the friendship of the first of kings,[14] he retired at the age of sixty with a plentiful fortune to a free and beautiful country, and resided two winters (1757 and 1758) in the town or neighbourhood of Lausanne. My desire of beholding Voltaire, whom I then rated above his real magnitude, was easily gratified. He received me with civility as an English youth; but I cannot boast of any peculiar notice or distinction: *Virgilium vidi tantum*.[15] The ode which he composed on his first arrival on the banks of the Leman Lake:

O Maison d'Aristippe! O Jardin d'Epicure! etc.[16]

had been imparted as a secret to the gentleman by whom I was introduced. He allowed me to read it twice; I knew it by heart; and as my discretion was not equal to my memory, the author was soon displeased by the circulation of a copy. In writing this trivial anecdote I wished to observe whether my memory was impaired, and I have the comfort of finding that every line of the poem is still engraved in fresh and indelible characters.

The highest gratification which I derived from Voltaire's residence at Lausanne was the uncommon circumstance of hearing a great poet declaim his own productions on the stage. He had formed a troop of gentlemen and ladies, some of whom were not destitute of talents; a decent theatre was framed at Monrepos, a country house at the end of a suburb; dresses and scenes were provided at the expense of the actors; and the author directed the rehearsals with the zeal and attention of paternal love. In two successive winters his tragedies of *Zaïre*, *Alzire*, *Zulime*, and his sentimental comedy of the *Enfant prodigue* were played at the Theatre of Monrepos, but it was not without much reluctance and ill-humour that the envious bard allowed the representation of the *Iphigénie* of Racine. The parts of the young and fair were distorted by his fat and ugly niece Madame Denys, who could not, like our admirable Pritchard, make the spectators forget the defects of her age and person. For himself Voltaire reserved the characters best adapted to his years, Lusignan, Alvarez, Benassar, Euphemon; his declamation was fashioned to the pomp and cadence of the old stage, and he expressed the enthusiasm of poetry, rather than the feelings of nature. My ardour, which soon became conspicuous, seldom failed of procuring me a ticket. The habits of pleasure fortified my taste for the French theatre: and that taste has perhaps abated my idolatory for the gigantic genius of Shakespeare, which is inculcated from our infancy as the first duty of an Englishman. The wit and philosophy of Voltaire, his table and theatre refined in a visible degree the manners of Lausanne, and however addicted to study, I enjoyed my share of the amusements of society. After the representations of Monrepos I sometimes supped with the actors; I was now familiar in some, and acquainted in many houses; and my evenings were generally devoted to cards and conversation either in private parties or numerous assemblies.

I hesitate from the apprehension of ridicule, when I approach the delicate subject of my early love. By this word I do not mean the polite attention, the gallantry without hope or design, which has originated from the spirit of chivalry, and is interwoven with the texture of French manners. I do not confine myself to the grosser appetite which our pride may affect to disdain, because it has been implanted by Nature in the whole animal creation: *Amor omnibus idem.*[17] The discovery of a sixth sense, the first consciousness of manhood, is a very interesting moment of our lives: but it less properly belongs to the memoirs of an individual, than to the natural history of the species. I understand by this passion the union of desire, friendship and tenderness, which is inflamed by a single female, which prefers her to the rest of her sex, and which seeks her possession as the supreme or the sole happiness of our being. I need not blush at recollecting the object of my choice, and though my love was disappointed of success, I am rather proud that I was once capable of feeling such a pure and exalted sentiment. The personal attractions of Mademoiselle Suzanne Curchod were embellished by the virtues and talents of the mind. Her fortune was humble but her family was respectable: her mother, a native of France, had preferred her religion to her country; the profession of her father did not extinguish the moderation and philosophy of his temper, and he lived content with a small salary and laborious duty in the obscure lot of minister of Crassy, in the mountains that separate the Pays de Vaud from the County of Burgundy. In the solitude of a sequestered village he bestowed a liberal and even learned education on his only daughter; she surpassed his hopes by her proficiency in the sciences and languages; and in her short visits to some relations at Lausanne, the wit and beauty and erudition of Mademoiselle Curchod were the theme of universal applause. The report of such a prodigy awakened my curiosity; I saw and loved. I found her learned without pedantry, lively in conversation, pure in sentiment, and elegant in manners; and the first sudden emotion was fortified by the habits and knowledge of a more familiar acquaintance. She permitted me to make her two or three visits at her father's house: I passed some happy days in the mountains of Burgundy; and her parents honourably encouraged a connection which might raise their daughter above want and dependence. In a calm retirement the gay vanity of youth no longer fluttered in her bosom: she listened to the voice of truth and passion; and I might presume to hope that I had made some impression on a virtuous heart.

At Crassy and Lausanne I indulged my dream of felicity; but on my return to England I soon discovered that my father would not hear of this strange alliance, and that without his consent I was myself destitute and helpless. After a painful struggle I yielded to my fate: the remedies of absence and time were at length effectual;[18] and my love subsided in friendship and esteem. The minister of Crassy soon afterwards died; his stipend died with him. His daughter retired to Geneva where, by teaching young ladies, she earned a hard subsistence for herself and her mother; but in her lowest distress she maintained a spotless reputation and a dignified behaviour. The Duchess of Grafton (now Lady Ossory) has often told me that she had nearly engaged Mademoiselle Curchod as a governess, and her declining a life of servitude was most probably blamed by the wisdom of her short-sighted friends. A rich banker of Paris, a citizen of Geneva, had the good fortune and good sense to discover and possess this inestimable treasure; and in the capital of taste and luxury, she resisted the temptations of wealth as she had sustained the hardships of indigence. The genius of her husband has exalted him to the most conspicuous station in Europe; in every change of prosperity and disgrace he has reclined on the bosom of a faithful friend; and Mademoiselle Curchod is now the wife of M. Necker, the Minister and perhaps the legislator of the French Monarchy.[19]

Such as I am in genius or learning or in manners, I owe my creation to Lausanne. It was in that school, that the statue was discovered in the block of marble; and my own religious folly and my father's blind resolution produced the effects of the most deliberate wisdom. One mischief, however, and in the eyes of my countrymen a serious and irreparable mischief, was derived from the success of my Swiss education: I had ceased to be an Englishman. At the flexible period of youth, from the age of sixteen to twenty-one, my opinions, habits and sentiments were cast in a foreign mould; the faint and distant remembrance of England was almost obliterated; my native language was grown less familiar; and I should have cheerfully accepted the offer of a moderate independent fortune on the terms of perpetual exile. By the good sense and temper of Pavilliard my yoke was insensibly lightened. He left me master of my time and actions; but he could neither change my situation, nor increase my allowance, and with the progress of my years and reason I impatiently sighed for the moment of my deliverance.

At length, in the spring of the year one thousand seven hundred and fifty-eight, my father signified his permission and his pleasure that I should immediately return home. We were then in the midst of a war:[20] the resentment of the French at our taking their ships without a declaration had rendered that polite nation somewhat peevish and difficult; they denied a passage to English travellers; and the road through Germany was circuitous, toilsome, and perhaps in the neighbourhood of the armies exposed to some danger. In this perplexity two Swiss officers[21] of my acquaintance in the Dutch service, who were returning to their garrisons, offered to conduct me through France as one of their companions; nor did we sufficiently reflect that my borrowed name and regimentals might have been considered in case of a discovery in a very serious light. I took my leave of Lausanne on the 11th of April 1758, with a mixture of joy and regret, in the firm resolution of revisiting as a man the persons and places which had been so dear to my youth. We travelled slowly but pleasantly in a hired coach over the hills of Franche-Comté and the fertile province of Lorraine, and passed without accident or enquiry through several fortified towns of the French frontier. From thence we entered the wild Ardennes of the Austrian duchy of Luxemburg,[22] and after crossing the Meuse at Liège, we traversed the heaths of Brabant, and reached on the fifteenth day our Dutch garrison of Bois-le-Duc. In our passage through Nancy, my eye was gratified by the aspect of a regular and beautiful city, the work of Stanislaus, who after the storms of Polish royalty reposed in the love and gratitude of his new subjects of Lorraine.[23] In our halt at Maestricht I visited M. de Beaufort, a learned critic who was known to me by his specious arguments against the five first centuries of the Roman history. After dropping my regimental companions I stepped aside to visit Rotterdam and the Hague. I wished to have observed a country, the monument of freedom and industry; but my days were numbered, and a longer delay would have been ungraceful. I hastened to embark at the Brill, landed the next day at Harwich, and proceeded to London where my father awaited my arrival. The whole term of my first absence from England was four years, ten months, and fifteen days.

Chapter V

Essai · Service in Militia
(1758–62)

In the prayers of the Church our personal concerns are judiciously reduced to the threefold distinction of *mind*, *body* and *estate*.[1] The sentiments of the mind excite and exercise our social sympathy: the review of my moral and literary character is the most interesting to myself and to the public; and I may expatiate without reproach on my private studies, since they have produced the public writings which can alone entitle me to the esteem and friendship of my readers. The pains and pleasures of the body, how important soever to ourselves are an indelicate topic of conversation ...[2] The experience of the World inculcates a discreet reserve on the subject of our estate; and we soon learn that a free disclosure of our riches or poverty, would provoke the malice of envy, or encourage the insolence of contempt. Yet I am tempted to glance in a few words on the state of my private circumstances, as I am persuaded that had I been more indigent or more wealthy, I should not have possessed the leisure or the perseverance to prepare and execute my voluminous history. My father's impatience for my return to England was not wholly of the disinterested kind. I have already hinted that he had been impoverished by his two sisters, and that his gay character and mode of life were less adapted to the acquisition than the expenditure of wealth. A large and legitimate debt for the supply of naval stores was lost by the injustice of the Court of Spain. His elegant hospitality at Putney exceeded the measure of his income; the honour of being chosen a member of the Old Club at White's had been dearly paid, and a more pernicious species of gaming, the contest for Southampton, exhausted his sickly finances. His retirement into Hampshire on my mother's death was coloured by a pious motive; some years of solitude allowed him to breathe; but it was only by his son's majority that he could be restored to the command of an entailed estate.

The time of my recall had been so nicely computed that I arrived in London three days before I was of age: the priests and the altar had been prepared, and the victim was unconscious of the impending stroke. According to the forms and fictions of our law I levied a fine and suffered a recovery.³ The entail was cut off: a sum of ten thousand pounds was raised on mortgage for my father's use; and he repaid the obligation by settling on me an annuity for life of three hundred pounds a year. My submission at the time was blind and almost involuntary, but it has been justified by duty and interest to my cooler thoughts; and I could only regret that the receipt of some appropriated fund was not given into my own hands. My annuity, though somewhat more valuable thirty years ago, was however inadequate to the style of a young Englishman of fashion in the most wealthy metropolis of Europe; but I was rich in my indifference, or more properly my aversion, for the active and costly pleasures of my age and country. Some arrears, especially my bookseller's bill, were occasionally discharged; and the extraordinaries of my travels into France and Italy amounted, by previous agreement, to the sum of twelve hundred pounds. But the ordinary scale of my expense was proportioned to my ordinary revenue; my desires were regulated by temper as much as by philosophy; and as soon as my purse was empty I had the courage to retire into Hampshire, where I found in my father's house a liberal maintenance, and in my own studies an inexhaustible source of amusement. With a credit which might have been largely abused, I may assume the singular merit that I never lost or borrowed twenty pounds in the twelve years which elapsed between my return from Switzerland and my father's death.

The only person in England whom I was impatient to see was my aunt Porten, the affectionate guardian of my tender years. I hastened to her house in College Street, Westminster, and the evening was spent in the effusions of joy and confidence. It was not without some awe and apprehension that I approached the presence of my father. My infancy, to speak the truth, had been neglected at home; the severity of his look and language at our last parting still dwelt on my memory; nor could I form any notion of *his* character, or *my* probable reception. They were both more agreeable than I could expect. The domestic discipline of our ancestors has been relaxed by the philosophy and softness of the age: and if my father remembered that *he* had trembled before a stern parent, it was only to adopt with his own son an opposite mode of behaviour. He received me as a man and a friend: all constraint was banished at our first interview, and we ever afterwards continued on the same terms of easy and equal politeness. He applauded the success of my education; every word and action was expressive of the most cordial affection; and our lives would have passed without a cloud, if his economy had been equal to his fortune, or if his fortune had been equal to his desires.

During my absence he had married his second wife, Miss Dorothea Patton, who was introduced to me with the most unfavourable prejudice. I considered his second marriage as an act of displeasure, and the rival who had usurped my mother's bed appeared in the light of a personal and domestic enemy. I will not say that I was apprehensive of the bowl or dagger, or that I had then weighed the sentence of Euripides –

Ἐχθρα γὰρ ἡ 'πιοῦσα μητρυιὰ τέκνοις
Τοῖς πρόσθ' ἐχίδνης οὐδὲν ἠπιοτέρα[4]

But I well knew that the *odium novercale* was proverbial in the language of antiquity; the Latin poets always couple with the name of stepmother the hateful epithets of *crudelis, saeva, scelerata*; and on the road I had often repeated the line of Virgil:

Est mihi namque domi pater, est injusta noverca.[5]

But the injustice was in my own fancy, and the imaginary monster was an amiable and deserving woman. I could not be mistaken in the first view of her understanding, her knowledge, and the elegant spirit of her conversation: her polite welcome, and her assiduous care to study and gratify my wishes announced at least that the surface would be smooth; and my suspicions of art and falsehood were gradually dispelled by the full discovery of her warm and exquisite sensibility. After some reserve on my side our minds associated in confidence and friendship, and as Mrs Gibbon had neither children nor the hopes of children, we more easily adopted the tender names and genuine characters of mother and of son. By the indulgence of these parents I was left at liberty to consult my taste or reason in the choice of place, of company and of amusements, and my excursions were only bounded by the limits of the island and the measure of my income. Some faint efforts were made to procure me an employment of secretary to a foreign embassy, and I listened to a scheme which would again have transported me to the continent. Mrs Gibbon, with seeming wisdom, exhorted me to take chambers in the Temple, and devote my leisure to the study of the law. I cannot repent of having neglected her advice: few men without the spur of necessity have resolution to force their way through the thorns and thickets of that gloomy labyrinth. Nature had not endowed me with the bold and ready eloquence which makes itself heard amidst the tumult of the bar:

Vincentem strepitus, et natum rebus agendis.[6]

and I should probably have been diverted from the labours of literature without acquiring the fame or fortune of a successful pleader. I had no need to call to my aid the regular duties of a profession; every day, every hour was agreeably filled; nor have I known, like so many of my countrymen, the tediousness of an idle life.

Of the two years (May 1758–May 1760) between my return to England and the embodying of the Hampshire militia, I passed about nine months in London and the remainder in the country. The metropolis affords many amusements which are open to all: it is itself an astonishing and perpetual spectacle to the curious eye; and each taste, each sense may be gratified by the variety of objects that will occur in the long circuit of a morning walk. I assiduously frequented the theatres at a very prosperous era of the stage, when a constellation of excellent actors, both in tragedy and comedy, was eclipsed by the meridian brightness of Garrick in the maturity of his judgement and vigour of his performance. The pleasures of a town life, the daily round from the tavern to the play, from the play to the coffee-house, from the coffee-house to the bagnio[7] are within the reach of every man who is regardless of his health, his money and his company. By the contagion of example I was sometimes seduced; but the better habits which I had formed at Lausanne induced me to seek a more elegant and rational society; and if my search was less easy and successful than I might have hoped, I shall at present impute the failure to the disadvantages of my situation and character. Had the rank and fortune of my parents given them an annual establishment in London, their own house would have introduced me to a numerous and polite circle of acquaintance. But my father's taste had always preferred the highest and the lowest company, for which he was equally qualified; and after a twelve years' retirement he was no longer in the memory of the great with whom he had associated. I found myself a stranger in the midst of a vast and unknown city, and at my entrance into life I was reduced to some dull family parties, and some scattered connections which were not such as I should have chosen for myself. The most useful friends of my father were the Mallets: they received me with civility and kindness at first on his account, and afterwards on my own; and (if I may use Lord Chesterfield's word) I was soon *domesticated*[8] in their house. Mr Mallet, a name among the English poets, is praised by an unforgiving enemy[9] for the ease and elegance of his conversation, and whatsoever might be the defects of his wife, she was not destitute of wit or learning. By his assistance I was introduced to Lady Hervey, the mother of the present Earl of Bristol. Her age and infirmities confined her at home; her dinners were select; in the evening her house was open to the best company of both sexes and all nations; nor was I displeased at her preference and even affectation of the manners, the language and the literature of France. But my progress in the English world was in general left to my own efforts, and those efforts were languid and slow. I had not been endowed by art or nature with those happy gifts of confidence and address which unlock every door and every bosom; nor would it be reasonable to complain of the just consequences of my sickly childhood, foreign education, and reserved temper. While coaches were rattling through Bond Street,[10] I have passed many a solitary evening in my lodging with my books; my studies were sometimes interrupted by a sigh which I breathed towards Lausanne; and on the approach of spring I withdrew without reluctance from the noisy and expensive scene of crowds without company, and dissipation without pleasure. In each of the twenty-five years of my acquaintance with London (1758–1783) the prospect gradually brightened; and this unfavourable picture most properly belongs to the first period after my return from Switzerland.

My father's residence in Hampshire, where I have passed many light and some heavy hours, was at Buriton near Petersfield, one mile from the Portsmouth road, and at the easy distance of fifty-eight miles from London. An old mansion in a state of decay had been converted into the fashion and convenience of a modern house; and if strangers had nothing to see, the inhabitants had little to desire. The spot was not happily chosen at the end of the village and the bottom of the hill; but the aspect of the adjacent grounds was various and cheerful: the downs commanded a noble prospect, and the long hanging woods in sight of the house could not perhaps have been improved by art or expense. My father kept in his own hands the whole of his estate, and even rented some additional land; and whatsoever might be the balance of profit and loss, the farm supplied him with amusement and plenty. The produce maintained a number of men and horses, which were multiplied by the inter-mixture of domestic and rural servants; and in the intervals of labour, the favourite team, a handsome set of bays or greys, was harnessed to the coach. The economy of the house was regulated by the taste and prudence of Mrs Gibbon; she prided herself in the elegance of her occasional dinners; and from the uncleanly avarice of Madame Pavilliard, I was suddenly transported to the daily neatness and luxury of an English table. Our immediate neighbourhood was rare and rustic; but from the verge of our hills as far as Chichester and Goodwood, the western district of Sussex was interspersed with noble seats and hospitable families, with whom we cultivated a friendly, and might have enjoyed a very frequent inter-course. As my stay at Buriton was always voluntary, I was received and dismissed with smiles; but the comforts of my retirement did not depend on the ordinary pleasures of the country. My father could never inspire me with his love and knowledge of farming. When he galloped away on a fleet hunter to follow the Duke of Richmond's foxhounds, I saw him depart without a wish to join in the sport; and in the command of an ample manor, I valued the supply of the kitchen much more than the exercise of the field. I never handled a gun, I seldom mounted a horse; and my philosophic walks were soon terminated by a shady bench, where I was long detained by the sedentary amusement of reading or meditation. At home I occupied a pleasant and spacious apartment; the library on the same floor was soon considered as my peculiar domain; and I might say with truth that I was never less alone than when by myself.[11]

My sole complaint, which I piously suppressed, arose from the kind restraint imposed on the freedom of my time. By the habit of early rising I always secured a sacred portion of the day, and many scattered moments were stolen and employed by my studious industry. But the family hours of breakfast, of dinner, of tea and of supper were regular and long; after breakfast Mrs Gibbon expected my company in her dressing-room; after tea my father claimed my conversation and the perusal of the newspapers; and in the midst of an interesting work I was often called down to receive the visit of some idle neighbours. Their dinners and visits required in due season a similar return, and I dreaded the period of the full moon which was usually reserved for our more distant excursions. I could not refuse attending my father in the summer of 1759 to the races at Stockbridge, Reading and Odiham, where he had entered a horse for the hunter's plate; and I was not displeased with the sight of our Olympic games, the beauty of the spot, the fleetness of the horses, and the gay tumult of the numerous spectators. As soon as the Militia business was agitated, many days were tediously consumed in meetings of Deputy-Lieutenants at Petersfield, Alton and Winchester. In the close of the same year 1759, Sir Simeon (then Mr) Stewart attempted an unsuccessful contest for the county of Southampton against Mr Legge, Chancellor of the Exchequer: a well known contest in which Lord Bute's influence was first exerted and censured. Our canvass at Portsmouth and Gosport lasted several days; but the interruption of my studies was compensated in some degree by the spectacle of English manners, and the acquisition of some practical knowledge.

If in a more domestic or more dissipated scene my application was somewhat relaxed, the love of knowledge was inflamed and gratified by the command of books, and I compared the poverty of Lausanne with the plenty of London. My father's study at Buriton was stuffed with much trash of the last age, with much high-church divinity and politics which have long since gone to their proper place; yet it contained some valuable editions of the Classics and the Fathers, the choice as it should seem of Mr Law; and many English publications of the times had been occasionally added. From this slender beginning I have gradually formed a numerous and select library, the foundation of my works, and the best comfort of my life both at home and abroad. On the receipt of the first quarter a large share of my allowance was appropriate to my literary wants. I cannot forget the joy with which I exchanged a bank-note of twenty pounds for the twenty volumes of the Memoirs of the Academy of Inscriptions; nor would it have been easy by any other expenditure of the same sum to have procured so large and lasting a fund of rational amusement. At a time when I most assiduously frequented this school of ancient literature I thus expressed my opinion of a learned and various collection, which since the year 1759 has been doubled in magnitude though not equally in merit. *'Une de ces sociétés qui ont mieux immortalisé Louis XIV qu'une ambition souvent pernicieuse aux hommes, commençoit déjà ces recherches qui réunissent la justesse de l'esprit, l'aménité et l'érudition: où l'on voit tant de découvertes, et quelquefois, ce qui ne cède qu'à peine aux découvertes, une* ignorance *modeste et* savante.[12]

The review of my library must be reserved for the period of its maturity: but in this place I may allow myself to observe that I am not conscious of having ever bought a book from a motive of ostentation, that every volume before it was deposited on the shelf was either read or sufficiently examined, and that I soon adopted the tolerating maxim of the elder Pliny, *nullum esse librum tam malum ut non ex aliqua parte prodesset.*[13] I could not yet find leisure or courage to renew the pursuit of the Greek language except by reading the lessons of the Old and New Testament every Sunday, when I attended the family to church. The series of my Latin authors was less strenuously completed; but the acquisition by inheritance or purchase of the best editions of Cicero, Quintilian, Livy, Tacitus, Ovid etc. afforded a fair opportunity which I seldom neglected. I persevered in the useful method of abstracts and observations and a single example may suffice of a note which had almost swelled into a work. The solution of a passage of Livy (xxxviii, 38)[14] involved me in the dry and dark treatises of Greaves, Arbuthnot, Hooper, Bernard, Eisenschmidt, Gronovius, La Barre, Fréret etc., and in my French essay (chapter xx), I ridiculously send the reader to my own manuscript remarks on the weights, coins, and measures of the ancients, which were abruptly terminated by the militia drum.

As I am now entering on a more ample field of society and study, I can only hope to avoid a vain and prolix garrulity by overlooking the vulgar crowd of my acquaintance, and confining myself to such intimate friends, among books and men, as are best entitled to my notice, by their own merit and reputation or by the deep impression which they have left on my mind. Yet I will embrace this occasion of recommending to the young student a practice which about this time I adopted myself. After glancing my eye over the design and order of a new book, I suspended the perusal till I had finished the task of self-examination, till I had revolved in a solitary walk all that I knew or believed or had thought on the subject of the whole work, or of some particular chapter. I was then qualified to discern how much the author added to my original stock; and if I was sometimes satisfied by the agreement, I was sometimes armed by the opposition of our ideas. The favourite companions of my leisure were our English writers since the Revolution: they breathe the spirit of reason and liberty, and they most seasonably contributed to restore the purity of my own language, which had been corrupted by the long use of a foreign idiom. By the judicious advice of Mr Mallet I was directed to the writings of Swift and Addison. Wit and simplicity are their common attributes: but the style of Swift is supported by manly original vigour, that of Addision is adorned by the female graces of elegance and mildness; and the contrast of too coarse, or too thin a texture is visible even in the defects of these celebrated authors. The old reproach, that no British altars had been raised to the Muse of history, was recently disproved by the first performances of Robertson and Hume, the histories of Scotland and of the Stuarts. I will assume the presumption to say that I was not unworthy to read them; nor will I disguise my different feelings in the repeated perusals. The perfect composition, the nervous language, the well-turned periods of Dr Robertson inflamed me to the ambitious hope that I might one day tread in his footsteps; the calm philosophy, the careless inimitable beauties of his friend and rival often forced me to close the volume, with a mixed sensation of delight and despair.

The design of my first work, the *Essay on the Study of Literature*, was suggested by a refinement of vanity, the desire of justifying and praising the object of a favourite pursuit. In France, to which my ideas were confined, the learning and language of Greece and Rome were neglected by a philosophic age. The guardian of those studies, the Academy of

Inscriptions, was degraded to the lowest rank among the three Royal societies of Paris:[15] the new appellation of *Erudits* was contemptuously applied to the successors of Lipsius and Casaubon; and I was provoked to hear (see M. d'Alembert's *Discours préliminaire à l'Encyclopédie*) that the exercise of the memory, their sole merit, had been superseded by the nobler faculties of the imagination and the judgement. I was ambitious of proving by my own example as well as by my precepts that all the faculties of the mind may be exercised and displayed by the study of ancient literature. I began to select and adorn the various proofs and illustrations which had offered themselves in reading the classics, and the first pages or chapters of my essay were composed before my departure from Lausanne. The hurry of the journey and of the first weeks of my English life suspended all thoughts of serious application; but my object was ever before my eyes, and no more than ten days, from the first to the eleventh of July, were suffered to elapse after my summer establishment at Buriton. My essay was finished in about six weeks, and as soon as a fair copy had been transcribed by one of the French prisoners at Petersfield I looked round for a critic and a judge of my first performance. A writer can seldom be content with the doubtful recompense of solitary approbation, but a youth ignorant of the world and of himself must desire to weigh his talents in some scales less partial than his own. My conduct was natural, my motive laudable, my choice of Dr Maty judicious and fortunate. By descent and education, Dr Maty, though born in Holland, might be considered as a Frenchman; but he was fixed in London by the practice of physic, and an office in the British Museum. His reputation was justly founded on the eighteen Volumes of the *Journal Britannique* which he had supported almost alone with perseverance and success. This humble though useful labour, which had once been dignified by the genius of Bayle and the learning of Le Clerc, was not disgraced by the taste, the knowledge and the judgement of Maty: he exhibits a candid and pleasing view of the state of literature in England during a period of six years (January 1750–December 1755); and far different from his angry son, he handles the rod of criticism with the tenderness and reluctance of a parent. The author of the *Journal Britannique* sometimes aspires to the character of a poet and philosopher: his style is pure and elegant, and in his virtues or even his defects, he may be ranked as one of the last disciples of the school of Fontenelle.[16]

His answer to my first letter was prompt and polite: after a careful examination he returned my manuscript with some animadversion and much applause, and when I visited London, in the ensuing winter, we discussed the design and execution in several free and familiar conversations. In a short excursion to Buriton, I reviewed my essay according to his friendly advice, and after suppressing a third, adding a third and altering a third, I consummated my first labour by a short preface, which is dated February 3rd 1759. Yet I still shrunk from the press with the terrors of virgin modesty. The manuscript was safely deposited in my desk; and as my attention was engaged by new objects, the delay might have been prolonged till I had fulfilled the precept of Horace, *nonumque prematur in annum.*[17] Father Sirmond, a learned Jesuit, was still more rigid, since he advised a young friend to expect the mature age of fifty before he gave himself or his writings to the public (Olivet, *Histoire de l'Académie Françoise,* tome ii, p. 143). The counsel was singular, but it is still more singular that it should have been approved by the example of the author. Sirmond was himself fifty-five years of age when he published (in 1614) his first work, an edition of Sidonius Apollinaris, with many valuable annotations. (See his life, before the great edition of his works in five volumes in folio, Paris, 1696, *e Typographia Regia.*)

Two years elapsed in silence; but in the spring of 1761, I yielded to the authority of a parent, and complied like a pious son with the wish of my own heart. My private resolves were influenced by the state of Europe. About this time the belligerent powers had made and accepted overtures of peace; our English plenipotentiaries were named to assist at the Congress of Augsbourg, which never met.[18] I wished to attend them as a gentleman or a secretary, and my father fondly believed that the proof of some literary talents might introduce me to public notice and second the recommendations of my friends. After a last revisal I consulted with Mr Mallet and Dr Maty, who approved the design and promoted the execution. Mr Mallet, after hearing me read my manuscript, received it from my hands and delivered it into those of Becket, with whom he made an agreement in my name: an easy agreement. I required only a certain number of copies, and without transferring my property, I devolved on the bookseller the charges and profits of the edition. Dr Maty undertook in my absence to correct the sheets. He inserted without my knowledge an elegant and flattering epistle to the author: which is composed, however, with so much art that in case of a defeat, his favourable report might have been ascribed to the indulgence of a friend for the rash attempt of a *young English Gentleman.*[19] The work was printed and published under the title of *Essai sur l'étude de la littérature, à Londres, chez T. Becket et P. A. de Hondt,* 1761, in a small volume in duodecimo. My dedication to my father, a proper and pious address, was composed the 28th of May; Dr Maty's letter is dated the 16th of June; and I received the first copy (June the 23rd) at Alresford, two days before I marched with the Hampshire militia. Some weeks afterwards, on the same ground, I presented my book to the late Duke of York, who breakfasted in Colonel Pitt's tent; and as the regiment was just returned from a field day, the author appeared before his Royal Highness, somewhat disordered with sweat and dust, in the cap, dress and accoutrements of a Captain of Grenadiers. By my father's direction and Mallet's advice, a number of copies were given to several of their acquaintance and my own; to the Duke of Richmond, the Marquis of Carnarvon, the Earls of Litchfield, Waldegrave, Egremont, Shelburne, Bute, Hardwicke, Bath, Granville, and Chesterfield, Lady Hervey, Sir Joseph Yorke, Sir Matthew Fetherstone, Messieurs Walpole, Scott, Wray, etc. Two books were sent to the Count de Caylus and the Duchess d'Aiguillon at Paris; I had reserved twenty for my friends at Lausanne, as the first fruits of my education and a grateful token of my remembrance; and on all these persons I levied an unavoidable tax of civility and compliment.

It is not surprising that a work of which the style and sentiments were so totally foreign should have been more successful abroad than at home. I was delighted by the copious extracts, the warm commendations, and the flattering predictions of the journals of France and Holland; and the next year (1762), a new edition (I believe at Geneva) extended the fame or at least the circulation of the work. In England it was received with cold indifference, little read and speedily forgotten. A small impression was slowly dispersed; the bookseller murmured, and the author (had his feelings been more exquisite) might have wept over the blunders and the baldness of the English translation. The publication of my History fifteen years afterwards revived the memory of my first performance, and the essay was eagerly sought in the shops. But I refused the permission which Becket solicited of reprinting it; the public curiosity was imperfectly satisfied by a pirated copy of the booksellers of Dublin; and when a copy of the original edition has been discovered in a sale, the primitive value of half a crown has risen to the fanciful price of a guinea or thirty shillings. Such is the power of a name.

I have expatiated on the loss of my literary maidenhead; a memorable era in the life of a student, when he ventures to reveal the measure of his mind. His hopes and fears are multiplied by the idea of self-importance, and he believes for a while, that the eyes of mankind are fixed on his person and performance. Whatsoever may be my present reputation, it no longer rests on the merit of this first essay, and at the end of twenty-eight years,[20] I may appreciate my juvenile work with the impartiality, and almost with the indifference of a stranger. In his answer to Lady Hervey, the Count de Caylus admires or affects to admire *'les livres sans nombre que M. Gibbon a lus et très bien lus'*. But, alas, my stock of erudition at that time was scanty and superficial; and if I allow myself the liberty of naming the Greek masters, my genuine and personal acquaintance was confined to the Latin classics. The most serious defect of my essay is a kind of obscurity and abruptness which always fatigues and may often elude the attention of the reader. Instead of a precise and proper definition, the title itself, the sense of the word *Littérature* is loosely and variously applied: a number of remarks, and examples historical, critical, philosophical, are heaped on each other without method or connection, and if we except some introductory pages, all the remaining chapters might indifferently be reversed or transposed. The obscurity of many passages is often affected: *brevis esse laboro, obscurus fio*;[21] the desire of expressing perhaps a common idea with sententious and oracular brevity. Alas, how fatal has been the imitation of Montesquieu! But this obscurity sometimes proceeds from a mixture of light and darkness in the author's mind, from a partial ray which strikes upon an angle, instead of spreading itself over the surface of an object. After this fair confession I shall presume to say that the essay does credit to a young writer of two and twenty years of age, who had read with taste, who thinks with freedom, and who writes in a foreign language with spirit and elegance. The defence of the early history of Rome and the new Chronology of Sir Isaac Newton form a specious argument.[22] The patriotic and political design of the Georgics is happily conceived; and any probable conjecture which tends to raise the dignity of the poet and the poem deserves to be adopted without a rigid scrutiny.

Some dawning of a philosophic spirit enlightens the general remarks on the study of history and of man. I am not displeased with the enquiry into the origin and nature of the gods of polytheism. In a riper season of judgement and knowledge, I am tempted to review the curious question whether these fabulous deities were mortal men or allegorical beings: perhaps the two systems might be blended in one; perhaps the distance between them is in a great measure verbal and apparent. In the rapid course of this narrative I have only time to scatter two or three hasty observations. *That* in the perusal of Homer, a naturalist would pronounce his gods and men to be of the same species, since they were capable of engendering together a fruitful progeny. *That* before the Reformation St Francis and the Virgin Mary had almost attained a similar apotheosis;

and that the saints and angels so different in their origin were worshipped with the same rites by the same nations. *That* the current of superstition and science flowed from India to Egypt, from Egypt to Greece and Italy; and that the incarnations of the celestial deities so darkly shadowed in our fragments of Egyptian theology are copiously explained in the sacred books of the Hindoos. Fifteen centuries before Christ, the great Osiris, the invisible agent of the universe, was born or manifested at Thebes in Boeotia under the name of Bacchus; the idea of Bishen is a metaphysical abstraction, the adventures of Kishen, his perfect image, are those of a man who lived and died about five thousand years ago in the neighbourhood of Delhi. Upon the whole I may apply to the first labour of my pen the speech of a far superior artist when he surveyed the first productions of his pencil. After viewing some portraits which he had painted in his youth, my friend Sir Joshua Reynolds acknowledged to me that he was rather humbled than flattered by the comparison with his present works; and that after so much time and study he had conceived his improvement to be much greater than he found it to have been.

At Lausanne I composed the first chapters of my essay in French, the familiar language of my conversation and studies, in which it was easier for me to write than in my mother tongue. After my return to England I continued the same practice without any affectation or design of repudiating (as Dr Bentley would say[23]) my vernacular idiom. But I should have escaped some anti-Gallican clamour had I been content with the more natural character of an English author; I should have been more consistent had I rejected Mallet's foolish advice of prefixing an English dedication to a French book: a confusion of tongues which seemed to accuse the ignorance of my patron. The use of a foreign dialect might be excused by the hope of being employed as a negotiator, by the desire of being generally understood on the continent; but my true motive was doubtless the ambition of new and singular fame, an Englishman claiming a place among the writers of France. The Latin tongue had been consecrated by the service of the Church; it was refined by the imitation of the ancients; and in the XVth and XVIth centuries the scholars of Europe enjoyed the advantage which they have gradually resigned, of conversing and writing in a common and learned idiom. As that idiom was no longer in any country the vulgar speech, they all stood on a level with each other; yet a citizen of old Rome might have smiled at the best Latinity of the Germans and Britons, and we may learn from the *Ciceronianus* of Erasmus how difficult it was found to steer a middle course between pedantry and barbarism. The Romans themselves had sometimes attempted a more perilous task, of writing in a living language, and appealing to the taste and judgement of the natives. The vanity of Tully was doubly interested in the *Greek* memoirs of his own consulship; and if he modestly supposes that some Latinisms might be detected in his style, he is confident of his own skill in the art of Isocrates and Aristotle; and he requests his friend Atticus to disperse the copies of his work at Athens and in the other cities of Greece (*ad Atticum*, I, 19; II, 1²⁴). But it must not be forgot that from infancy to manhood Cicero and his contemporaries had read and declaimed and composed with equal diligence in both languages, and that he was not allowed to frequent a Latin school till he had imbibed the lessons of the Greek grammarians and rhetoricians.

In modern times the language of France has been diffused by the merit of her writers, the social manners of the natives, the influence of the monarchy, and the exile of the Protestants. Several foreigners have seized the opportunity of speaking to Europe in this common dialect, and Germany may plead the authority of Leibnitz and Frederic, of the first of her philosophers and the greatest of her kings. The just pride and laudable prejudice of England has restrained this communication of idioms; and of all the nations on this side of the Alps, my countrymen are the least practised and least perfect in the exercise of the French tongue. By Sir William Temple and Lord Chesterfield it was only used on occasions of civility and business, and their printed letters will not be quoted as models of composition. Lord Bolingbroke may have published in French a sketch of his *Reflections on Exile*: but his reputation now reposes on the address of Voltaire, '*Docte sermones utriusque linguae*';²⁵ and by his English dedication to Queen Caroline, and his *Essay on Epic Poetry*, it should seem that Voltaire himself wished to deserve a return of the same compliment. The exception of Count Hamilton cannot fairly be urged; though an Irishman by birth, he was educated in France from his childhood. Yet I *am* surprised that a long residence in England, and the habits of domestic conversation did not affect the ease and purity of his inimitable style; and I regret the omission of his English verses which might have afforded an amusing object of comparison. I might therefore assume the *primus ego in patriam meam*,²⁶ etc.; but with what success I have explored this untrodden path must be left to the decision of my French readers. Dr Maty, who might himself be questioned as a foreigner, has secured his retreat at my expense: '*Je ne crois pas que vous vous piquiez d'être moins facile à reconnoître pour un Anglois que Lucullus pour un Romain.*'²⁷ My friends at Paris have been more indulgent: they received me as a countryman, or at least as a provincial, but they were friends and Parisians. The defects which Maty insinuates, *'Ces traits saillants, ces figures hardies, ce sacrifice de la règle au sentiment, et de la cadence à la force,'* are the faults of the youth rather than of the stranger: and after the long and laborious exercise of my own language, I am conscious that my French style has been ripened and improved.

I have already hinted that the publication of my essay was delayed till I had embraced the military profession. I shall now amuse myself with the recollection of an active scene which bears no affinity to any other period of my studious and social life. From the general idea of a militia I shall descend to the militia of England in the war before the last;[28] to the state of the regiment in which I served, and to the influence of that service on my personal situation and character.

The defence of the State may be imposed on the body of the people, or it may be delegated to a select number of mercenaries; the exercise of arms may be an occasional duty or a separate trade; and it is this difference which forms the distinction between a militia and a standing army. Since the union of England and Scotland the public safety has never been attacked and has seldom been threatened by a foreign invader; but the sea was long the sole safeguard of our isle. If the reign of the Tudors or the Stuarts was often signalized by the valour of our soldiers and sailors, they were dismissed at the end of the campaign or the expedition for which they had been levied. The national spirit at home had subsided in the peaceful occupations of trade, manufactures and husbandry, and if the obsolete forms of a militia were preserved, their discipline in the last age was less the object of confidence than of ridicule.

> The country rings around with loud alarms,
> And raw in fields, the rude Militia swarms:
> Mouths without hands maintained at vast expense
> In peace a charge, in war a weak defence.
> Stout once a month they march, a blust'ring band,
> And ever but in times of need at hand.
> This was the morn when, issuing on the guard,
> Drawn up in rank and file they stood prepar'd
> Of seeming arms to make a short essay;
> Then hasten to be drunk, the business of the day.[29]

The impotence of such unworthy soldiers was supplied from the era of the Restoration by the establishment of a body of mercenaries: the conclusion of each war increased the numbers that were kept on foot, and although their progress was checked by the jealousy of opposition, time and necessity reconciled, or at least accustomed a free country to the annual perpetuity of a standing army.

The zeal of our patriots, both in and out of Parliament (I cannot add both in and out of office), complained that the sword had been stolen from the hands of the people. They appealed to the victorious example of the Greeks and Romans, among whom every citizen was a soldier; and they applauded the happiness and independence of Switzerland which, in the midst of the great monarchies of Europe, is sufficiently defended by a constitutional and effective militia. But their enthusiasm overlooked the modern changes in the art of war, and the insuperable difference of government and manners. The liberty of the Swiss is maintained by the concurrence of political causes: the superior discipline of their militia arises from the numerous intermixture of officers and soldiers whose youth has been trained in foreign service; and the annual exercise of a few days is the *sole* tax which is imposed on a martial people, consisting for the most part of shepherds and husbandmen. In the primitive ages of Greece and Rome, a war was determined by a battle, and a battle was decided by the personal qualities of strength, courage and dexterity, which every citizen derived from his domestic education. The public quarrel was his own; he had himself voted in the assembly of the people; and the private passions of the majority had pronounced the general decree of the Republic. On the event of the contest each freeman had staked his fortune and family, his liberty and life; and if the enemy prevailed he must expect to share in the common calamity of the ruin or servitude of his native city. By such irresistible motives were the first Greeks and Romans summoned to the field: but when the art was improved, when the war was protracted, their militia was transformed into a standing army, or their freedom was oppressed by the more regular forces of an ambitious neighbour.

Two disgraceful events, the progress in the year forty-five of some naked highlanders,[30] the invitation of the Hessians and Hanoverians in fifty-six,[31] had betrayed and insulted the weakness of an unarmed people. The country gentlemen of England unanimously demanded the establishment of a militia: a patriot was expected,

> Otia qui rumpet patriae, residesque movebit
> ... in arma viros.[32]

and the merit of the plan or at least of the execution was assumed by Mr Pitt, who was then in the full splendour of his popularity and power.[33] In the new model the choice of the officers was founded on the most constitutional principle, since they were all obliged, from the colonel to the ensign, to prove a certain qualification, to give a landed security to the country, which entrusted them for her defence with the use of arms. But in the first steps of this institution, the legislators of the militia despaired of imitating the practice of Switzerland. Instead of summoning to the standard *all* the inhabitants of the Kingdom who were not disabled by age, or excused by some indispensable avocation, they directed that a moderate proportion should be chosen by lot for the term of three years, at the end of which their places were to be supplied by a new and similar ballot. Every man who was drawn had the option of serving in person, of finding a substitute, or of paying ten pounds; and in a country already burthened, this honourable duty was degraded into an additional tax. It is reported that the subjects of Queen Elizabeth amounted to 1,172,674 men able to bear arms (Hume's *History of England*, vol. V, p. 482 of the last octavo edition); and if in the war before the last many active and vigorous hands were employed in the fleet and army, the difference must have been amply compensated by the general increase of population, and we may smile at this mighty effort which reduced the national defence to the puny establishment of thirty-two thousand men. The Sunday afternoons had first been appointed for their exercise, but superstition clamoured against the profanation of the sabbath, and a useful day was subtracted from the labour of the week. Whatever was the day, such rare and superficial practice could never have entitled them to the character of soldiers. But the King was invested with the power of calling the militia into actual service on the event or the danger of rebellion or invasion; and in the year 1759 the British islands were seriously threatened by the armaments of France. At this crisis the national spirit most gloriously disproved the charge of effeminacy which, in a popular estimate, had been imputed to the times; a martial enthusiasm seemed to have pervaded the land, and a constitutional army was formed under the command of the nobility and gentry of England. After the naval victory of Sir Edward Hawke[34] (November 20 1759) the danger no longer subsisted; yet instead of disbanding the first regiments of militia, the remainder was embodied the ensuing year, and public unanimity applauded their illegal continuance in the field till the end of the war.

In this new mode of service they were subject like the regulars to martial law; they received the same advantages of pay and clothing, and the families, at least of the principals, were maintained at the charge of the parish. At a distance from their respective counties, these provincial corps were stationed and removed and encamped by the command of the

Secretary at War; the officers and men were trained in the habits of subordination, nor is it surprising that some regiments should have assumed the discipline and appearance of veteran troops. With the skill they soon imbibed the spirit of mercenaries; the character of a militia was lost; and, under that specious[35] name, the crown had acquired a second army more costly and less useful than the first. The most beneficial effect of this institution was to eradicate among the country gentlemen the relics of Tory or rather of Jacobite prejudice. The accession of a British king[36] reconciled them to the government and even to the court; but they have been since accused of transferring their passive loyalty from the Stuarts to the family of Brunswick; and I have heard Mr Burke exclaim in the House of Commons, 'They have changed the idol, but they have preserved the idolatry!'

By the general ardour of the times, my father, a new Cincinnatus, was drawn from the plough; his authority and advice prevailed on me to relinquish my studies; a general meeting was held at Winchester; and before we knew the consequences of an irretrievable step, we accepted (June 12th 1759) our respective commissions of major and captain in the South Battalion of the Hampshire. The proportion of the County of Southampton had been fixed at nine hundred and sixty men who were divided into the two regiments of the North and South, each consisting of eight companies. By the special exemption of the Isle of Wight we lost a company; our Colonel resigned, and we were reduced to the legal definition of an independent battalion, of a lieutenant colonel Commandant (Sir Thomas Worsley, Baronet), a major, five captains, seven lieutenants, seven ensigns, twenty-one serjeants, fourteen drummers, and four hundred and twenty rank and file. I will not renew our prolix and passionate dispute with the Duke of Bolton, our Lord Lieutenant, which at that time appeared to me an object of the most serious importance: by the interpretation of an Act of Parliament we contested his right of naming himself Colonel of the two battalions; after the final decision of the Attorney General, and Secretary at War, his poor revenge was confined to the use and abuse of his power in the choice of an adjutant and the promotion of officers. In the year 1759 our ballot was slowly completed, and as the fear of an invasion passed away, we began to hope, my father and myself, that our campaigns would extend no farther than Petersfield and Alton, the seat of our particular companies. We were undeceived by the King's sign manual for our embodying, which was issued May 10th 1760. It was too late to retreat; it was too soon to repent; the battalion, on the 4th of June, assembled at Winchester, from whence in about a fortnight we were removed at our own request for the benefit of a foreign education.[37] In a new raised militia the neighbourhood of home was always found inconvenient to the officers and mischievous to the men.

The battalion continued in actual service above two years and a half, from May 10, 1760 to December 23, 1762. In this period of a military life, I have neither sieges nor battles to relate; but, like my brother Major Sturgeon,[38] I shall describe our marches and counter-marches as they are faithfully recorded in my own journal or commentary of the times.

i. Our first and most agreeable station was at Blandford in Dorsetshire, where we enjoyed about two months (June 17–August 23) the beauty of the country, the hospitality of the neighbouring gentlemen, the novelty of command and exercise, and the consciousness of our daily and rapid improvements.

ii. From this school we were led against the enemy, a body of French, three thousand two hundred strong, who had occupied Portchester Castle, near Portsmouth. It must not indeed be dissembled that our enemies were naked unarmed prisoners, the object of pity rather than of terror; their misery was somewhat alleviated by public and private bounty; but their sufferings exhibited the evils of war, and their noisy spirits the character of the nation. During the months of September, October and November 1760 we performed this disagreeable duty by large detachments of a captain, four subalterns, and two hundred and thirty men, at first from Hilsea Barracks, and afterwards from our quarters at Tichfield and Fareham. The barracks within the Portsmouth lines are a square of low ill-built huts in a damp and dreary situation. On this unwholesome spot we lost many men by fevers and the small-pox; and our dispute with the Duke of Bolton, which produced a series of arrests, memorials and court-martials, was not less pernicious to the discipline than to the peace of the regiment.

iii. Rejoicing in our escape from this sink of distemper and discord, we performed with alacrity a long march (December 1–11) to Cranbrook in the weald of Kent, where we had been sent to guard eighteen hundred French prisoners at Sissinghurst. The inconceivable dirtiness of the season, the country and the spot aggravated the hardships of a duty too heavy for our numbers; but these hardships were of short duration, and before the end of the month we were relieved by the interest of our Tory friends under the new reign.

iv. At Dover, in the space of five months, we began to breathe (December 27, 1760–May 31, 1761): for the men the quarters were healthy and plentiful, and our dull leisure was enlivened by the society of the fourteenth Regiment in the Castle, and some sea parties in the spring. Our persecutions were at an end; the command was settled; we smiled at our own prowess, as we exercised each morning in sight of the French coast; and before we left Dover we had recovered the union and discipline which we possessed at our departure from Blandford.

v. In the summer of 1761 a camp was formed near Winchester in which we solicited and obtained a place. Our march from Dover to Alton in Hampshire was a pleasant walk (June 1–12): I was appointed captain of the new company of Grenadiers, and with proper clothing and accoutrements we assumed somewhat of the appearance of regular troops. The four months (June 25–October 21) of this encampment were the most splendid and useful period of our military life. Our establishment amounted to near five thousand men, the thirty-fourth regiment of foot, and six militia corps, the Wiltshire, Dorsetshire, South Hampshire, Berkshire, and the North and South Gloucestershire. The regulars were satisfied with their ideal pre-eminence; the Gloucestershire, Berkshire and Dorsetshire approached by successive steps the superior merit of the Wiltshire, the pride and pattern of the militia, an active, steady, well-appointed regiment of eight hundred men, which had been formed by the strict and skilful discipline of their Colonel, Lord Bruce. At our entrance into camp *we* were indisputably the last and worst: but we were excited by a generous shame:

Extremos pudeat rediisse[39]

and such was our indefatigable labour, that in the general reviews, the South Hampshire were rather a credit than a disgrace to the line. A friendly emulation, ready to teach and eager to learn, assisted our mutual progress; but the great evolutions, the exercise of acting and moving as an army, which constitutes the best lessons of a camp, never entered the thoughts of the Earl of Effingham, our drowsy General.

vi. The Devizes, our winter quarters during four months (October 23, 1761–February 28, 1762) are a populous town full of disorder and disease. The men who were allowed to work earned too much money; and their drunken quarrels with the townsmen and Colonel Barré's black musqueteers were painfully repressed by the sharp sentences of one and twenty court-martials. The Devizes afforded, however, a great number of fine young recruits whom we enlisted from the regimental stock-purse without much regard to the forms or the spirit of the Militia laws.

vii. After a short march and halt at Salisbury we paid a second visit of ten weeks (March 9–May 31) to our old friends at Blandford, where in that garden of England we again experienced the warm and constant hospitality of the natives. The spring was favourable to our military exercise, and the Dorsetshire gentlemen who had cherished our infancy now applauded a regiment, in appearance and discipline, not inferior to their own.

viii. The necessity of discharging a great number of men, whose term of three years was expired, forbade our encampment in the summer of 1762, and the colours were stationed at Southampton in the last six or seven months (June–December) of our actual service. But after so long an indulgence we could not complain that during many of the first and last weeks of this period, a detachment almost equal to the whole was required to guard the French prisoners at Forton and Fareham. The operation of the ballot was slow and tedious. In the months of August and September our life at Southampton was indeed gay and busy; the battalion had been renewed in youth and vigour; and so rapid was the improvement, that had the militia lasted another year we should not have yielded to the most perfect of our brethren. The preliminaries of peace and the suspension of arms determined our fate. We were dismissed with the thanks of the King and Parliament; and on the 23rd of December 1762, the companies were disembodied at their respective homes. The officers possessed of property rejoiced in their freedom; those who had none lamented the loss of their pay and profession; but it was found by experience that the greatest part of the men were rather civilized than corrupted by the habits of military subordination.

A young mind, unless it be of a cold and languid temper, is dazzled even by the play of arms; and in the first sallies of my enthusiasm I had seriously wished and tried to embrace the regular profession of a soldier. This military fever was cooled by the enjoyment of our mimic Bellona, who gradually unveiled her naked deformity. How often did I sigh for my true situation of a private gentleman and a man of letters: how often did I repeat the complaint of Cicero, 'Clitellae bovi sunt impositae. Est incredibile quam me negotii taedat … Ille cursus animi et industriae meae praeclara opera cessat. Lucem, libros, urbem, domum, vos desidero. Sed feram ut potero, sit modo annuum. Si prorogatur, actum est.'[40] From a service without danger I might indeed have retired without disgrace; but as often as I hinted a wish of resigning, my fetters were riveted by my father's authority, the entreaties of Sir Thomas Worsley, and some regard for the welfare of a corps of which I was the principal support. My proper province was the care of my own, and afterwards of the Grenadier company: but, with the rank of first captain, I possessed the confidence, and supplied the place, of the colonel and major. In their presence or in their absence I acted as the commanding officer: every memorial and letter relative to our disputes was the work of my pen; the detachments or court-martials of any delicacy or importance were my extraordinary duties; and to supersede the Duke of Bolton's adjutant I always exercised the battalion in the field. Sir Thomas Worsley was an easy good-humoured man, fond of the table and of his bed; our conferences were marked by every stroke of the midnight and morning hours, and the same drum which invited him to rest has often summoned me to the parade. His example encouraged the daily practice of hard and even excessive drinking which has sown in my constitution the seeds of the gout; the loss of so many busy and idle hours was not compensated by any elegant pleasure; and my temper was insensibly soured by the society of our rustic officers, who were alike deficient in the knowledge of scholars and the manners of gentlemen.

In every state there exists, however, a balance of good and evil. The habits of a sedentary life were usefully broken by the duties of an active profession. In the healthful exercise of the field I hunted with a battalion instead of a pack; and at that time I was ready at any hour of the day or night to fly from quarters to London, from London to quarters, on the slightest call of private or regimental business. But my principal obligation to the militia was the making me an Englishman and a soldier. After my foreign education, with my reserved temper, I should long have continued a stranger in my native country had I not been shaken in this various scene of new faces and new friends; had not experience forced me to feel the characters of our leading men, the state of parties, the forms of office, and the operation of our civil and military system. In this peaceful service I imbibed the rudiments of the language and science of tactics, which opened a new field of study and observation. I diligently read and meditated the *Mémoires militaires* of Quintus Icilius (M. Guichardt), the only writer who has united the merits of a professor and a veteran. The discipline and evolutions of a modern battalion gave me a clearer notion of the phalanx and the legion, and the captain of the Hampshire Grenadiers (the reader may smile) has not been useless to the historian of the Roman Empire.

When I complain of the loss of time, justice to myself and to the militia must throw the greatest part of that reproach on the first seven or eight months, while I was obliged to learn as well as to teach. The dissipation of Blandford and the disputes of Portsmouth consumed the hours which were not employed in the field; and amid the perpetual hurry of an inn, a barrack or a guard-room, all literary ideas were banished from my mind. After this long fast, the longest which I have ever known, I once more tasted at Dover the pleasures of reading and thinking; and the hungry appetite with which I opened a volume of Tully's philosophical works[41] is still present to my memory. The last review of my essay before its publication had prompted me to investigate the *Nature of the Gods*; my enquiries led me to the *Histoire critique du Manichéisme* of Beausobre, who discusses many deep questions of pagan and Christian theology; and from this rich treasury of facts and opinions I deduced my own consequences beyond the holy circle of the author. After this recovery, I never relapsed into indolence, and my example might prove that in the life most adverse to study some hours may be stolen, some minutes may be snatched. Amidst the tumult of Winchester camp I sometimes thought and read in my tent; in the more settled quarters of the Devizes, Blandford and Southampton, I always secured a separate lodging and the necessary books; and in the summer of 1762, while the new militia was raising, I enjoyed at Buriton two or three months of literary repose. In forming a new plan of study I hesitated between the mathematics and the Greek language, both of which I had neglected since my return from Lausanne. I consulted a learned and friendly mathematician, Mr George Scott, a pupil of de Moivre; and his map of a country which I have never explored may perhaps be more serviceable to others.

As soon as I had given the preference to Greek, the example of Scaliger and my own reason determined me on the choice of Homer, the father of poetry, and the Bible of the ancients: but Scaliger ran through the Iliad in one and twenty days, and I was not dissatisfied with my own diligence for performing the same labour in an equal number of weeks. After the first difficulties were surmounted, the language of nature and harmony soon became easy and familiar, and each day I sailed on the ocean with a brisker gale and a more steady course.

> Ἐν δ' ἄνεμος πρῆσεν μέσον ἱστίον, ἀμφὶ δὲ κῦμα
> Στείρῃ πορφύρεον μεγάλ' ἴαχε, νηὸς ἰούσης.
> Ἡ δ' ἔθεεν κατὰ κῦμα διαπρήσσουσα κέλευθον.[42]

In the study of a poet who has since become the most intimate of my friends, I successively applied many passages and fragments of Greek writers; and among these I shall notice a life of Homer in the *Opuscula mythologica* of Gale, several books of the *Geography* of Strabo, and the entire treatise of Longinus which, from the title and the style is equally worthy of the epithet of *Sublime*. My grammatical skill was improved, my vocabulary was enlarged; and in the militia, I acquired a just and indelible knowledge of the first of languages. On every march, in every journey, Horace was always in my pocket and often in my hand; but I should not mention his two critical Epistles, the amusement of a morning, had they not been accompanied by the elaborate commentary of Dr Hurd, now Bishop of Worcester. On the interesting subjects of composition and imitation of epic and dramatic poetry, I presumed to think for myself, and fifty close-written pages in folio[43] could scarcely comprise my full and free discussion of the sense of the master and the pedantry of the servant.

After his oracle Dr Johnson, my friend Sir Joshua Reynolds denies all original genius, any natural propensity of the mind to one art or science rather than another.[44] Without engaging in a metaphysical or rather verbal dispute, I *know* by experience that from my early youth I aspired to the character of an historian. While I served in the militia, before and after the publication of my essay, this idea ripened in my mind; nor can I paint in more lively colours the feelings of the moment, than by transcribing some passages, under their respective dates, from a Journal which I kept at that time.

Buriton, April 14, 1761

(In a short excursion from Dover.)

Having thought of several subjects for a historical composition, I chose the expedition of Charles VIII of France into Italy. I read two memoirs of M. de Foncemagne in the Academy of Inscriptions (Tome xvii, pp. 539–607) and abstracted them. I likewise finished this day a dissertation,[45] in which I examine the right of Charles VIII to the crown of Naples, and the rival claims of the houses of Anjou and Aragon. It consists of ten folio pages, besides large notes.

Buriton, August 4, 1761

(In a week's excursion from Winchester Camp.)

After having long revolved subjects for my intended historical essay, I renounced my first thought of the expedition of Charles VIII as too remote from us, and rather an introduction to great events than great and important in itself. I successively chose and rejected the Crusade of Richard the First, the Barons' wars against John and Henry III, the history of Edward the Black Prince, the lives and comparison of Henry V and the Emperor Titus, the life of Sir Philip Sidney, or of the Marquis of Montrose. At length I have fixed on Sir Walter Raleigh for my hero. His eventful story is varied by the characters of the soldier and sailor, the courtier and historian, and it may afford such a fund of materials as I desire which have not yet been properly manufactured. At present I cannot attempt the execution of this work. Free leisure and the opportunity of consulting many books, both printed and manuscript, are as necessary as they are impossible to be attained in my present way of life. However, to acquire a general insight into my subject and resources, I read the Life of Sir Walter Raleigh by Dr Birch, his copious article in the *General Dictionary* by the same hand, and the reigns of Queen Elizabeth and James the First in Hume's *History of England.*

Buriton, January 1762

(In a month's absence from the Devizes.)

During this interval of repose I again turned my thoughts to Sir Walter Raleigh, and looked more closely into my materials. I read the two volumes in quarto of the *Bacon papers*[46] published by Dr Birch, the *Fragmenta Regalia* of Sir Robert Naunton, Mallet's *Life of Lord Bacon* and the political treatises of that great man in the first volume of his works, with many of his letters in the second; Sir William Monson's *Naval Tracts*, and the elaborate *Life of Sir Walter Raleigh* which Mr Oldys has prefixed to the best edition of his *History of the World.* My subject opens upon me and in general improves on a nearer prospect.

Buriton, July 26, 1762

(During my summer residence.)

I am afraid of being reduced to drop my hero: but my time has not, however, been lost in the research of his story and of a memorable era of our English annals. This *Life of Sir Walter Raleigh* by Oldys is a very poor performance: a servile panegyric or flat apology, tediously minute, and composed in a dull and affected style. Yet the author was a man of diligence and learning, who had read everything relative to his object, and whose ample collections are arranged with perspicuity and method. Except some anecdotes lately revealed in the Sidney and Bacon papers I know not what I should be able to add.

My ambition (exclusive of the uncertain merit of style and sentiment) must be confined to the hope of giving a good abridgement of Oldys. I have even the disappointment of finding some parts of this copious work very dry and barren, and these parts are unluckily some of the most characteristic: Raleigh's colony of Virginia, his quarrels with Essex, the true secret of his conspiracy, and above all the detail of his private life, the most essential and important to a biographer. My best resource would be in the circumjacent history of the times, and perhaps in some digressions artfully introduced, like the fortunes of the Peripatetic philosophy in the portrait of Lord Bacon. But the reigns of Elizabeth and James I are the period of English history which has been the most variously illustrated: and what new lights could I reflect on a subject which has exercised the accurate industry of *Birch*, the lively and curious acuteness of *Walpole*, the critical spirit of *Hurd*, the vigorous sense of *Mallet* and *Robertson*, and the impartial philosophy of *Hume*? Could I even surmount these obstacles, I should shrink with terror from the modern history of England, where every character is a problem and every reader a friend or an enemy; where a writer is supposed to hoist a flag of party, and is devoted to damnation by the adverse faction. Such would be *my* reception at home; and abroad the historian of Raleigh must encounter an indifference far more bitter than censure or reproach. The events of his life are interesting; but his character is ambiguous, his actions are obscure, his writings are English, and his fame is confined to the narrow limits of our language and our island. I must embrace a safer and more extensive theme.

There is one which I should prefer to all others, *The History of the Liberty of the Swiss*, of that independence which a brave people rescued from the house of Austria, defended against a Dauphin of France, and finally sealed with the blood of Charles of Burgundy. From such a theme, so full of public spirit, of military glory, of examples of virtue, of lessons of government, the dullest stranger would catch fire. What might not *I* hope, whose talents, whatsoever they may be, would be inflamed by the zeal of patriotism. But the materials of this history are inaccessible to me, fast locked in the obscurity of an old, barbarous German dialect of which I am totally ignorant, and which I cannot resolve to learn for this sole and peculiar purpose.

I have another subject in view which is the contrast of the former history: the one a poor, warlike, virtuous republic which emerges into glory and freedom; the other a commonwealth, soft, opulent and corrupt, which by just degrees is precipitated from the abuse to the loss of her liberty: both lessons are perhaps equally instructive. This second subject is *The History of the Republic of Florence under the House of Medicis*: a period of one hundred and fifty years, which rises or descends from the dregs of the Florentine democracy to the title and dominion of Cosmo de Medicis[47] in the Grand Duchy of Tuscany. I might deduce a chain of revolutions not unworthy of the pen of Vertot: singular men and singular events; the Medicis four times expelled, and as often recalled, and the genius of freedom reluctantly yielding to the arms of Charles V and the policy of Cosmo. The character and fate of Savonarola, and the revival of arts and letters in Italy will be essentially connected with the elevation of the family and the fall of the republic. The Medicis, *stirps quasi fataliter nata ad instauranda vel fovenda studia*[48] (Lipsius *ad Germanos et Gallos, Epist.* vii), were illustrated by the patronage of learning, and enthusiasm was the most formidable weapon of their adversaries. On this spendid subject I shall most probably fix; but *when*, or *where* or *how* will it be executed? I behold in a dark and doubtful perspective

Res alta terra et caligine mersa.[49]

Chapter VI[1]

Grand Tour · Buriton–London · Father's Death
(1763–70)

The youthful habits of the language and manners of France had left in my mind an ardent desire of revisiting the continent on a larger and more liberal plan. According to the law of custom and perhaps of reason, foreign travel completes the education of an English gentleman; my father had consented to my wish, but I was detained above four years by my rash engagement in the militia. I eagerly grasped the first moments of freedom; three or four weeks in Hampshire and London were employed in the preparations of my journey and the farewell visits of friendship and civility. My last act in town was to applaud Mallet's new tragedy of *Elvira*; a post-chaise conveyed me to Dover, the packet to Boulogne,[2] and such was my diligence, that I reached Paris on the 28th of January 1763, only thirty-six days after the disbanding of the militia. Two or three years were loosely defined for the term of my absence; and I was left at liberty to spend that time in such places and in such a manner as was most agreeable to my taste and judgement.

In this first visit I passed three months and a half (January 28–May 9) at Paris, and a much longer space might have been agreeably filled without any intercourse with the natives. At home we are content to move in the daily round of pleasure and business; and a scene which is always present is supposed to be within our knowledge or at least within our power. But in a foreign country, curiosity is our business and our pleasure; and the traveller, conscious of his ignorance and covetous of his time, is diligent in the search and the view of every object that can deserve his attention. I devoted many hours of the morning to the circuit of Paris and the neighbourhood, to the visit of churches and palaces conspicuous by their architecture, to the royal manufactures, collections of books and pictures, and all the various treasures of art, of learning, and of luxury. An Englishman may hear without reluctance that in these curious and costly articles Paris is superior to London, since the opulence of the French capital arises from the defects of its government and religion. In the absence of Louis XIV and his successors, the Louvre has been left unfinished: but the millions which have been lavished on the sands of Versailles and the morass of Marli could not be supplied by the legal allowance of a British king. The splendour of the French nobles is confined to their town-residence; that of the English is more usefully distributed in their country seats; and we should be astonished at our own riches, if the labours of architecture, the spoils of Italy and Greece, which are now scattered from Inverary to Wilton,[3] were accumulated in a few streets between Marylebone and Westminster. All superfluous ornament is rejected by the cold frugality of the Protestants; but the Catholic superstition, which is always the enemy of reason, is often the parent of taste. The wealthy communities of priests and monks expend their revenues in stately edifices, and the parish church of St Sulpice, one of the noblest structures in Paris, was built and adorned by the private industry of a late curate.[4] In this outset and still more in the sequel of my tour, my eye was amused; but the pleasing vision cannot be fixed by the pen; the particular images are darkly seen through the medium of five and twenty years, and the narrative of my life must not degenerate into a book of travels.

But the principal end of my journey was to enjoy the society of a polished and amiable people in whose favour I was strongly prejudiced, and to converse with some authors, whose conversation as I fondly imagined, must be far more pleasing and instructive than their writings. The moment was happily chosen. At the close of a successful war, the British name was respected on the continent:

> Clarum et venerabile nomen
> Gentibus.[5]

Our opinions, our fashions, even our games were adopted in France; a ray of national glory illuminated each individual, and every Englishman was supposed to be born a patriot and a philosopher. For myself I carried a personal recommendation: my name and my essay were already known; the compliment of writing in the French language entitled me to some returns of civility and gratitude. I was considered as a man of letters, or rather as a gentleman who wrote for his amusement; my appearance, dress and equipage distinguished me from the tribe of authors who even at Paris are secretly envied and despised by those who possess the advantages of birth and fortune. Before my departure I had obtained from the Duke de Nivernois, Lady Hervey, the Mallets, Mr Walpole, etc., many letters of recommendation to their private or literary friends. Of these epistles the reception and success was determined by the character and situation of the persons by whom and to whom they were addressed: the seed was sometimes cast on a barren rock, and it sometimes multiplied a hundred fold in the production of new shoots, spreading branches and exquisite fruit. But upon the whole I had reason to praise the national urbanity, which from the court has diffused its gentle influence to the shop, the cottage and the schools.

Of the men of genius of the age, Montesquieu and Fontenelle were no more; Voltaire resided on his own estate near Geneva; Rousseau in the preceding year had been driven from his hermitage of Montmorency, and I blush at my neglecting to seek, in this journey, the acquaintance of Buffon. Among the men of letters whom I saw, d'Alembert and Diderot held the foremost rank, in merit, or at least in fame. These two associates were the elements of water and fire; but the eruption was clouded with smoke, and the stream though devoid of grace was limpid and copious. I shall content myself with enumerating the well-known names of the Count de Caylus, of the Abbés de la Bléterie, Barthélémy, Raynal, Arnaud, of Messieurs de la Condamine, Duclos, de Ste Palaye, de Bougainville, Caperonnier, de Guignes, Suard, etc., without attempting to discriminate the shades of their characters, or the degrees of our connection. Alone in a morning visit I commonly found the wits and authors of Paris less vain and more reasonable than in the circles of their equals, with whom they mingle in the houses of the rich. Four days in the week I had a place without invitation at the hospitable tables of Mesdames Geoffrin and du Bocage, of the celebrated Helvétius, and of the Baron d'Olbach. In these *Symposia* the pleasures of the table were improved by lively and liberal conversation; the company was select, though various and voluntary, and each unbidden guest might mutter a proud and ungrateful sentence

’Αυτόματοι δ’ἀγαθοὶ δειλῶν ἐπὶ δαῖτας ἴασιν.[6]

Yet I was often disgusted with the capricious tyranny of Madame Geoffrin, nor could I approve the intolerant zeal of the philosophers and Encyclopedists, the friends of d'Olbach and Helvétius: they laughed at the scepticism of Hume, preached the tenets of atheism with the bigotry of dogmatists, and damned all believers with ridicule and contempt. The society of Madame du Bocage was more soft and moderate than that of her rivals; and the evening conversations of M. de Foncemagne were supported by the good sense and learning of the principal members of the Academy of Inscriptions. The opera and the Italians[7] I occasionally visited: but the French theatre, both in tragedy and comedy, was my daily and favourite amusement. Two famous actresses then divided the public applause: for my own part I preferred the consummate art of the Clairon to the intemperate sallies of the Dumesnil, which were extolled by her admirers as the genuine voice of nature and passion.

I have reserved for the last the most pleasing connection which I formed at Paris, the acquisition of a female friend by whom I was sure of being received every evening with the smile of confidence and joy. I delivered a letter from Mrs Mallet to Madame Bontems, who had distinguished herself by a translation of Thomson's *Seasons* into French prose; at our first interview we felt a sympathy which banished all reserve, and opened our bosoms to each other. In every light, in every attitude, Madame B. was a sensible and amiable companion; an author careless of literary honours, a devotee untainted with religious gall. She managed a small income with elegant economy; her apartment on the Quai des Théatins commanded the river, the bridges, and the Louvre; her familiar suppers were adorned with freedom and taste; and I attended her in my carriage to the houses of her acquaintance, to the sermons of the most popular preachers, and in pleasant excursions to St Denys, St Germain, and Versailles. In the middle season of life, her beauty was still an object of desire. The Marquis de Mirabeau, a celebrated name, was neither her first nor her last lover; but if her heart was tender, if her passions were warm, a veil of decency was cast over her frailties. Fourteen weeks insensibly stole away; but had I been rich and independent, I should have prolonged and perhaps have fixed my residence at Paris.

Between the expensive style of Paris and of Italy, it was prudent to interpose some months of tranquil simplicity; and at the thoughts of Lausanne, I again lived in the pleasures and studies of my early youth. Shaping my course through Dijon and Besançon, in the last of which places I was kindly entertained by my cousin Acton, I arrived in the month of May 1763 on the banks of the Leman Lake. It had been my intention to pass the Alps in the autumn; but such are the simple attractions of the place, that the annual circle was almost revolved before my departure from Lausanne in the ensuing spring. An absence of five years had not made much alteration in manners or even in persons. My old friends of both sexes hailed my voluntary return, the most genuine proof of my attachment; they had been flattered by the present of my book, the produce of their soil, and the good Pavilliard shed tears of joy as he embraced a pupil with whose success his vanity as well as friendship might be delighted. To my old list I added some new acquaintance, who in my former residence had not been on the spot, or in my way, and among the strangers I shall distinguish Prince Lewis of Wirtemberg, the brother of the reigning Duke, at whose country house near Lausanne I frequently dined. A wandering meteor and at length a falling star, his light and ambitious spirit had successively dropped from the firmament of Prussia, of France and of Austria; and his faults, which he styled his misfortunes, had driven him into philosophic exile in the Pays de Vaud. He could now moralize on the vanity of the world, the equality of mankind, and the happiness of a private station: his address was affable and polite, and as he had shone in courts and armies, his memory could supply, and his eloquence could adorn a copious fund of interesting anecdotes. His first enthusiasm was that of charity and agriculture, but the sage gradually lapsed in the saint, and Prince Lewis of Wirtemberg is now buried in a hermitage near Mayence in the last stage of mystic devotion.

By some ecclesiastical quarrel Voltaire had been provoked to withdraw himself from Lausanne; but the theatre which he had founded, the actors whom he had formed survived the loss of their master; and recent from Paris I assisted[8] with pleasure at the representation of several tragedies and comedies. I shall not descend to specify particular names and characters; but I cannot forget a private institution which will display the innocent freedom of Swiss manners. My favourite society had assumed from the age of its members the proud denomination of the spring (*la société du printemps*). It consisted of fifteen or twenty young unmarried ladies of genteel though not of the very first families; the eldest perhaps about twenty, all agreeable, several handsome, and two or three of exquisite beauty. At each others' houses they assembled almost every day: without the control or even the presence of a mother or an aunt, they were trusted to their own prudence, among a crowd of young men of every nation in Europe. They laughed, they sung, they danced, they played at cards, they acted comedies; but in the midst of this careless gaiety, they respected themselves, and were respected by the men. The invisible line between liberty and licentiousness was never transgressed by a gesture, a word or a look, and their virgin chastity was never sullied by the breath of scandal or suspicion.

After tasting the luxury of England and Paris, I could not have returned with patience to the table and table-cloth of Madame Pavilliard, nor was her husband offended that I now entered myself as a *pensionnaire* or boarder in the more elegant house of M. de Mésery, which may be entitled to a short remembrance, as it has stood above twenty years, perhaps, without a parallel in Europe. The house in which we lodged was spacious and convenient in the best street, and commanding from behind a noble prospect over the country and the lake. Our table was served with neatness and plenty; the boarders were numerous; we had the liberty of inviting any guests at a stated price; and in the summer the scene was occasionally transferred to a pleasant villa about a league from Lausanne. The characters of the master and mistress were happily suited to each other and to their situation. At the age of seventy-five Madame de Mésery, who had survived her husband, is still a graceful, I had almost said a handsome woman: she was alike qualified to preside in her kitchen and her drawing-room, and such was the equal propriety of her conduct that of two or three hundred foreigners, none ever failed in respect, none could complain of her neglect, and none could ever boast of her favour. Mésery himself, of the noble family of de Crousaz, was a man of the world, a jovial companion, whose easy manners and natural sallies maintained the cheerfulness of his house. His wit could laugh at his own ignorance; he disguised by an air of profusion a strict attention to his interest; and in the exercise of a mean trade he appeared like a nobleman, who spent his fortune and entertained his friends. In this agreeable family I resided near eleven months (May 1763–April 1764). But the habits of the militia and the example of my countrymen betrayed me into some riotous acts[9] of intemperance; and before my departure, I had deservedly forfeited the public opinion which had been acquired by the virtues of my better days. Yet in this second visit to Lausanne, among a crowd of my English companions, I knew and esteemed Mr Holroyd,[10] late captain in the Royal Foresters, and our mutual attachment was renewed and fortified in the subsequent stages of our Italian journey. Our lives are in the power of chance, and a slight variation on either side, in time or place, might have deprived me of a friend whose activity in the ardour of youth was always prompted by a benevolent heart, and directed by a strong understanding.

If my studies at Paris had been confined to the study of the world, three or four months would not have been unprofitably spent. My visits, however superficial, to the Cabinet of Medals and the public libraries opened a new field of enquiry, and the view of so many manuscripts of different ages and characters induced me to consult the two great Benedictine works, the *Diplomatica* of Mabillon, and the *Palæographica* of Montfaucon. I studied the theory, without attaining the practice of the art; nor should I complain of the intricacy of Greek abbreviations and Gothic alphabets since every day, in a familiar language, I am at a loss to decipher the hieroglyphics of a female note. In a tranquil scene, which revived the memory of my first studies, idleness would have been less pardonable: the public libraries of Lausanne and Geneva liberally supplied me with books, and if many hours were lost in dissipation, many more were employed in literary labour. In the country, Horace and Virgil, Juvenal and Ovid were my assiduous companions; but in town I formed and executed a plan of study for the use of my Transalpine expedition: the topography of old Rome, the ancient geography of Italy, and the science of Medals.

1. I diligently read, almost always with my pen in my hand, the elaborate treatises of Nardini, Donatus, etc., which fill the fourth volume of the *Roman Antiquities* of Graevius.

2. I next undertook and finished the *Italia Antiqua* of Cluverius, a learned native of Prussia, who had measured on foot every spot, and has compiled and digested every passage of the ancient writers. These passages in Greek or Latin I perused in the text of Cluverius in two folio volumes; but I separately read the descriptions of Italy by Strabo, Pliny and Pomponius Mela, the Catalogues of the Epic poets, the itineraries of Wesseling's Antoninus, and the coasting voyage of Rutilius Numatianus; and I studied two kindred subjects in the *Mésures itinéraires* of d'Anville and the copious work of Bergier, *Histoire des grands chemins de l'Empire Romain*. From these materials I formed a table of roads and distances reduced to our English measure; filled a folio common-place book with my collections and remarks on the geography of Italy, and inserted in my journal many long and learned notes on the *insulae* and populousness of Rome, the Social War, the passage of the Alps by Hannibal, etc.[11]

3. After glancing my eye over Addison's agreeable Dialogues, I more seriously read the great work of Ezechiel Spanheim, *De præstantia et usu Numismatum*, and applied with him the medals of the kings and emperors, the families and colonies, to the illustration of ancient history – And thus was I armed for my Italian journey. Perhaps I might boast that few travellers more completely armed and instructed have ever followed the footsteps of Hannibal. As soon as the return of spring had unlocked the mountains, I departed from Lausanne (April 18, 1764) with an English companion (Mr, afterwards Sir William, Guise) whose partnership divided and alleviated the expenses of the journey.

I shall advance with rapid brevity in the narrative of my Italian tour, in which somewhat more than a year (April 1764–May 1765) was agreeably employed. Content with tracing my line of march, and slightly touching on my personal feelings, I shall waive the minute investigation of the scenes which have been viewed by thousands and described by hundreds of our modern travellers. ROME is the great object of our pilgrimage, and i. the Journey, ii. the residence, and iii. the return will form the most proper and perspicuous division.

i. I climbed Mount Cenis and descended into the plain of Piedmont, not on the back of an elephant, but on a light osier seat in the hands of the dexterous and intrepid chairmen of the Alps. The architecture and government of Turin presented the same aspect of tame and tiresome uniformity: but the court was regulated with decent and splendid economy; and I was introduced to his Sardinian majesty, Charles Emanuel, who after the incomparable Frederic, held the second rank (*proximus longo tamen intervallo*[12]) among the kings of Europe. The size and populousness of Milan could not surprise an inhabitant of London: the Dome or Cathedral is an unfinished monument of Gothic superstition and wealth; but the fancy is amused by a visit to the Borromean islands, an enchanted palace, a work of the fairies in the midst of a lake encompassed with mountains, and far removed from the haunts of men. I was less amused by the marble palaces of Genoa than by the recent memorials of her deliverance (in December 1746) from the Austrian tyranny; and I took a military survey of every scene of action within the enclosure of her double walls. My steps were detained at Parma and Modena by the precious relics of the Farnese and Este collections; but, alas! the far greater part had been already transported by inheritance or purchase to Naples and Dresden. By the road of Bologna and the Apennine I at last reached Florence, where I reposed from June to September during the heat of the summer months. In the gallery, and especially in the Tribune, I first acknowledged, at the feet of the Venus of Medicis, that the chisel may dispute the pre-eminence with the pencil, a truth in the fine arts which cannot, on this side of the Alps, be felt or understood. At home I had taken some lessons of Italian; on the spot I read with a learned native the classics of the Tuscan idiom; but the shortness of my time, and the use of the French language, prevented my acquiring any facility of speaking; and I was a silent spectator in the conversations[13] of our envoy, Sir Horace Mann, whose most serious business was that of entertaining the English at his hospitable table. After leaving Florence I compared the solitude of Pisa with the industry of Lucca and Leghorn, and continued my journey through Sienna to Rome, where I arrived in the beginning of October.

ii. My temper is not very susceptible of enthusiasm, and the enthusiasm which I do not feel I have ever scorned to affect. But at the distance of twenty-five years, I can neither forget nor express the strong emotions which agitated my mind as I first approached and entered the *eternal City*. After a sleepless night I trod with a lofty step the ruins of the Forum; each memorable spot where Romulus *stood*,[14] or Tully spoke, or Caesar fell was at once present to my eye; and several days of intoxication were lost or enjoyed before I could descend to a cool and minute investigation. My guide was Mr Byers, a Scotch antiquary of experience and taste; but in the daily labour of eighteen weeks the powers of attention were sometimes fatigued, till I was myself qualified in a last review to select and study the capital works of ancient and modern art. Six weeks were borrowed for my tour of Naples, the most populous of cities relative to its size, whose luxurious inhabitants seem to dwell on the confines of paradise and hell-fire. I was presented to the boy-king[15] by our new envoy, Sir William Hamilton, who, wisely diverting his correspondence from the Secretary of State to the Royal Society and British Museum, has elucidated a country of such inestimable value to the naturalist and antiquarian. On my return I fondly embraced for the last time the miracles of Rome; but I departed without kissing the feet of Rezzonico (Clement XIII), who neither possessed the wit of his predecessor Lambertini, nor the virtue of his successor Ganganelli.

iii. In my pilgrimage from Rome to Loretto, I again crossed the Apennine; from the coast of the Adriatic I traversed a fruitful and populous country which would alone disprove the paradox of Montesquieu, that modern Italy is a desert.[16] Without adopting the exclusive prejudice of the natives I sincerely admired the paintings of the Bologna school. I hastened to escape from the sad solitude of Ferrara, which in the age of Caesar was still more desolate. The spectacle of Venice afforded some hours of astonishment and some days of disgust; the university of Padua is a dying taper; but Verona still boasts her amphitheatre, and his native Vicenza is adorned by the classic architecture of Palladio. The road of Lombardy and Piedmont (did Montesquieu find them without inhabitants?) led me back to Milan, Turin, and the passage of Mount Cenis, where I again crossed the Alps in my way to Lyons.

The use of foreign travel has been often debated as a general question; but the conclusion must be finally applied to the character and circumstances of each individual. With the education of boys, *where*, or *how* they may pass over some juvenile years with the least mischief to themselves or others, I have no concern. But after supposing the previous and indispensable requisites of age, judgement, a competent knowledge of men and books, and a freedom from domestic prejudices, I will briefly describe the qualifications which I deem most essential to a traveller. He should be endowed with an active, indefatigable vigour of mind and body, which can seize every mode of conveyance, and support with a careless smile every hardship of the road, the weather or the inn. I must stimulate him with a restless curiosity, impatient of ease, covetous of time and fearless of danger; which drives him forth at any hour of the day or night, to brave the flood, to climb the mountain, or to fathom the mine, on the most doubtful promise of entertainment or instruction. The arts of common life are not studied in the closet; with a copious stock of classical and historical learning, my traveller must blend the practical knowledge of husbandry and manufactures; he should be a chemist, a botanist, and a master of mechanics. A musical ear will multiply the pleasures of his Italian tour; but a correct and exquisite eye, which commands the landscape of a country, discerns the merits of a picture, and measures the proportions of a building, is more closely connected with the finer feelings of the mind; and the fleeting image should be fixed and realized by the dexterity of the pencil. I have reserved for the last a virtue which borders on a vice: the flexible temper which can assimilate itself to every tone of society, from the court to the cottage; the happy flow of spirits which can amuse and be amused in every company and situation. With the advantage of an independent fortune and the ready use of national and provincial idioms, the traveller should unite the pleasing aspect and decent familiarity which makes every stranger an acquaintance; and the art of conversing with ignorance and dullness on some topic of local or professional information.

The benefits of foreign travel will correspond with the degrees of these various qualifications: but in this sketch of ideal perfection, those to whom I am known will not accuse me of framing my own panegyric. Yet the historian of the Decline and Fall must not regret his time or expense, since it was the view of Italy and Rome which determined the choice of the subject. In my Journal the place and moment of conception are recorded;[17] the fifteenth of October 1764, in the close of evening, as I sat musing in the Church of the Zoccolanti or Franciscan friars, while they were singing Vespers in the Temple of Jupiter on the ruins of the Capitol. But my original plan was circumscribed to the decay of the City, rather than of the Empire: and, though my reading and reflections began to point towards the object, some years elapsed and several avocations intervened before I was seriously engaged in the execution of that laborious work.

I had not totally renounced the southern provinces of France; but the letters which I found at Lyons were expressive of some impatience.[18] The measure of absence and expense was filled; Rome and Italy had satiated my curious appetite, and the excessive heat of the weather decided the sage resolution of turning my face to the north, and seeking the peaceful retreat of my family and books. After a happy fortnight I tore myself from the embraces of Paris, embarked at Calais, again landed at Dover, after an interval of two years and five months, and hastily drove through the

summer dust and solitude of London. On the 25th of June 1765 I reached
the rural mansion of my parents, to whom I was endeared by my long
absence and cheerful submission.

After my first (1758) and my second return to England (1765) the forms
of the pictures were nearly the same: but the colours had been darkened
by time; and the five years and a half between my travels and my father's
death (1770) are the portion of my life which I passed with the least
enjoyment, and which I remember with the least satisfaction. I have
nothing to change (for there was not any change) in the annual distribution of my summers and winters, between my domestic residence in
Hampshire and a casual lodging at the west end of the town; though, once,
from the trial of some months I was tempted to substitute the tranquil
dissipation of Bath instead of the smoke, the expense and the tumult of the
metropolis, *fumum, et opes, strepitumque Romae.*[19] Every spring I attended
the monthly meeting and exercise of the militia at Southampton; and by
the resignation of my father and the death of Sir Thomas Worsley, I was
successively promoted to the rank of major and lieutenant-colonel commandant. Under the care (may I presume to say?) of a veteran officer, the
South Battalion of the Hampshire militia acquired the degree of skill and
discipline which was compatible with the brevity of time and the looseness
of peaceful subordination; but I was each year more disgusted with the
inn, the wine, the company, and the tiresome repetition of annual attendance and daily exercise. At home, the economy of the family and farm still
maintained the same creditable appearance. I was received, entertained
and dismissed with similar kindness and indulgence. My connection with
Mrs Gibbon was mellowed into a warm and solid attachment; my growing
years abolished the distance that might yet remain between a parent and
a son, and my behaviour satisfied my father, who was proud of the success,
however imperfect in his own lifetime, of my literary talents.

Our solitude was soon and often enlivened by the visit of the friend
of my youth, M. Deyverdun, whose absence from Lausanne I had sincerely
lamented. About three years after my first departure he had migrated
from his native lake to the banks of the Oder in Germany. The *res angusta
domi*,[20] the waste of a decent patrimony by an improvident father, obliged
him, like many of his countrymen, to confide in his own industry: and
he was entrusted with the education of a young prince, the grandson
of the Margrave of Schwedt of the Royal family of Prussia. Our friendship
was never cooled; our correspondence was sometimes interrupted; but
I rather wished than hoped to obtain M. Deyverdun for the companion
of my Italian tour. An unhappy though honourable passion drove him

from his German court; and the attractions of hope and curiosity were fortified by the expectation of my speedy return to England. I was allowed to offer him the hospitality of the house; during four successive summers he passed several weeks or months at Buriton, and our free conversations on every topic that could interest the heart or understanding would have reconciled me to a desert or a prison. In the winter months of London my sphere of knowledge and action was somewhat enlarged by the many new acquaintance which I had contracted in the militia and abroad; and I must regret as more than an acquaintance Mr Godfrey Clarke of Derbyshire, an amiable and worthy young man, who was snatched away by an untimely death. A weekly convivial meeting was instituted by myself and my fellow travellers under the name of the Roman Club; and I was soon balloted into Boodle's (the school of virtue, as the Earl of Shelburne had first named it) where I found the daily resource of excellent dinners, mixed company and moderate play. I must own, however, with a blush, that my virtues of temperance and sobriety had not completely recovered themselves from the wounds of the militia, that my connections were much less among women than men; and that these men, though far from contemptible in rank and fortune, were not of the first eminence in the literary or political world.

The renewal, or perhaps the improvement, of my English life was embittered by the alteration of my own feelings. At the age of twenty-one, I was in my proper station of a youth, delivered from the yoke of education, and delighted with the comparative state of liberty and affluence. My filial obedience was natural and easy; and in the gay prospect of futurity, my ambition did not extend beyond the enjoyment of my books, my leisure, and my patrimonial estate, undisturbed by the cares of a family and the duties of a profession. But in the militia I was armed with power, in my travels I was exempt from control; and as I approached, as I gradually transcended my thirtieth year, I began to feel the desire of being master in my own house. The most gentle authority will sometimes frown without reason, the most cheerful submission will sometimes murmur without cause; and such is the law of our imperfect nature, that we must either command or obey, that our personal liberty is supported by the obsequiousness of our own dependents. While so many of my acquaintance were married, or in parliament, or advancing with a rapid step in the various roads of honours and fortune, I stood alone, immoveable and insignificant; for after the monthly meeting of 1770 I had even withdrawn myself from the militia by the resignation of an empty and barren commission.

My temper is not susceptible of envy, and the view of successful merit has always excited my warmest applause. A matrimonial alliance has ever been the object of my terror rather than of my wishes. I was not very strongly pressed by my family or my passions to propagate the name and race of the Gibbons, and if some reasonable temptations occurred in the neighbourhood, the vague idea never proceeded to the length of a serious negotiation. The miseries of a vacant life were never known to a man whose hours were insufficient for the inexhaustible pleasures of study. But I lamented that at the proper age I had not embraced the lucrative pursuits of the law or of trade, the chances of civil office or India adventure, or even the fat slumbers of the Church; and my repentance became more lively as the loss of time was more irretrievable. Experience showed me the use of grafting my private consequence on the importance of a great professional body; the benefits of those firm connections, which are cemented by hope and interest, by gratitude and emulation, by the mutual exchange of services and favours. From the emoluments of a profession I might have derived an ample fortune or a competent income, instead of being stinted to the same narrow allowance, to be increased only by an event which I sincerely deprecated. The progress and the knowledge of our domestic disorders aggravated my anxiety, and I began to apprehend that I might be left in my old age without the fruits either of industry or inheritance.

In the first summer after my return, whilst I enjoyed at Buriton the society of my friend Deyverdun, our daily conversations expatiated over the field of ancient and modern literature, and we freely discussed my studies, my first essay, and my future projects. The Decline and Fall of Rome I still contemplated at an awful distance; but the two historical designs which had balanced my choice were submitted to his taste; and in the parallel between the revolutions of Florence and Switzerland, our common partiality for a country which was *his* by birth and *mine* by adoption inclined the scale in favour of the latter. According to the plan, which was soon conceived and digested, I embraced a period of two hundred years from the association of the three peasants of the Alps[21] to the plenitude and prosperity of the Helvetic body in the sixteenth century. I should have described the deliverance and victory of the Swiss, who have never shed the blood of their tyrants but in a field of battle; the laws and manners of the confederate states; the splendid trophies of the Austrian, Burgundian and Italian wars; and the wisdom of a nation, who after some sallies of martial adventure has been content to guard the blessings of peace with the sword of freedom.

... Manus haec inimica tyrannis
Ense petit placidam sub libertate quietem.[22]

My judgement as well as my enthusiasm was satisfied with the glorious theme, and the assistance of Deyverdun seemed to remove an insuperable obstacle. The French or Latin memorials, of which I was not ignorant, are inconsiderable in number and weight; but in the perfect acquaintance of my friend with the German language, I found the key of a more valuable collection. The most necessary books were procured: he translated for my use the folio volume of Schilling, a copious and contemporary relation of the war of Burgundy; we read and marked the most interesting parts of the great chronicle of Tschudi; and by his labour or that of an inferior assistant, large extracts were made from the history of Lauffer, and the dictionary of Leu.

Yet such was the distance and delay that two years elapsed in these preparatory steps; and it was late in the third summer (1767) before I entered with these slender materials on the more agreeable task of composition. A specimen of my history, the first book, was read the following winter in a literary society of foreigners in London; and as the author was unknown, I listened without observation, to the free strictures and unfavourable sentence of my judges. The momentary sensation was painful; but their condemnation was ratified by my cooler thoughts. I delivered my imperfect sheets to the flames;[23] and for ever renounced a design in which some expense, much labour, and more time had been so vainly consumed. I cannot regret the loss of a slight and superficial essay: for such the work must have been in the hands of a stranger, uninformed by the scholars and statesmen, remote from the libraries and archives of the Swiss republics. My ancient habits and the presence of Deyverdun encouraged me to write in French, for the continent of Europe; but I was conscious myself, that my style, above prose and below poetry, degenerated into a verbose and turgid declamation. Perhaps I may impute the failure to the injudicious choice of a foreign language. Perhaps I may suspect that the language itself is ill adapted to sustain the vigour and dignity of an important narrative. But if France, so rich in literary merit, had produced a great original historian, his genius would have formed and fixed the idiom to the proper tone, the peculiar mode of historical eloquence.

It was in search of some liberal and lucrative employment that my friend Deyverdun had visited England. His remittances from home were scanty and precarious; my purse was always open but it was often empty, and I bitterly felt the want of riches and power, which might have enabled me to correct the errors of his fortune. His wishes and qualifications solicited the station of the travelling governor of some wealthy pupil: but every vacancy provoked so many eager candidates, that for a long time I struggled without success; nor was it till after much application that I could even place him as a clerk in the office of the Secretary of State. In a residence of several years he never acquired the just pronunciation and familiar use of the English tongue; but he read our most difficult authors with ease and taste, his critical knowledge of our language and poetry was such as few foreigners have possessed; and few of our countrymen could enjoy the theatre of Shakespeare and Garrick with more exquisite feeling and discernment. The consciousness of his own strength and the assurance of my aid emboldened him to imitate the example of Dr Maty, whose *Journal Britannique* was esteemed and regretted; and to improve his model by uniting with the transactions of literature a philosophic view of the arts and manners of the British nation. Our Journal for the year 1767, under the title of *Mémoires littéraires de la Grande Bretagne*, was soon finished and sent to the press. For the first article, Lord Lyttleton's *History of Henry II*, I must own myself responsible; but the public has ratified my judgement of that voluminous work, in which sense and learning are not illuminated by a ray of genius. The next specimen was the choice of my friend, *The Bath Guide*,[24] a light and whimsical performance of local and even verbal pleasantry. I started at the attempt; he smiled at my fears. His courage was justified by success, and a master of both languages will applaud the curious felicity with which he has transfused into French prose the spirit and even humour of the English verse. It is not my wish to deny how deeply I was interested in these Memoirs, of which I need not surely be ashamed; but at the distance of more than twenty years, it would be impossible for me to ascertain the respective shares of the two associates. A long and intimate communication of ideas had cast our sentiments and style in the same mould. In our social labours we composed and corrected by turns; and the praise which I might honestly bestow would fall perhaps on some article or passage most properly my own.

A second volume (for the year 1768) was published of these Memoirs. I will presume to say that their merit was superior to their reputation; but it is not less true that they were productive of more reputation than emolument. They introduced my friend to the protection, and myself to the acquaintance, of the Earl of Chesterfield, whose age and infirmities secluded him from the world; and of Mr David Hume, who was Under-

Secretary to the office in which Deyverdun was more humbly employed. The former accepted a dedication (April 12, 1769) and reserved the author for the future education of his successor: the latter enriched the Journal with a reply to Mr Walpole's historical doubts, which he afterwards shaped into the form of a note.[25] The materials of the third volume were almost completed, when I recommended Deyverdun as governor to Sir Richard Worsley, a youth, the son of my old lieutenant-colonel, who was lately deceased. They set forwards on their travels; nor did they return to England till some time after my father's death.

My next publication was an accidental sally of love and resentment; of my reverence for modest genius, and my aversion for insolent pedantry. The sixth book of the Aeneid is the most pleasing and perfect composition of Latin poetry. The descent of Aeneas and the Sibyl to the infernal regions, to the world of spirits, expands an awful and boundless prospect, from the nocturnal gloom of the Cumaean grot

> Ibant obscuri sola sub nocte per umbram,

to the meridian brightness of the Elysian fields;

> Largior hic campos aether et lumine vestit
> Purpureo;

from the dreams of simple nature to the dreams, alas! of Egyptian theology and the philosophy of the Greeks. But the final dismission of the hero through the ivory gate from whence

> Falsa ad coelum mittunt insomnia manes[26]

seems to dissolve the whole enchantment, and leaves the reader in a state of cold and anxious scepticism. This most lame and impotent conclusion has been variously imputed to the haste or irreligion of Virgil; but according to the more elaborate interpretation of Bishop Warburton, the descent to Hell is not a false but a mimic scene, which represents the initiation of Aeneas, in the character of a lawgiver, to the Eleusinian mysteries. This hypothesis, a singular chapter in the *Divine Legation of Moses*, had been admitted by many as true, it was praised by all as ingenious; nor had it been exposed in a space of thirty years to a fair and critical discussion. The learning and abilities of the author had raised him to a just eminence; but he reigned the dictator and tyrant of the world of Literature. The real merit of Warburton was degraded by the pride and presumption with which he pronounced his infallible decrees; in his polemic writings he lashed his antagonists without mercy or moderation;

and his servile flatterers (see the base and malignant *Delicacy of Friendship*[27]), exalting the master critic far above Aristotle and Longinus, assaulted every modest dissenter who refused to consult the oracle and to adore the idol. In a land of liberty, such despotism must provoke a general opposition, and the zeal of opposition is seldom candid or impartial. A late professor of Oxford (Dr Lowth), in a pointed and polished epistle (August 31, 1765) defended himself and attacked the Bishop; and whatsoever might be the merits of an insignificant controversy, his victory was clearly established by the silent confusion of Warburton and his slaves. *I* too, without any private offence, was ambitious of breaking a lance against the giant's shield: and in the beginning of the year 1770, my *Critical Observations on the Sixth Book of the Aeneid* were sent without my name to the press.

In this short essay, my first English publication, I aimed my strokes against the person and the hypothesis of Bishop Warburton. I proved, at least to my own satisfaction, *that* the ancient lawgivers did not invent the mysteries, and *that* Aeneas was never invested with the office of lawgiver; *that*, there is not any argument, any circumstance, which can melt a fable into allegory, or remove the scene from the Lake Avernus to the Temple of Ceres; *that* such a wild supposition is equally injurious to the poet and the man; *that* if Virgil was not initiated he could not, if he were he would not reveal the secrets of the initiation; *that* the anathema of Horace (*Vetabo qui Cereris sacrum vulgarit*,[28] etc.) at once attests his own ignorance and the innocence of his friend.

As the Bishop of Gloucester and his party maintained a discreet silence, my critical disquisition was soon lost among the pamphlets of the day; but the public coldness was over-balanced to my feelings by the weighty approbation of the last and best editor of Virgil, Professor Heyne of Göttingen, who acquiesces in my confutation, and styles the unknown author *doctus ... et elegantissimus Britannus.*[29] But I cannot resist the temptation of transcribing the favourable judgement of Mr Hayley, himself a poet and a scholar.

An intricate hypothesis, twisted into a long and laboured chain of quotation and argument, the dissertation on the sixth book of Virgil, remained some time unrefuted. ... At length a superior but anonymous critic arose; who, in one of the most judicious and spirited essays that our nation has produced on a point of classical literature, completely overturned this ill-founded edifice, and exposed the arrogance and futility of its assuming architect.

He even condescends to justify an acrimony of style, which had been gently blamed by the more unbiassed German, '*Paullo acrius quam velis ... perstrinxit*'.[30] But I cannot forgive myself the contemptuous treatment of a man who, with all his faults, was entitled to my esteem; and I can less forgive, in a personal attack, the cowardly concealment of my name and character.

In the fifteen years between my *Essay on the Study of Literature* and the first volume of the *Decline and Fall* (1761–1776), this criticism on Warburton and some articles in the Journal were my sole publications. It is more specially incumbent on me to mark the employment, or to confess the waste of time from my travels to my father's death, an interval in which I was not diverted by any professional duties from the labours and pleasures of a studious life.

i. As soon as I was released from the fruitless task of the Swiss revolutions, I more seriously undertook (1768) to methodize the form, and to collect the substance of my Roman decay, of whose limits and extent I had yet a very inadequate notion. The classics as low as Tacitus, the younger Pliny and Juvenal were my old and familiar companions. I insensibly plunged into the ocean of the Augustan History,[31] and in the descending series I investigated, with my pen almost always in my hand, the original records, both Greek and Latin, from Dion Cassius to Ammianus Marcellinus, from the reign of Trajan to the last age of the Western Caesars. The subsidiary rays of medals and inscriptions, of geography and chronology were thrown on their proper objects; and I applied the collections of Tillemont, whose inimitable accuracy almost assumes the character of genius, to fix and arrange within my reach the loose and scattered atoms of historical information. Through the darkness of the Middle Ages I explored my way in the *Annals* and *Antiquities of Italy* of the learned Muratori; and diligently compared them with the parallel or transverse lines of Sigonius and Maffei, Baronius and Pagi, till I almost grasped the ruins of Rome in the fourteenth century, without suspecting that this final chapter must be attained by the labour of six quartos and twenty years. Among the books which I purchased, the Theodosian Code with the commentary of James Godefroy must be gratefully remembered. I used it (and much I used it) as a work of history, rather than of jurisprudence: but in every light it may be considered as a full and capacious repository of the political state of the Empire in the fourth and fifth centuries. As I believed, and as I still believe, that the propagation of the gospel and triumph of the Church are inseparably connected with the decline of the Roman monarchy, I weighed the causes and effects of the revolution, and contrasted the narratives and apologies of the Christians themselves with the glances of candour or enmity which the Pagans have cast on the rising sect. The Jewish and Heathen testimonies, as they are collected and illustrated by Dr Lardner, directed without superseding my search of the originals; and in an ample dissertation on the miraculous darkness of the Passion, I privately drew my conclusions from the silence of an unbelieving age. I have assembled the preparatory studies directly or indirectly relative to my history; but in strict equity they must be spread beyond this period of my life, over the two summers (1771 and 1772) that elapsed between my father's death and my settlement in London.

ii. In a free conversation with books and men, it would be endless to enumerate the names and characters of all who are introduced to our acquaintance; but in this general acquaintance we may select the degrees of friendship and esteem. According to the wise maxim *Multum legere potius quam multa*[32] I reviewed again and again the immortal works of the French and English, the Latin and Italian classics. My Greek studies (though less assiduous than I designed) maintained and extended my knowledge of that incomparable idiom. Homer and Xenophon were still my favourite authors; and I had almost prepared for the press an essay on the *Cyropaedia*, which in my own judgement is not unhappily laboured. After a certain age the new publications of merit are the sole food of the many; and the most austere student will be often tempted to break the line for the sake of indulging his own curiosity and of providing the topics of fashionable currency. A more respectable motive may be assigned for the triple perusal of Blackstone's *Commentaries*, and a copious and critical abstract of that English work was my first serious production in my native language.

iii. My literary leisure was much less complete and independent than it might appear to the eye of a stranger. In the hurry of London I was destitute of books; in the solitude of Hampshire I was not master of my time. By the habit of early rising I always secured a sacred portion of the day, and many precious moments were stolen and saved by my rational avarice. But the family hours of breakfast and dinner, of tea and supper were regular and tedious; after breakfast Mrs Gibbon expected my company in her dressing room; after tea my father claimed my conversation and the perusal of the newspapers. In the heat of some interesting pursuit, I was called down to receive the visits of our idle neighbours; their civilities required a suitable return; and I dreaded the period of the full moon, which was usually reserved for our more distant excursions.[33] My quiet was gradually disturbed by our domestic anxiety; and I should be ashamed of my unfeeling philosophy, had I found much time or taste for study in the last fatal summer (1770) of my father's decay and dissolution.

The disembodying of the militia at the close of the war (1762) had restored the Major, a new Cincinnatus, to a life of agriculture. His labours were useful, his pleasures innocent, his wishes moderate: and my father *seemed* to enjoy the state of happiness which is celebrated by poets and philosophers as the most agreeable to Nature, and the least accessible to Fortune:

> Beatus ille, qui procul negotiis
> (Ut prisca gens mortalium)
> Paterna rura bubus exercet suis,
> Solutus omni foenore.[34]

But the last indispensable condition, the freedom from debt, was wanting to my father's felicity; and the vanities of his youth were severely punished by the solicitude and sorrow of his declining age. The first mortgage on my return from Lausanne (1758) had afforded him a partial and transient relief. The annual demand of interest and allowance was a heavy deduction from his income; the militia was a source of expense; the farm in his hands was not a profitable adventure; he was loaded with the costs and damages of an obsolete lawsuit; and each year multiplied the number and exhausted the patience of his creditors. Under these painful circumstances, my own behaviour was not only guiltless but meritorious. Without stipulating any personal advantages, I consented at a mature and well-informed age to an additional mortgage, to the sale of Putney, and to every sacrifice that could alleviate his distress. But he was no longer capable of a rational effort, and his reluctant delays postponed not the evils themselves, but the remedies of those evils (*remedia malorum potius quam mala differebat*[35]). The pangs of shame, tenderness and self-reproach incessantly preyed on his vitals; his constitution was broken; he lost his strength and his sight; the rapid progress of a dropsy admonished him of his end, and he sunk into the grave on the tenth of November 1770, in the sixty-fourth year of his age.

A family tradition insinuates that Mr William Law has drawn his pupil in the light and inconstant character of *Flatus*, who is ever confident and ever disappointed in the chase of happiness. But these constitutional failings were amply compensated by the virtues of the head and heart, by the warmest sentiments of honour and humanity. His graceful person, polite address, gentle manners, and unaffected cheerfulness recommended him to the favour of every company; and in the change of times and opinions, his liberal spirit had long since delivered him from the zeal and prejudice of a Tory education. The tears of a son are seldom lasting; I submitted to the order of Nature; and my grief was soothed by the conscious satisfaction, that I had discharged all the duties of filial piety. Few, perhaps, are the children who, after the expiration of some months or years, would sincerely rejoice in the resurrection of their parents; and it is a melancholy truth, that my father's death, not unhappy for himself, was the only event that could save me from a hopeless life of obscurity and indigence.

Chapter VII[1]

London Life · Parliament · *Decline and Fall*
(1770–83)

As soon as I had paid the last solemn duties to my father and obtained
from time and reason a tolerable composure of mind, I began to form
the plan of an independent life most adapted to my circumstances and
inclination. Yet so intricate was the net, my efforts were so awkward
and feeble, that near two years (*November 1770–October 1772*) were
suffered to elapse before I could disentangle myself from the management
of the farm, and transfer my residence from Buriton to a house in London.
During this interval I continued to divide my year between town and
the country; but my new freedom was brightened by hope; nor could
I refuse the advantages of a change, which had never (I have scrutinized
my conscience), which had never been the object of my secret wishes.
Without indulging the vanity and extravagance of a thoughtless heir,
I assumed some additional latitude and lodging, attendance and equipage.
I no longer numbered with the same anxious parsimony my dinners at
the club or tavern; my stay in London was prolonged into the summer;
and the uniformity of the summer was occasionally broken by visits and
excursions at a distance from home. That home, the house and estate
at Buriton, were now my own. I could invite without control the persons
most agreeable to my taste; the horses and servants were at my disposal;
and in all their operations my rustic ministers solicited the commands,
and smiled at the ignorance of their master. I will not deny that my pride
was flattered by the local importance of a country gentleman: the busy
scene of the farm, productive of seeming plenty, was embellished in my
eyes by the partial sentiment of property; and still adhering to my original
plan, I expected the adequate offers of a tenant and postponed without
much impatience the moment of my departure. My friendship for Mrs
Gibbon long resisted the idea of our final separation. After my father's
decease, she preserved the tenderness, without the authority of a parent;
the family and even the farm were entrusted to her care; and as the habits

of fifteen years had attached her to the spot, she was herself persuaded, and she tried to persuade *me* of the pleasures and benefits of a country life. But as I could not afford to maintain a double establishment, my favourite project of a house in London was incompatible with the farm at Buriton, and it was soon apparent that a woman and a philosopher could not direct with any prospect of advantage such a complex and costly machine. In the second summer my resolution was declared and effected. The advertisement of the farm attracted many competitors; the fairest terms were preferred; the proper leases were executed; I abandoned the mansion to the principal tenant, and Mrs G with some reluctance departed for Bath, the most fashionable asylum for the sober singleness of widowhood. But the produce of the effects and stock was barely sufficient to clear my accounts in the country and my first settlement in town. From the mischievous extravagance of the tenant I sustained many subsequent injuries; and a change of ministry could not be accomplished without much trouble and expense.

Besides the debts for which my honour and piety were engaged, my father had left a weighty mortgage of seventeen thousand pounds. It could only be discharged by a landed sacrifice, and my estate at Lenborough near Buckingham was a devoted victim. At first the appearances were favourable; but my hopes were too sanguine, my demands were too high. After slighting some offers by no means contemptible, I rashly signed an agreement with a worthless fellow[2] (half knave and half madman) who, in three years of vexatious chicanery, refused either to consummate or to relinquish his bargain. After I had broken my fetters, the opportunity was lost. The public distress had reduced the value of land; I waited the return of peace and prosperity; and my last secession to Lausanne preceded the sale of my Buckinghamshire estate. The delay of fifteen years, which I may impute to myself, my friends and the times, was accompanied with the loss of many thousand pounds. A delicious morsel, a share in the New River Company, was cast with many a sigh into the gulf of principal, interest, and annual expense; and the far greater part of the inadequate price of poor Lenborough was finally devoured by the insatiate monster. Such remembrance is bitter; but the temper of a mind exempt from avarice suggests some reasonable topics of consolation. My patrimony has been diminished in the enjoyment of life.[3] The gratification of my desires (they were not immoderate) has been seldom disappointed by the want of money or credit; my pride was never insulted by the visit of an importunate tradesman; and any transient anxiety for the past or future was soon dispelled by the studious or social occupation of the present hour. My conscience does not accuse me of any act of extravagance or injustice: the remnant of my estate affords an ample and honourable provision for my declining age, and my spontaneous bounty must be received with implicit gratitude by the heirs of my choice.[4]

I shall not expatiate more minutely on my economical affairs which cannot be instructive or amusing to the reader. It is a rule of prudence, as well as of politeness, to reserve such confidence for the ear of a private friend, without exposing our situation to the envy or pity of strangers; for envy is productive of hatred, and pity borders too nearly on contempt. Yet I may believe and even assert that in circumstances more indigent or more wealthy, I should never have accomplished the task or acquired the fame, of an historian; that my spirit would have been broken by poverty and contempt; and that my industry might have been relaxed in the labour and luxury of a superfluous fortune. Few works of merit and importance have been executed either in a garret or a palace. A gentleman possessed of leisure and independence, of books and talents, may be encouraged to write by the distant prospect of honour and reward; but wretched is the author, and wretched will be the work, where daily diligence is stimulated by daily hunger.

At the time of my father's decease – 1770, *November* 10 –[5] I was upwards of thirty-three years of age, the ordinary term of a human generation. My grief was sincere for the loss of an affectionate parent, an agreeable companion, and a worthy man. But the ample fortune which my grandfather had left was deeply impaired, and would have been gradually consumed by the easy and generous nature of his son. I revere the memory of my father, his errors I forgive, nor can I repent of the important sacrifices which were cheerfully offered by filial piety. Domestic command, the free distribution of time and place, and a more liberal measure of expense were the immediate consequences of my new situation; but two years rolled away before I could disentangle myself from the web of rural economy – 1772, *October* – and adopt a mode of life agreeable to my wishes. From Buriton Mrs Gibbon withdrew to Bath; while I removed myself and my books into my new house in Bentinck Street, Cavendish Square, in which I continued to reside near eleven years. The clear untainted remains of my patrimony have been always sufficient to support the rank of a gentleman, and to satisfy the desires of a philosopher.

1773, January–1783, September – I had now attained the solid comforts of life, a convenient well-furnished house, a domestic table, half a dozen chosen servants, my own carriage, and all those decent luxuries whose value is the more sensibly felt the longer they are enjoyed. These advantages were crowned by the first of earthly blessings, independence. I was the absolute master of my hours and actions; nor was I deceived in the hope that the establishment of my library in town would allow me to divide the day between study and society. Each year the circle of my acquaintance, the number of my dead and living companions was enlarged. To a lover of books the shops and sales in London present irresistible temptations; and the manufacture of my History required a various and growing stock of materials. The militia, my travels, the House of Commons, the fame of an author contributed to multiply my connections: I was chosen a member of the fashionable clubs (27)[6]; and before I left England there were few persons of any eminence in the literary or political world to whom I was a stranger (28). By my own choice I passed in town the greatest part of the year; but whenever I was desirous of breathing the air of the country, I possessed an hospitable retreat at Sheffield Place in Sussex, in the family of Mr Holroyd, a valuable friend, whose character, under the name of Lord Sheffield, has since been more conspicuous to the public.

1773, February, etc. – No sooner was I settled in my house and library than I undertook the composition of the first volume of my History. At the outset all was dark and doubtful: even the title of the work, the true era of the Decline and Fall of the Empire, the limits of the introduction, the division of the chapters, and the order of the narrative; and I was often tempted to cast away the labour of seven years. The style of an author should be the image of his mind; but the choice and command of language is the fruit of exercise. Many experiments were made before I could hit the middle tone between a dull chronicle and a rhetorical declamation; three times did I compose the first chapter, and twice the second and third, before I was tolerably satisfied with their effect. In the remainder of the way I advanced with a more equal and easy pace: but the fifteenth and sixteenth chapters have been reduced by three successive revisals from a large volume to their present size; and they might still be compressed without any loss of facts or sentiments. An opposite fault may be imputed to the concise and superficial narrative of the first reigns from Commodus to Alexander, a fault of which I have never heard except from Mr Hume in his last journey to London. Such an oracle might have been consulted and obeyed with rational devotion: but I was soon disgusted with the modest practice of reading the manuscript to my friends. Of such friends some will praise from politeness, and some will criticise from vanity. The author himself is the best judge of his own performance: none has so deeply meditated on the subject, none is so sincerely interested in the event.

1774, September – By the friendship of Mr (now Lord) Eliot, who had married my first cousin (29), I was returned at the general election for the borough of Liskeard. I took my seat at the beginning of the memorable contest between Great Britain and America; and supported with many a sincere and silent vote the rights, though not, perhaps, the interest of the mother country. After a fleeting illusive hope, prudence condemned me to acquiesce in the humble station of a mute. I was not armed by nature or education with the intrepid energy of mind and voice,

> Vincentem strepitus, et natum rebus agendis.[7]

Timidity was fortified by pride; and even the success of my pen discouraged the trial of my voice. But I assisted at the debates of a free assembly, which agitated the most important questions, of peace and war, of justice and policy; I listened to the attack and defence of eloquence and reason; I had a near prospect of the characters, views, and passions of the first men of the age. The eight sessions that I sat in Parliament were a school of civil prudence, the first and most essential virtue of an historian.

1775, June – The volume of my History, which had been somewhat delayed by the novelty and tumult of a first session, was now ready for the press. After the perilous adventure had been declined by my timid friend Mr Elmsley, I agreed, on very easy terms, with Mr Thomas Cadell, a respectable bookseller, and Mr William Strahan, an eminent printer; and they undertook the care and risk of the publication, which derived more credit from the name of the shop than from that of the author. The last revisal of the proofs was submitted to my vigilance: and many blemishes of style, which had been invisible in the manuscript, were discovered and corrected in the printed sheet. So moderate were our hopes that the original impression had been stinted to five hundred, till the number was doubled by the prophetic taste of Mr Strahan. During this awful interval I was neither elated by the ambition of fame, nor depressed by the apprehension of contempt. My diligence and accuracy were attested by my own conscience. History is the most popular species of writing, since it can adapt itself to the highest or the lowest capacity. I had chosen an illustrious subject; Rome is familiar to the schoolboy and the statesman; and my narrative was deduced from the last period of classical reading. I had likewise flattered myself that an age of light and liberty would receive without scandal an enquiry into the *human* causes of the progress and establishment of Christianity.

1776, February 17 – I am at a loss how to describe the success of the work, without betraying the vanity of the writer. The first impression was exhausted in a few days; a second and third edition were scarcely adequate to the demand; and the bookseller's property was twice invaded by the pirates of Dublin. My book was on every table, and almost on every toilette; the historian was crowned by the taste or fashion of the day; nor was the general voice disturbed by the barking of any *profane* critic. The favour of mankind is most freely bestowed on a new acquaintance of any original merit; and the mutual surprise of the public and their favourite is productive of those warm sensibilities, which, at a second meeting, can no longer be rekindled. If I listened to the music of praise, I was more seriously satisfied with the approbation of my judges. The candour of Dr Robertson embraced his disciple; a letter from Mr Hume (30) overpaid the labour of ten years; but I have never presumed to accept a place in the triumvirate of British historians.

1777, May–November – My second excursion to Paris was determined by the pressing invitation of M. and Madame Necker, who had visited England in the preceding summer. On my arrival I found M. Necker, Director General of the Finances, in the first bloom of power and popularity. His private fortune enabled him to support a liberal establishment; and his wife, whose talents and virtues I had long admired, was admirably qualified to preside in the conversation of her table and drawing-room. As their friend I was introduced to the best company of both sexes; to the foreign ministers of all nations; and to the first names and characters of France, who distinguished me by such marks of civility and kindness as gratitude will not suffer me to forget, and modesty will not allow me to enumerate. The fashionable suppers often broke into the morning hours: yet I occasionally consulted the Royal Library, and that of the Abbey of St Germain; and in the free use of their books at home I had always reason to praise the liberality of those institutions. The society of men of letters I neither courted nor declined; but I was happy in the acquaintance of M. de Buffon, who united with a sublime genius the most amiable simplicity of mind and manners. At the table of my old friend M. de Foncemagne I was involved in a dispute (31) with the Abbé de Mably (32): and his jealous, irascible spirit revenged itself on a work which he was incapable of reading in the original (33).

1777, December, etc. – Near two years had elapsed between the publication of my first and the commencement of my second volume; and the causes must be assigned of this long delay.

1. After a short holiday, I indulged my curiosity in some studies of a very different nature, a course of anatomy which was demonstrated by Dr Hunter, and some lessons of chemistry which were delivered by Mr

Higgins. The principles of these sciences, and a taste for books of natural history contributed to multiply my ideas and images; and the anatomist or chemist may sometimes track me in their own snow.

2. I dived perhaps too deeply into the mud of the Arian controversy: and many days of reading, thinking and writing were consumed in the pursuit of a phantom.

3. It is difficult to arrange with order and perspicuity the various transactions of the age of Constantine:[8] and so much was I displeased with the first essay that I committed to the flames above fifty sheets.

4. The six months of Paris and pleasure must be deducted from the account. But when I resumed my task I felt my improvement. I was now master of my style and subject; and while the measure of my daily performance was enlarged, I discovered less reason to cancel or correct. It has always been my practice to cast a long paragraph in a single mould, to try it by my ear, to deposit it in my memory, but to suspend the action of the pen till I had given the last polish to my work. Shall I add that I never found my mind more vigorous, or my composition more happy, than in the winter hurry of society and parliament?

1779, February 3 – Had I believed that the majority of English readers were so fondly attached even to the name and shadow of Christianity; had I foreseen that the pious, the timid and the prudent would feel or affect to feel with such exquisite sensibility, I might, perhaps, have softened the two invidious chapters,[9] which would create many enemies, and conciliate few friends. But the shaft was shot, the alarm was sounded, and I could only rejoice, that if the voice of our priests was clamorous and bitter, their hands were disarmed of the powers of persecution. I adhered to the wise resolution of trusting myself and my writings to the candour of the public, till Mr Davies of Oxford presumed to attack not the faith, but the good faith, of the historian. My *Vindication* (34), expressive of less anger than contempt, amused for a moment the busy and idle metropolis; and the most rational part of the laity and even of the clergy appears to have been satisfied of my innocence and accuracy. My antagonists, however, were rewarded in this world: poor Chelsum was indeed neglected, and I dare not boast the making Dr Watson a bishop (35); but I enjoyed the pleasure of giving a royal pension to Mr Davies, and of collating Dr Apthorpe to an archiepiscopal living. Their success encouraged the zeal of Taylor the Arian (36) and Milner the Methodist (37), with many others whom it would be difficult to remember and tedious to rehearse. The list of my adversaries was graced with the more respectable names of Dr Priestley (38), Sir David Dalrymple (39), and Dr White (40); and every polemic of

either university discharged his sermon or pamphlet against the impene-
trable silence of the Roman historian (41). Let me frankly own that I was
startled at the first volleys of this ecclesiastical ordnance; but as soon as I
found that this empty noise was mischievous only in the intention, my
fear was converted to indignation; and every feeling of indignation or
curiosity has long since subsided in pure and placid indifference.

1779, May – The prosecution of my history was soon afterwards
checked by another controversy of a very different kind. At the request of
the Chancellor, and of Lord Weymouth, then Secretary of State, I vindi-
cated against the French manifesto the justice of the British arms. The
whole correspondence of Lord Stormont our late Ambassador at Paris, was
submitted to my inspection; and the *Mémoire justificatif*, which I composed
in French, was first approved by the Cabinet Ministers, and then delivered
as a state paper to the Courts of Europe.[10] The style and manner are praised
by Beaumarchais himself, who, in his private quarrel, attempted a reply;
but he flatters me by ascribing the *Mémoire* to Lord Stormont; and the
grossness of his invective betrays the loss of temper and of wit (42).

1779, July 3 – Among the honourable connections which I had formed,
I may justly be proud of the friendship of Mr Wedderburne, at that time
Attorney General: who now illustrates the title of Lord Loughborough, and
the office of Chief Justice of the Common Pleas. By his strong recommendation, and the favourable disposition of Lord North, I was appointed one of
the Lords Commissioners of Trade and Plantations; and my private
income was enlarged by a clear addition of between seven and eight
hundred pounds a year. The fancy of a hostile Orator may paint in the
strong colours of ridicule 'the perpetual virtual adjournment and the
unbroken sitting vacation of the Board of Trade' (43); but it must be
allowed that our duty was not intolerably severe, and that I enjoyed
many days and weeks of repose without being called away from my library
to the office. My acceptance of a place provoked some of the leaders of
opposition with whom I lived in habits of intimacy; and I was most
unjustly accused of deserting a party in which I had never been enlisted.

The aspect of the next session of Parliament was stormy and perilous;
county meetings, petitions, and committees of correspondence announced
the public discontent; and instead of voting with a triumphant majority,
the friends of government were often exposed to a struggle and sometimes
to a defeat. The House of Commons adopted Mr Dunning's motion 'that
the influence of the Crown had increased, was increasing, and ought to
be diminished', and Mr Burke's Bill of Reform was framed with skill,

introduced with eloquence, and supported by numbers. Our late president, the American Secretary of State,[11] very narrowly escaped the sentence of proscription; but the unfortunate Board of Trade was abolished in the committee by a small majority (207 to 199) of eight votes – AD 1780, *March* 13. – The storm however blew over for a time. A large defection of country gentlemen eluded the sanguine hopes of the patriots; the Lords of Trade were revived; administration recovered their strength and spirit; and the flames of London – *June* 2, etc. – which were kindled by a mischievous madman,[12] admonished all thinking men of the danger of an appeal to the people. In the premature dissolution which followed this session of Parliament, I lost my seat – September 1. – Mr Eliot was now deeply engaged in the measures of opposition, and the electors of Liskeard are commonly of the same opinion as Mr Eliot.

In this interval of my senatorial life I published – 1781, *March* 1 – the second and third volumes of the Decline and Fall. My ecclesiastical history still breathed the same spirit of freedom: but Protestant zeal is more indifferent to the characters and controversies of the fourth and fifth centuries. My obstinate silence had damped the ardour of the polemics; Dr Watson, the most candid of my adversaries, assured me that he had no thoughts of renewing the attack, and my impartial balance of the virtues and vices of Julian was generally praised. This truce was interrupted only by some animadversions of the Catholics of Italy (44), and by some angry letters from Mr Travis (45), who made me personally responsible for condemning with the best critics the spurious text of the three heavenly witnesses.[13] The bigoted advocate of Popes and monks may be turned over even to the bigots of Oxford, and the wretched Travis still howls under the lash of the merciless Porson (46). But I perceived, and without surprise, the coldness and even prejudice of the town: nor could a whisper escape my ear that, in the judgement of many readers, my continuation was much inferior to the original attempt. An author who cannot ascend will always appear to sink; envy was now prepared for my reception, and the zeal of my religious (47) was fortified by the malice of my political enemies. I was however encouraged by some domestic and foreign testimonies of applause, and the second and third volumes insensibly rose in sale and reputation to a level with the first. But the public is seldom wrong; and I am inclined to believe that especially in the beginning they are more prolix and less entertaining than the first; my efforts had not been relaxed by success, and I had rather deviated into the opposite fault of minute and superfluous diligence. On the continent my name and writings were slowly diffused: a French translation of the first volume had disappointed the booksellers of Paris; and a passage in the third was construed as a personal reflection on the reigning Monarch (48).

AD 1781, June – Before I could apply for a seat at the general election the list was already full; but Lord North's promise was sincere, his recommendation was effectual, and I was soon chosen on a vacancy for the borough of Lymington in Hampshire. In the first session of the new Parliament the administration stood their ground: their final overthrow was reserved for the second. The American war had once been the favourite of the country; the pride of England was irritated by the resistance of her colonies; and the executive power was driven by national clamour into the most vigorous and coercive measures. But the length of a fruitless contest, the loss of armies, the accumulation of debt and taxes, and the hostile confederacy of France, Spain and Holland indisposed the public to the American war and the persons by whom it was conducted. The representatives of the people followed at a slow distance the changes of their opinion; and the ministers who refused to bend were broken by the tempest. As soon as Lord North had lost or was about to lose a majority in the House of Commons, he surrendered his office, and retired to a private station, with the tranquil assurance of a clear conscience and a cheerful temper. The old fabric was dissolved, and the posts of government were occupied by the victorious and veteran troops of opposition. The Lords of Trade were not immediately dismissed; but the Board itself was abolished by Mr Burke's bill, which decency compelled the patriots to revive; and I was stripped of a convenient salary after I had enjoyed it about three years – 1782, *May* 1.

So flexible is the title of my History that the final era might be fixed at my own choice; and I long hesitated whether I should be content with the three volumes, the fall of the Western Empire, which fulfilled my first engagement with the public. In this interval of suspense, near a twelve-month, I returned by a natural impulse to the Greek authors of antiquity. In my library at Bentinck Street, at my summer lodgings at Brighthelmstone, at a country house which I hired at Hampton Court,[14] I read with new pleasure the Iliad and Odyssey, the histories of Herodotus, Thucydides and Xenophon, a large portion of the tragic and comic theatre of Athens, and many interesting dialogues of the Socratic school. Yet in the luxury of freedom I began to wish for the daily task, the active pursuit which gave a value to every book and an object to every enquiry; the preface of a new edition – 1782, *March* 1 – announced my design, and I dropped without reluctance from the age of Plato to that of Justinian. The original texts of Procopius and Agathias supplied the events and even the characters of his reign; but a laborious winter was devoted to the Codes, the Pandects and the modern interpreters before I presumed to form an abstract of the Civil law. My skill was improved by practice; my diligence perhaps was quickened by the loss of office, and except the last chapter, I had finished my fourth volume before I sought a retreat on the banks of the Leman Lake.

It is not the purpose of this narrative to expatiate on the public or secret history of the times: the schism which followed the death of the Marquis of Rockingham, the appointment of the Earl of Shelburne, the resignation of Mr Fox, and his famous coalition with Lord North – 1783. But I may affirm with some degree of assurance, that in their political conflict those great antagonists had never felt any personal animosity to each other, that their reconciliation was easy and sincere; and that their friendship had never been clouded by the shadow of suspicion or jealousy. The most violent or venal of their respective followers embraced this fair occasion of revolt, but their alliance still commanded a majority in the House of Commons; the peace was censured, Lord Shelburne resigned; and the two friends knelt on the same cushion to take the oath of Secretary of State. From a principle of gratitude I adhered to the coalition: my vote was counted in the day of battle, but I was overlooked in the division of the spoil. There were many claimants more deserving and importunate than myself; the Board of Trade could not be restored; and while the list of places was curtailed the number of candidates was doubled. An easy dismission to a secure seat at the Board of Customs or Excise was promised on the first vacancy, but the chance was distant and doubtful; nor could I solicit with much ardour an ignoble servitude which would have robbed me of the most valuable of my studious hours. At the same time the tumult of London and the attendance on Parliament were grown more irksome; and without some additional income I could not long or prudently maintain the style of expense to which I was accustomed.

Chapter VIII

Lausanne
(1783–93)

1783, May 20 – From my early acquaintance with Lausanne I had always cherished a secret wish that the school of my youth might become the retreat of my declining age. A moderate fortune would secure the blessings of ease, leisure and independence; the country, the people, the manners, the language were congenial to my taste; and I might indulge the hope of passing some years in the domestic society of a friend. After travelling with several English, M. Deyverdun was now settled at home in a pleasant habitation, the gift of his deceased aunt; we had long been separated, we had long been silent; yet in my first letter I exposed with the most perfect confidence my situation, my sentiments and my designs. His immediate answer was a warm and joyful acceptance; the picture of our future life provoked my impatience; and the terms of arrangement were short and simple, as he possessed the property, and I undertook the expense, of our common house. Before I could break my English chain, it was incumbent on me to struggle with the feelings of my heart, the indolence of my temper, and the opinion of the world, which unanimously condemned this voluntary banishment. In the disposal of my effects, the library, a sacred deposit, was alone excepted. As my post-chaise moved over Westminster bridge, I bid a long farewell to the *fumum, et opes, strepitumque Romae;*[1] my journey – *September 15–27* – by the direct road through France was not attended with any accident, and I arrived at Lausanne, near twenty years after my second departure. Within less than three months the Coalition struck on some hidden rocks; had I remained aboard I should have perished in the general shipwreck.

AD 1783, September 27–1787, July 29 – Since my establishment at Lausanne, more than seven years[2] have elapsed; and if every day had not been equally soft and serene, not a day, not a moment has occurred in which I have repented of my choice. During my absence, a long portion of human life, many changes had happened: my elder acquaintance had left the stage; virgins were ripened into matrons, and children grown to the age of manhood. But the same manners were transmitted from one generation to another; my friend alone was an inestimable treasure; my name was not totally forgotten, and all were ambitious to welcome the arrival of a stranger, and the return of a fellow-citizen. The first winter was given to a general embrace, without any nice discrimination of persons and characters; after a more regular settlement,[3] a more accurate survey, I discovered three solid and permanent benefits of my new situation.

1. My personal freedom had been somewhat impaired by the House of Commons and the Board of Trade; but I was now delivered from the chain of duty and dependence, from the hopes and fears of political adventure; my sober mind was no longer intoxicated by the fumes of party, and I rejoiced in my escape, as often as I read of the midnight debates which preceded the dissolution of Parliament.

2. My English economy had been that of a solitary bachelor who might afford some occasional dinners. In Switzerland I enjoyed at every meal, at every hour, the free and pleasant conversation of the friend of my youth; and my daily table was always provided for the reception of one or two extraordinary guests. Our importance in society is less a positive than a relative weight: in London I was lost in the crowd; I ranked with the first families of Lausanne, and my style of prudent expense enabled me to maintain a fair balance of reciprocal civilities.

3. Instead of a small house between a street and a stable-yard, I began to occupy a spacious and convenient mansion, connected on the north side with the city, and open on the south to a beautiful and boundless horizon. A garden of four acres had been laid out by the taste of M. Deyverdun; from the garden a rich scenery of meadows and vineyards descends to the Leman Lake, and the prospect far beyond the lake is crowned by the stupendous mountains of Savoy. My books and my acquaintance had been first united in London; but this happy position of my library in town *and* country was finally reserved for Lausanne. Possessed of every comfort in this triple alliance, I could not be tempted to change my habitation with the changes of the seasons.

My friends had been kindly apprehensive that I should not be able to exist in a Swiss town at the foot of the Alps, after so long conversing with the first men of the first cities of the world. Such lofty connections may attract the curious and gratify the vain; but I am too modest or too proud to rate my own value by that of my associates; and whatsoever may be the fame of learning or genius, experience has shown me that the cheaper qualifications of politeness and good sense are of more useful currency in the commerce of life. By many, conversation is esteemed as a theatre or a school; but after the morning has been occupied by the labours of the library, I wish to unbend rather than to exercise my mind; and in the interval between tea and supper I am far from disdaining the innocent amusement of a game at cards. Lausanne is peopled by a numerous gentry whose companionable idleness is seldom disturbed by the pursuits of avarice or ambition; the women, though confined to a domestic education, are endowed for the most part with more taste and knowledge than their husbands or brothers; but the decent freedom of both sexes is equally remote from the extremes of simplicity and refinement. I shall add as a misfortune rather than a merit that the situation and beauty of the Pays de Vaud, the long habits of the English, the medical reputation of Dr Tissot, and the fashion of viewing the mountains and glaciers have opened us on all sides to the incursions of foreigners. The visits of M. and Madame Necker (49), of Prince Henry of Prussia (50), and of Mr Fox (51) may form some pleasing exceptions: but in general Lausanne has appeared most agreeable in my eyes when we have been abandoned to our own society.

AD 1784, July – My transmigration from London to Lausanne could not be effected without interrupting the course of my historical labours. The hurry of my departure, the joy of my arrival, the delay of my tools suspended their progress; and a full twelvemonth was lost before I could resume the thread of regular and daily industry. A number of books most requisite and least common had been previously selected; the academical library of Lausanne, which I could use as my own, contains at least the Fathers and Councils, and I have derived some occasional succour from the public collections of Bern and Geneva. The fourth volume was soon terminated by an abstract of the controversies of the Incarnation[4] (52), which the learned Dr Prideaux was apprehensive of exposing to profane eyes (53). In the fifth and sixth volumes, the revolutions of the Empire and the world are most rapid, various and instructive; and the Greek or Roman historians are checked by the hostile narratives of the barbarians of the East and West.

It was not till after many designs and many trials, that I preferred, as I still prefer, the method of grouping my picture by nations (54); and the seeming neglect of chronological order is surely compensated by the superior merits of interest and perspicuity. The style of the first volume is, in my opinion, somewhat crude and elaborate; in the second and third it is ripened into ease, correctness and numbers; but in the three last, I may have been seduced by the facility of my pen, and the constant habit of speaking one language and writing another may have infused some mixture of Gallic idioms. Happily for my eyes, I have always closed my studies with the day, and commonly with the morning; and a long but temperate labour has been accomplished without fatiguing either the mind or body. But when I computed the remainder of my time and my task, it was apparent that, according to the season of publication, the delay of a month would be productive of that of a year. I was now straining for the goal, and in the last winter many evenings were borrowed from the social pleasures of Lausanne. I could now wish that a pause, an interval, had been allowed for a serious revisal.

1787, June 27 – I have presumed to mark the moment of conception; I shall now commemorate the hour of my final deliverance. It was on the day or rather the night of the 27th June 1787, between the hours of eleven and twelve, that I wrote the last lines of the last page in a summer-house in my garden. After laying down my pen, I took several turns in a *berceau* or covered walk of acacias which commands a prospect of the country, the lake and the mountains. The air was temperate, the sky was serene; the silver orb of the moon was reflected from the waters, and all Nature was silent. I will not dissemble the first emotions of joy on the recovery of my freedom, and perhaps the establishment of my fame. But my pride was soon humbled, and a sober melancholy was spread over my mind by the idea that I had taken my everlasting leave of an old and agreeable companion, and that, whatsoever might be the future date of my History, the life of the historian must be short and precarious. I will add two facts which have seldom occurred in the composition of six, or at least of five quartos.

1. My first rough manuscript, without any intermediate copy, has been sent to the press (55).

2. Not a sheet has been seen by any human eyes except those of the author and the printer: the faults and the merits are exclusively my own.

AD 1787, July 29 – After a quiet residence of four years, during which I had never moved ten miles from Lausanne, it was not without some reluctance and terror that I undertook, in a journey of two hundred leagues, to cross the mountains and the sea. Yet this formidable adventure was achieved without danger or fatigue, and at the end of a fortnight I found myself in Lord Sheffield's house and library, safe, happy and at home. The character of my friend (Mr Holroyd) had recommended him to a seat in Parliament for Coventry, the command of a regiment of light dragoons, and an Irish peerage. The sense and spirit of his political writings have decided the public opinion on the great questions of our commercial intercourse with America (56) and Ireland (57). He fell (in 1784) with the unpopular coalition, but his merit has been acknowledged at the last general election (1790) by the honourable invitation and free choice of the city of Bristol. During the whole time of my residence in England I was entertained at Sheffield Place and in Downing Street[5] by his hospitable kindness, and the most pleasant period was that which I passed in the domestic society of the family.

In the larger circle of the metropolis, I observed the country and the inhabitants with the knowledge and without the prejudices of an Englishman; but I rejoiced in the apparent increase of wealth and prosperity which might be fairly divided between the spirit of the nation and the wisdom of the minister. All party resentment was now lost in oblivion; since I was no man's rival, no man was my enemy; I felt the dignity of independence, and as I asked no more, I was satisfied with the general civilities of the world. The house in London which I frequented with the most pleasure and assiduity was that of Lord North. After the loss of power and of sight he was still happy in himself and his friends, and my public tribute of gratitude and esteem could no longer be suspected of any interested motive. Before my departure from England I assisted at the august spectacle of Mr Hastings's trial in Westminster Hall – 1788, *June* – I shall not absolve or condemn the Governor of India; but Mr Sheridan's eloquence demanded my applause, nor could I hear without emotion the personal compliment which he paid me in the presence of the British nation (58).

As the publication of my three last volumes was the principal object, so it was the first care of my English journey – 1787, *August*–1788, *April*. The previous arrangements with the bookseller and the printer were settled in my passage through London, and the proofs, which I returned more correct, were transmitted every post from the press to Sheffield Place. The length of the operation and the leisure of the country allowed some time to review my manuscript. Several rare and useful books, *Assises de Jerusalem*, Ramusius *De bello Constantinopolitano*, the Greek Acts of the Synod of Florence, the *Statuta Urbis Romae*, etc. were procured, and I introduced in their proper places the supplements which they afforded. The impression of the fourth volume had consumed three months; our common interest required that we should move with a quicker pace; and Mr Strahan fulfilled his engagement, which few printers could sustain, of delivering every week three thousand copies of nine sheets. The day of publication was however delayed that it might coincide with the fifty-first anniversary of my own birthday – 1788, *May* 8. – The double festival was celebrated by a cheerful literary dinner at Cadell's house; and I seemed to blush while they read an elegant compliment from Mr Hayley (59), whose poetical talent had more than once been employed in the praise of his friend. As most of the former purchasers were naturally desirous of completing their sets, the sale of the quarto edition was quick and easy, and an octavo size was printed to satisfy at a cheaper rate the public demand. The conclusion of my work appears to have diffused a strong sensation: it was generally read and variously judged. The style has been exposed to much academical criticism; a religious clamour was revived; and the reproach of indecency has been loudly echoed by the rigid censors of morals (60). Yet upon the whole the History of the Decline and Fall seems to have struck a root both at home (61) and abroad (62), and may, perhaps a hundred years hence, still continue to be abused. The French, Italian, and German translations (63) have been executed with various success; but instead of patronizing, I should willingly suppress such imperfect copies which injure the character while they propagate the name of the author. The Irish pirates are at once my friends and my enemies; but I cannot be displeased with the two numerous and correct impressions of the English original, which have been published for the use of the continent at Basil in Switzerland (64). The conquests of our language and literature are not confined to Europe alone; and the writer who succeeds in London is speedily read on the banks of the Delaware and the Ganges.

In the preface of the fourth volume, while I gloried in the name of an Englishman, I announced my approaching return to the neighbourhood of the Lake of Lausanne. This last trial confirmed my assurance that I had wisely chosen for my own happiness; nor did I once, in a year's visit, entertain a wish of settling in my native country. Britain is the free and fortunate island; but where is the spot in which I could unite the comforts and beauties of my establishment at Lausanne? The tumult of London astonished my eyes and ears; the amusements of public places were no longer adequate to the trouble; the clubs and assemblies were filled with new faces and young men; and our best society, our long and late dinners would soon have been prejudicial to my health. Without any share in the political wheel I must be idle and insignificant: yet the most splendid temptations would not have enlisted me a second time in the servitude of Parliament or office. At Tunbridge, some weeks after the publication of my History, I tore myself from the embraces of Lord and Lady Sheffield, and with a young Swiss friend[6] whom I had introduced to the English world, I pursued the road of Dover and Lausanne – AD 1788, *July* 21–30. My habitation was embellished in my absence, and the last division of books, which followed my steps, increased my chosen library to the number of six or seven thousand volumes. My seraglio was ample, my choice was free, my appetite was keen. After a full repast on Homer and Aristophanes, I involved myself in the philosophic maze of the writings of Plato, of which the dramatic is perhaps more interesting than the argumentative part; but I stepped aside into every path of enquiry which reading or reflection accidentally opened.

Alas! the joy of my return and my studious ardour were soon damped by the melancholy state of my friend M. Deyverdun. His health and spirits had long suffered a gradual decline; a succession of apoplectic fits announced his dissolution, and before he expired – 1789, *July* 5 – those who loved him could not wish for the continuance of his life. The voice of reason might congratulate his deliverance, but the feelings of nature and friendship could be subdued only by time. His amiable character was still alive in my remembrance; each room, each walk was imprinted with our common footsteps, and I should blush at my own philosophy if a long interval[7] of study had not preceded and followed the death of my friend. By his last will he left me the option of purchasing his house and garden or of possessing them during my life, on the payment either of a stipulated price, or of an easy retribution to his kinsman and heir. I should probably have been tempted by the demon of property (65), if some legal difficulties had not been started against my title. A contest would have been vexatious, doubtful and invidious; and the heir most gratefully subscribed an agreement which rendered my life-possession more perfect, and his future condition more advantageous. The certainty of my tenure has allowed me to lay out a considerable sum in improvements and alterations; they have been executed with skill and taste; and few men of letters, perhaps, in Europe, are so desirably lodged as myself. But I feel, and with the decline of years I shall more painfully feel, that I am alone in paradise. Among the circle of my acquaintance at Lausanne, I have gradually acquired the solid and tender friendship of a respectable family: the four persons of whom it is composed are all endowed with the virtues best adapted to their age and situation; and I am encouraged to love the parents as a brother, and the children as a father. Every day we seek and find the opportunities of meeting; yet even this valuable connection cannot supply the loss of domestic society.

Within the last two or three years our tranquillity has been clouded by the disorders of France. Many families of Lausanne were alarmed and affected by the terrors of an impending bankruptcy; but the revolution, or rather the dissolution, of the kingdom (66) has been heard and felt in the adjacent lands. A swarm of emigrants of both sexes, who escaped from the public ruin, has been attracted by the vicinity, the manners and the language of Lausanne; and our narrow habitations in town and country are now occupied by the first names and titles of the departed monarchy. These noble fugitives are entitled to our pity; they may claim our esteem; but they cannot, in the present state of their mind and fortune, much contribute to our amusement. Instead of looking down as calm and idle spectators on the theatre of Europe, our domestic harmony is somewhat embittered by the infusion of party spirit; our ladies and gentlemen assume the character of self-taught politicians; and the sober dictates of wisdom and experience are silenced by the clamours of the triumphant *démocrates*. The fanatic missionaries of sedition have scattered the seeds of discontent in our cities and villages, which had flourished above two hundred and fifty years[8] without fearing the approach of war, or feeling the weight of government. Many individuals, and some communities appear to be infected with the French disease, the wild theories of equal and boundless freedom; but I trust that the body of the people will be faithful to their sovereign and themselves; and I am satisfied that the failure or success of a revolt would equally terminate in the ruin of the country. While the aristocracy of Bern protects the happiness, it is superfluous to enquire whether it be founded in the rights of man: the economy of the state is liberally supplied without the aid of taxes (67); and the magistrates *must* reign with prudence and equity, since they are unarmed in the midst of an armed nation. For myself (may the omen be averted), I can only declare that the first stroke of a rebel drum would be the signal of my immediate departure.

When I contemplate the common lot of mortality, I must acknowledge that I have drawn a high prize in the lottery of life. The far greater part of the globe is overspread with barbarism or slavery; in the civilized world the most numerous class is condemned to ignorance and poverty; and the double fortune of my birth in a free and enlightened country, in an honourable and wealthy family, is the lucky chance of a unit against millions. The general probability is about three to one that a new-born infant will not live to complete his fiftieth year (68). I have now passed that age, and may fairly estimate the present value of my existence in the three-fold division of mind, body and estate.

i. The first indispensable requisite of happiness is a clear conscience unsullied by the reproach or remembrance of an unworthy action:

> Hic murus aheneus esto,
> Nil conscire sibi, nulla pallescere culpa.[9]

I am endowed with a cheerful temper, a moderate sensibility, and a natural disposition to repose rather than to action; some mischievous appetites and habits have perhaps been corrected by philosophy or time. The love of study, a passion which derives fresh vigour from enjoyment, supplies each day, each hour, with a perpetual source of independent and rational pleasure; and I am not sensible of any decay of the mental faculties. The original soil has been highly improved by labour and manure; but it may be questioned whether some flowers of fancy, some grateful errors, have not been eradicated with the weeds of prejudice.

ii. Since I have escaped from the long perils of my childhood, the serious advice of a physician has seldom been requisite. 'The madness of superfluous health'[10] I have never known; but my tender constitution has been fortified by time; the play of the animal machine still continues to be easy and regular; and the inestimable gift of the sound and peaceful slumbers of infancy may be imputed both to the mind and body. About the age of forty I was first afflicted with the gout, which in the space of fourteen years had made seven or eight different attacks; their duration though not their intensity appears to increase; and after each fit I rise and walk with less strength and agility than before. But the gout has hitherto been confined to my feet and knees; the pain is never intolerable; I am surrounded by all the comforts that art and attendance can bestow; my sedentary life is amused with books and company, and in each step of my convalescence I pass through a progress of agreeable sensations.

iii. I have already described the merits of my society and situation: but these enjoyments would be tasteless and bitter if their possession were not assured by an annual and adequate supply. By the painful method of amputation, my father's debts have been completely discharged; the labour of my pen, the sale of lands, the inheritance of a maiden aunt (Mrs Hester Gibbon (69)) have improved my property, and it will be exonerated on some melancholy day from the payment of Mrs Gibbon's jointure.[11] According to the scale of Switzerland I am a rich man; and I am indeed rich, since my income is superior to my expense, and my expense is equal to my wishes. My friends, more especially Lord Sheffield, kindly relieve me from the cares to which my taste and temper are most adverse: the economy of my house is settled without avarice or profusion; at stated periods all my bills are regularly paid, and in the course of my life, I have never been reduced to appear, either as plaintiff or defendant, in a court of justice. Shall I add that since the failure of my first wishes, I have never entertained any serious thoughts of a matrimonial connection?

I am disgusted with the affectation of men of letters, who complain that they have renounced a substance for a shadow; and that their fame (which sometimes is no insupportable weight) affords a poor compensation for envy, censure and persecution (70). My own experience at least has taught me a very different lesson: twenty happy years have been animated by the labour of my history; and its success has given me a name, a rank, a character in the world to which I should not otherwise have been entitled. The freedom of my writings has indeed provoked an implacable tribe; but as I was safe from the stings, I was soon accustomed to the buzzing of the hornets; my nerves are not tremblingly alive; and my literary temper is so happily framed that I am less sensible of pain than of pleasure. The rational pride of an author may be offended rather than flattered by vague indiscriminate praise: but he cannot, he should not be indifferent to the fair testimonies of private and public esteem. Even his social sympathy may be gratified by the idea that now in the present hour, he is imparting some degree of amusement or knowledge to his friends in a distant land; that one day his mind will be familiar to the grandchildren of those who are yet unborn (71). I cannot boast of the friendship or favour of princes: the patronage of English literature has long since been devolved on our booksellers, and the measure of their liberality is the least ambiguous test of our common success. Perhaps the golden mediocrity[12] of my fortune has contributed to fortify my application; few books of merit and importance have been composed either in a garret or a palace. A gentleman, possessed of leisure and competency, may be encouraged by the assurance of an honourable reward; but wretched is the writer, and wretched will be the work, where daily diligence is stimulated by daily hunger.[13]

The present is a fleeting moment, the past is no more; and our prospect of futurity is dark and doubtful. This day may *possibly* be my last; but the laws of probability, so true in general, so fallacious in particular, still allow me about fifteen years (72); and I shall soon enter into the period, which, as the most agreeable of his long life, was selected by the judgement and experience of the sage Fontenelle.[14] His choice is approved by the eloquent historian of nature, who fixes our moral happiness to the mature season, in which our passions are supposed to be calmed, our duties fulfilled, our ambition satisfied, our fame and fortune established on a solid basis (73). I am far more inclined to embrace than to dispute this comfortable doctrine; I will not suppose any premature decay of the mind or body; but I must reluctantly observe that two causes, the abbreviation of time and the failure of hope, will always tinge with a browner shade the evening of life. The proportion of a part to the whole is the only standard by which we can measure the length of our existence. At the age of twenty, one year is a tenth perhaps of the time which has elapsed within our consciousness and memory; at the age of fifty it is no more than a fortieth, and this relative value continues to decrease till the last sands are shaken by the hand of death. This reasoning may seem metaphysical; but on a trial it will be found satisfactory and just. The warm desires, the long expectations of youth are founded on the ignorance of themselves and of the world. They are gradually damped by time and experience, by disappointment or possession; and after the middle season, the crowd must be content to remain at the foot of the mountain, while the few who have climbed the summit, aspire to descend or expect to fall. In old age, the consolation of hope is reserved for the tenderness of parents, who commence a new life in their children; the faith of enthusiasts who sing hallelujahs above the clouds (74); and the vanity of authors who presume the immortality of their name and writings.

Lausanne, March 2 1791

27. From the mixed, though polite company of Boodle's, White's and Brooks's I must honourably distinguish a weekly society which was instituted in the year 1764, and which still continues to flourish under the title of the Literary Club. (Hawkins's *Life of Johnson*, p. 415. Boswell's *Tour to the Hebrides*, p. 97.) The names of Dr Johnson, Mr Burke, Mr Garrick, Dr Goldsmith, Sir Joshua Reynolds, Mr Colman, Sir William Jones, Dr Percy, Mr Fox, Mr Sheridan, Dr Adam Smith, Mr Steevens, Mr Dunning, Sir Joseph Banks, Dr Warton and his brother Mr Thomas Warton, Dr Burney, etc. form a large and luminous constellation of British stars.

28. It would most assuredly be in my power to amuse the reader with a gallery of portraits, and a collection of anecdotes. But I have always condemned the practice of transforming a private memorial into a vehicle of satire or praise.

29. Catherine Elliston, whose mother Catherine Gibbon, was my grandfather's second daughter. The education of Lady Eliot, a rich heiress, had been entrusted to the Mallets; and she is thus invited to their Hymenaeal feast.

> Last comes a Virgin – Pray admire her!
> Cupid himself attends to squire her:
> A welcome guest! we much had missed her
> For 'tis our Kitty, or his sister.
> But Cupid, let no knave or fool
> Snap up this lamb to shear her wool;
> No Teague[1] of that unblushing band,
> Just landed or about to land;
> Thieves from the womb, and train'd at nurse
> To steal an heiress, or a purse.

No scraping, saving, saucy cit,
Sworn foe of breeding, worth and wit;
No half-form'd insect of a peer,
With neither land, nor conscience, clear;
Who, if he can, 'tis all he can do,
Just spell the motto on his Landau,
From all, from each of these defend her;
But thou and Hymen both befriend her,
With truth, taste, honour in a mate
And much good sense and some estate.

The poet's wishes were soon accomplished by her marriage with Mr Eliot, of Port Eliot in Cornwall. In the year 1784 he was raised to the honour of an English peerage; and their three sons are all members of the House of Commons.

30. That curious and original letter will amuse the reader; and his gratitude should shield my free communication from the reproach of vanity.

Edinburgh, 18 of March, 1776

Dear Sir,

As I ran through your volume of History with great avidity and impatience, I cannot forbear discovering somewhat of the same impatience in returning you thanks for your agreeable present, and expressing the satisfaction which the performance has given me. Whether I consider the dignity of your style, the depth of your matter, or the extensiveness of your learning, I must regard the work as equally the object of esteem, and I own that if I had not previously had the happiness of your personal acquaintance, such a performance from an Englishman in our age would have given me some surprise. You may smile at this sentiment, but as it seems to me, that your countrymen, for almost a whole generation have given themselves up to barbarous and absurd faction, and have totally neglected all polite letters, I no longer expected any valuable production ever to come from them. I know it will give you pleasure (as it did me) to find that all the men of letters in this place concur in their admiration of your work, and in their anxious desire of your continuing it.

When I heard of your undertaking (which was some time ago), I own that I was a little curious to see how you would extricate yourself from the subject of your last two chapters. I think you have observed a very prudent temperament; but it was impossible to treat the subject so as not to give grounds of suspicion against you, and you may expect that a clamour will arise. This, if anything, will retard your success with the public; for in every other respect your work is calculated to be popular. But, among many other marks of decline, the prevalence of superstition in England prognosticates the fall of philosophy and decay of taste;

and, though nobody be more capable than you to revive them, you will probably find a struggle in your first advances.

I see you entertain a great doubt with regard to the authenticity of the poems of Ossian. You are certainly right in so doing. It is indeed strange that any men of sense could have imagined it possible that above twenty thousand verses, along with numberless historical facts, could have been preserved by oral tradition during fifty generations by the rudest perhaps of all the European nations, the most necessitous, the most turbulent, and the most unsettled. Where a supposition is so contrary to common sense, any positive evidence for it ought never to be regarded. Men run with great avidity to give their evidence in favour of what flatters their passions and their national prejudices. You are therefore over and above indulgent to us, in speaking of the matter with hesitation.

I must inform you that we are all very anxious to hear that you have fully collected the materials for your second volume, and that you are even considerably advanced in the composition of it. I speak this more in the name of my friends than in my own; as I cannot expect to live so long as to see the publication of it. Your ensuing volume will be still more delicate than the preceding; but I trust in your prudence for extricating you from the difficulties; and in all events you have courage to despise the clamour of bigots.

> I am with great regard, Dear Sir,
> Your most obedient and most humble servant
> David Hume

Some weeks afterwards I had the melancholy pleasure of seeing Mr Hume in his passage through London; his body feeble, his mind firm. On the 25 of August of the same year (1776) he died at Edinburgh the death of a philosopher.

31. As I might be partial in my own cause, I shall transcribe the words of an unknown critic[2] (*Supplément à la manière d'écrire l'histoire*, p. 125, etc.), observing only that this dispute had been preceded by another on the English constitution at the house of the Countess de Froulay, an old Jansenist lady.

Vous étiez chez M. de Foncemagne, mon cher Théodon, le jour que M. l'Abbé de Mably et M. Gibbon y dinèrent en grande compagnie. La conversation roula presque entièrement sur l'histoire. L'Abbé, étant un profond politique, la tourna sur l'administration, quand on fut au dessert: et comme, par caractère, par humeur, par l'habitude d'admirer Tite-Live, il ne prise que le système républicain, il se mit à vanter l'excellence des républiques; bien persuadé que le savant Anglois l'approuveroit en tout et admireroit la profondeur de génie, qui avoit fait deviner tous ces avantages à un François. Mais M. Gibbon, instruit par expérience des inconvéniens d'un gouvernement populaire, ne fut point du tout de son avis, et il prit généreusement la défense du gouvernement monarchique. L'Abbé voulut le convaincre par Tite-Live, et par quelques argumens tirés de Plutarque en faveur des Spartiates. M. Gibbon, doué de la mémoire la plus heureuse et ayant tous les faits présens à la pensée, domina bientôt la conversation: l'Abbé se fâcha, il s'emporta, il dit des choses dures. L'Anglois, conservant le flegme de son pays, prenoit ses avantages, et pressoit l'Abbé avec d'autant plus de succès que la colère le troubloit de plus en plus. La conversation s'échauffoit, et M. de Foncemagne la rompit en se levant de table, et en passant dans le salon, où personne ne fut tenté de la renouer.

32. Of the voluminous writings of the Abbé de Mably (see his *Eloge* by the Abbé Brizard), the *Principes du droit public de l'Europe*, and the first part of the *Observations sur l'histoire de France* may be deservedly praised; and even the *Manière d'écrire l'histoire* contains several useful precepts and judicious remarks. Mably was a lover of virtue and freedom; but his virtue was austere, and his freedom was impatient of an equal. Kings, magistrates, nobles and successful writers were the objects of his contempt or hatred or envy; but his illiberal abuse of Voltaire, Hume, Buffon, the Abbé Raynal, Dr Robertson, and *tutti quanti* can be injurious only to himself.

33. '*Est-il rien de plus fastidieux* [says the polite Censor] *qu'un M. Guibbon, qui, dans son éternelle histoire des Empéreurs Romains, suspend à chaque instant son insipide et lente narration, pour vous expliquer la cause des faits que vous allez lire?*[3] (*Manière d'écrire l'histoire*, p. 184; see another passage, p. 280.) Yet I am indebted to the Abbé de Mably for two such advocates as the anonymous French critic (Supplément, pp. 125–34) and my friend Mr Hayley (vol. ii, pp. 261–3).

34. *A Vindication of some passages in the fifteenth and sixteenth Chapters of the history of the decline and fall of the Roman Empire, by the Author: London 1779 in octavo,*[4] for I would not print it in quarto lest it should be bound and preserved with the history itself. At the distance of twelve years I calmly affirm my judgement of Davies, Chelsum, etc. A victory over such antagonists was a sufficient humiliation.

35. Dr Watson, now Bishop of Llandaff, is a prelate of a large mind and liberal spirit. I should be happy to think that his *Apology for Christianity* had contributed, though at my expense, to clear his theological character. He has amply repaid the obligation by the amusement and instruction which I have received from the five volumes of his *Chemical Essays*. It is a great pity that an agreeable and useful science should not yet be reduced to a state of *fixity*.

36. The stupendous title, *Thoughts on the Causes of the Grand Apostacy* at first agitated my nerves, till I discovered that it was the apostacy of the whole Church, since the Council of Nice, from Mr Taylor's private religion. His book is a strange mixture of *high* enthusiasm, and *low* buffoonery, and the *Millennium* is a fundamental article of his creed.

37. From his grammar school at Kingston-upon-Hull, Mr Joseph Milner pronounces an anathema against all rational religion. *His* faith is a divine taste, a spiritual inspiration; *his* Church is a mystic and invisible body; the *natural* Christians, such as Mr Locke, who believe and interpret the Scriptures, are, in his judgement, no better than profane infidels.

38. In his *History of the Corruptions of Christianity* (vol. ii), Dr Priestley throws down his two gauntlets to Bishop Hurd and Mr Gibbon. I declined the challenge in a polite letter, exhorting my opponent to enlighten the world by his philosophical discoveries, and to remember that the merit of his predecessor Servetus is now reduced to a single passage, which indicates the smaller circulation of the blood through the lungs, from and to the heart. (Astruc, *De la structure du coeur*, tome i, pp. 77–9.) Instead of listening to this friendly advice, the dauntless philosopher of Birmingham continues to fire away his double battery against those who believe too little, and those who believe too much. From *my* replies he has nothing to hope or fear; but his Socinian[5] shield has repeatedly been pierced by the spear of the mighty Horsley; and his trumpet of sedition may at length awaken the magistrates of a free country.

39. The profession and rank of Sir David Dalrymple (now a Lord of Session) have given a more decent colour to his style. But he scrutinizes each separate passage of the two chapters with the dry minuteness of a special pleader, and as he is always solicitous to make, he may sometimes succeed in finding, a flaw. In his *Annals of Scotland*, he has shown himself a diligent collector and an accurate critic.

40. I have praised, and I still praise the eloquent sermons which were preached in St Mary's pulpit at Oxford by Dr White. If he assaults me with some degree of illiberal acrimony, in such a place and before such an audience, he was obliged to speak the language of the country. I smiled at a passage in one of his private letters to Mr Badcock. 'The part where we encounter Gibbon must be brilliant and striking.'

41. In a sermon lately preached before the University of Cambridge, Dr Edwards compliments a work, 'which can only perish with the language itself', and esteems the author as a formidable enemy. He is indeed astonished that more learning and ingenuity has not been shown in the defence of Israel, that the prelates and dignitaries of the Church (alas! good man) did not vie with each other, whose stone should sink the deepest in the forehead of this Goliath. 'But the force of truth will oblige us to confess that in the attacks which have been levelled against our sceptical historian we can discover but slender traces of profound and exquisite erudition – of solid criticism and accurate investigation; but are too frequently disgusted by vague and inconclusive reasoning; by unseasonable banter and senseless witticisms; by unlettered bigotry, and enthusiastic jargon; by futile cavils and illiberal invectives. Proud and elated by the weakness of his antagonists, he condescends not to handle the sword of controversy, etc. (*Monthly Review* for October 1790, vol. iii, p. 287).

42. See *Oeuvres de Beaumarchais*, tome iii, pp. 299–355. *'Le style ne serait pas sans grâces ni la logique sans justesse'*, etc., if the facts were true, which he undertakes to disprove. For these facts my credit is not pledged; I spoke as a lawyer from my brief: but the veracity of Beaumarchais may be estimated from the assertion that France, by the treaty of Paris (1763), was limited to a certain number of ships of war. On the application of the Duke of Choiseul he was obliged to retract this daring falsehood.

43. See Mr Burke's speech on the Bill of Reform, pp. 72–80. I can never forget the delight with which that diffusive and ingenious orator was heard by all sides of the House, and even by those whose existence he proscribed. The Lords of Trade blushed at their own insignificancy, and Mr Eden's appeal to the two thousand five hundred volumes of our reports served only to excite a general laugh. I take this opportunity of certifying the correctness of Mr Burke's printed speeches which I have heard and read.

44. The piety or prudence of my Italian translator has provided an antidote against the poison of his original.[6] The Vth and VIIth volumes are armed with five letters from an anonymous divine to his friends, Foothead and Kirk, two English students at Rome, and this meritorious service is commended by *Monsignore* Stonor, a prelate of the same nation, who discovers much venom in the *fluid* and nervous style of Gibbon. The critical essay at the end of the IIIrd volume was furnished by the Abbate Nicola

Spedalieri, whose zeal has gradually swelled to a more solid confutation in two quarto volumes. Shall I be excused for not having read them?

45. The brutal insolence of his challenge can only be excused by the absence of learning, judgement and humanity; and to that excuse he has the fairest or foulest title. Compared with Archdeacon Travis, Chelsum and Davis assume the character of respectable enemies.

46. I consider Mr Porson's answer to Archdeacon Travis, as the most acute and accurate piece of criticism which has appeared since the days of Bentley. His strictures are founded in argument, enriched with learning, and enlivened with wit; and his adversary neither deserves nor finds any quarter at his hands. The evidence of the three heavenly witnesses[7] would now be rejected in any court of justice: but prejudice is blind, authority is deaf, and our vulgar Bibles will ever be polluted by this spurious text, *sedet aeternumque sedebit*. The more learned ecclesiastics will indeed have the secret satisfaction of reprobating in the closet what they read in the church.

47. Bishop Newton (see his Life in *Posthumous Works*, vol. I, pp. 173, 174, octavo edition) was at full liberty to declare how much he himself and two eminent brethren were disgusted by Mr G's prolixity, tediousness and affectation. But the old man should not have indulged his zeal in a false and feeble charge against the historian who had faithfully and even cautiously rendered Dr Burnet's meaning by the alternative 'of sleep *or repose*'. That philosophic divine supposes that in the period between death and the resurrection human souls exist without a body, endowed with internal consciousness, but destitute of all active or passive connection with the external world. '*Secundum communem dictionem Sacrae Scripturae, mors dicitur somnus et morientes dicuntur* obdormire: *quod innuere mihi videtur statum mortis esse statum quietis silentii et* ἀεργασίας' (*De statu mortuorum*, Chapter V, p. 98).[8]

48. It may not be generally known that Louis XVI is a great reader, and a reader of English books. On the perusal of a passage of my History (vol. III, p. 636) which seems to compare him with Arcadius or Honorius,[9] he expressed his resentment to the Prince of B— from whom the intelligence was conveyed to me. I shall neither disclaim the allusion nor examine the likeness; but the situation of the *late* King of France excludes all suspicion of flattery; and I am ready to declare that the concluding observations

of my third volume were written before his accession to the throne.

49. I saw them frequently in the summer of 1784 at a country house near Lausanne, where M. Necker composed his treatise *Of the Administration of the Finances*. I have since (in October 1790) visited them in their present residence, the castle and barony of Coppet, near Geneva. Of the merits and measures of that statesman various opinions may be entertained; but all impartial men must agree in their esteem of his integrity and patriotism.

50. In the month of August 1784, Prince Henry of Prussia, in his way to Paris, passed three days at Lausanne. His military conduct is praised by professional men; his character has been vilified by the wit and malice of a demon[10] (*Mémoires secrets de la Cour de Berlin*), but I was flattered by his affability, and entertained by his conversation.

51. In his tour of Switzerland (September 1788) Mr Fox gave me two days of free and private society. He seemed to feel and even to envy the happiness of my situation; while I admired the powers of a superior man, as they are blended in his attractive character, with the softness and simplicity of a child. Perhaps no human being was ever more perfectly exempt from the taint of malevolence, vanity or falsehood.

52. In one of the *Dialogues of the Dead* (xvi) Lucian turns into ridicule the pagan theology concerning the double nature of Hercules, god and man (*Opera*, tome i, pp. 402–5, edition Reitz). As truth and falsehood have sometimes an apparent similitude, I am afraid that even the Synods of Ephesus and Chalcedon would not have been safe from the arrows of his profane wit.

53. It had been the original design of the learned Dean Prideaux to write the history of the ruin of the Eastern Church. In this work it would have been necessary not only to unravel all those controversies which the Christians made about the hypostatical union, but also to unfold all the niceties and subtle notions, which each sect did hold concerning it. The pious historian was apprehensive of exposing that incomprehensible mystery to the cavils and objections of unbelievers, and he durst not, considering the nature of this book, venture it abroad in so wanton and lewd an age. (See preface to the *Life of Mahomet*, pp. x–xi.)

54. I have followed the judicious precept of the Abbé de Mably (*Manière d'écrire l'histoire*, p. 110), who advises the historian not to dwell too minutely on the decay of the Eastern Empire; but to consider the barbarian conquerors as a more worthy subject of his narrative. *Fas est et ab hoste doceri.*[11]

55. I cannot help recollecting a much more extraordinary fact which is affirmed of himself by Rétif de la Bretonne, a voluminous and original writer of French novels. He laboured, and may still labour, in the humble office of corrector to a printing-house. But this office enabled him to transport an entire volume from his mind to the press; and his work was given to the public without ever having been written with a pen.

56. *Observations on the Commerce of the American States* by John, Lord Sheffield, the sixth edition, London, 1784, in octavo. Their sale was diffusive, their effect beneficial: the Navigation Act, the palladium[12] of Britain, was defended and perhaps saved by his pen; and he proves by the weight of fact and argument, that the mother-country may survive and flourish after the loss of America. My friend has never cultivated the arts of composition, but his materials are copious and correct, and he leaves on his paper the clear impression of an active and vigorous mind.

57. *Observations on the Trade, Manufactures and Present State of Ireland* by John, Lord Sheffield, the third edition, London, 1785, in octavo. Their useful aim was to guide the industry, to correct the prejudices and to assuage the passions of a country which seemed to forget that she could only be free and prosperous by a friendly connection with Great Britain. The concluding observations are expressed with so much ease and spirit that they may be read by those who are the least interested in the subject.

58. From this display of genius, which blazed four successive days, I shall stoop to a very mechanical circumstance. As I was waiting in the managers' box, I had the curiosity to enquire of the short-hand writer, how many words a ready and rapid orator might pronounce in an hour. From 7,000 to 7,500 was his answer. The medium of 7,200 will afford one hundred and twenty words in a minute, and two words in each second. But this computation will only apply to the English language.

59. Before Mr Hayley inscribed with my name his *Epistles on History*, I

was not personally acquainted with that amiable man and elegant poet. He afterwards thanked me in verse for my second and third volumes, and in the summer of 1781, the Roman eagle (a proud title) accepted the invitation of the English sparrow, who chirped in the groves of Eartham, near Chichester.

60. I never could understand the clamour which has been raised against the indecency of my three last volumes.

1. An equal degree of freedom in the former part, especially in the first volume, had passed without reproach.

2. I am justified in painting the manners of the times; the vices of Theodora form an essential feature in the reign and character of Justinian, and the most naked tale in my history is told by the Reverend Mr Joseph Warton, an instructor of youth[13] (*Essay on the Genius and Writings of Pope*, pp. 322–4).

3. My English text is chaste and all licentious passages are left in the obscurity of a learned language. '*Le Latin dans ses mots brave l'honnêteté*,'[14] says the correct Boileau, in a country and idiom more scrupulous than our own.

61. I am less flattered by Mr Porson's high encomium on the style and spirit of my history than I am satisfied with his honourable testimony to my attention, diligence and accuracy: those humble virtues which religious zeal has most audaciously denied. The sweetness of his praise is tempered by a reasonable mixture of acid. (See his preface, pp. xxviii–xxxii.)

62. As the book may not be common in England, I shall transcribe my own character from the *Bibliotheca historica* of Meuselius, a learned and laborious German (vol. iv, part i, pp. 342–4).

Summis aevi nostri historicis Gibbonus sine dubio adnumerandus est. Inter Capitolii ruinas stans primum hujus operis scribendi consilium cepit. Florentissimos vitae annos colligendo et laborando eidem impendit. Enatum inde monimentum aere perennius, licet passim appareant sinistre dicta, minus perfecta, veritati non satis consentanea. Videmus quidem ubique fere studium scrutandi veritatemque scribendi maximum: tamen sine Tillemontio duce, ubi scilicet hujus historia finitur, saepius noster titubat atque hallucinatur. Quod vel maxime fit, ubi de rebus ecclesiasticis vel de jurisprudentia Romana (tome iv) tradit, et in aliis locis. Attamen naevi hujus generis haud impediunt quo minus operis summam et δικονομίαν praeclare dispositam, delectum rerum sapientissimum, argutum quoque interdum, dictionemque seu stilum historico aeque ac philosopho dignissimum et vix a quoque alio Anglo, Humio ac Robertsono haud exceptis, praerepto [praereptum?], vehementer laudemus, atque saeculo nostro de hujusmodi historia gratulemur ... Gibbonus adversarios cum in tum extra patriam nactus est, quia propagationem religionis Christianae, non, ut vulgo fieri solet, aut more theologorum, sed ut historicum et philosophum decet exposuerat.[15]

63. The first volume had been feebly though faithfully translated into French by M. Le Clerc de Septchênes, a young gentleman of a studious character and liberal fortune. After his decease the work was continued by two manufacturers of Paris, M.M. Desmeuniers and Cantwell; but the former is now an active member in the National Assembly, and the undertaking languishes in the hands of his associate. The superior merit of the interpreter or his language inclines me to prefer the Italian version: but I wish it were in my power to read the German, which is praised by the best judges.

64. Of their fourteen octavo volumes, the two last include the whole body of the notes. The public importunity had forced *me* to remove them from the end of the volume to the bottom of the page: but I have often repented of my compliance.

65. Yet I had often revolved the judicious lines in which Pope answers the objection of his long-sighted friend:

> 'Pity to build without a child or wife!
> Why, you'll enjoy it *only* all your life.'
> Well, if the use be mine, does it concern one
> Whether the name belong to Pope or Vernon?[16]

66. I beg leave to subscribe my assent to Mr Burke's creed on the Revolution of France. I admire his eloquence, I approve his politics, I adore his chivalry, and I can almost excuse his reverence for church establishments. I have sometimes thought of writing a dialogue of the dead, in which Lucian, Erasmus and Voltaire should mutually acknowledge the danger of exposing an *old* superstition to the contempt of the blind and fanatic multitude.

67. The revenue of Bern (I except some small duties) is derived from Church lands, tithes, feudal rights, and interest of money. The Republic has near 500,000 pounds sterling in the English funds, and the amount of their treasure is unknown to the citizens themselves.

68. See Buffon, *Supplément à l'histoire naturelle*, tome vii, pp. 158–64. Of a given number of new-born infants, one half, by the fault of nature or man, is extinguished before the age of puberty and reason. A melancholy calculation!

69. My pious aunt and her profane sister are described under the names of Miranda and Flavia in Law's *Serious Call*, a popular and powerful book of devotion. Mr William Law, a nonjuror, a saint and a wit, had been my father's domestic tutor. He afterwards retired with his spiritual daughter Miranda to live and die in a hermitage at Cliffe in Northamptonshire.

70. M. d'Alembert relates that as he was walking in the gardens of Sans-souci with the King of Prussia, Frederic said to him, 'Do you see that old woman, a poor weeder, asleep on that sunny bank? She is probably a more happy being than either of us.' The king and the philosopher may speak for themselves; for my part I do not envy the old woman.

71. In the first of ancient or modern romances (*Tom Jones*, Book xiii, Chapter 1), this proud sentiment, this feast of fancy is enjoyed by the genius of Fielding: 'Foretell me that some future maid whose grandmother is yet unborn', etc. But the whole of this beautiful passage deserves to be read.

72. See Buffon, p. 224. From our disregard of the possibility of death within the four and twenty hours he concludes (pp. 56–8) that a chance which falls below or rises above ten thousand to one will never affect the hopes or fears of a reasonable man. The fact is true, but our courage is the effect of thoughtlessness rather than of reflection. If a public lottery was drawn for the choice of an immediate victim and if our name were inscribed on one of the ten thousand tickets, should we be perfectly easy?

73. See Buffon, p. 413. In private conversation, that great and amiable man added the weight of his own experience; and this autumnal felicity might be exemplified in the lives of Voltaire, Hume, and many other men of letters.

74. This celestial hope is confined to a small number of the elect, and we must deduct,
1. All the *mere* philosophers who can only speculate about the immortality of the soul.

2. All the *earthly* Christians, who repeat, without thought or feeling, the words of their catechism.

3. All the *gloomy* fanatics who are more strongly affected by the fear of Hell than by the hopes of Heaven. 'Strait is the way, and narrow is the gate, and *few* there be, who find it!'[17]

Appendix I

Lord Sheffield's Continuation
of the Memoirs[1]

Mr Gibbon's letters in general bear a strong resemblance to the style and turn of his conversation; the characteristics of which were vivacity, elegance, and precision, with knowledge astonishingly extensive and correct. He never ceased to be instructive and entertaining; and in general there was a vein of pleasantry in his conversation which prevented its becoming languid, even during a residence of many months with a family in the country.

It has been supposed that he always arranged what he intended to say, before he spoke. His quickness in conversation contradicts this notion; but it is very true, that before he sat down to write a note or letter, he completely arranged in his mind what he meant to express. He pursued the same method in respect to other composition; and he occasionally would walk several times about his apartment before he had rounded a period to his taste.[2] He has pleasantly remarked to me, that it sometimes cost him many a turn before he could throw a sentiment into a form that gratified his own criticism. His systematic habit of arrangement in point of style, assisted, in his instance, by an excellent memory and correct judgement, is much to be recommended to those who aspire to any perfection in writing.

It may, perhaps, not be quite uninteresting to the readers of these Memoirs, to know that I found Mr Gibbon at Lausanne[3] in possession of an excellent house; the view from which, and from the terrace, was so uncommonly beautiful, that even his own pen would with difficulty describe the scene which it commanded. This prospect comprehended everything vast and magnificent, which could be furnished by the finest mountains among the Alps, the most extensive view of the Lake of Geneva, with a beautifully varied and cultivated country, adorned by numerous villas, and picturesque buildings, intermixed with beautiful masses of stately trees. Here my friend received us with a hospitality and kindness which I can never forget. The best apartments of the house were appropriated to our use; the choicest society of the place was sought for, to enliven our visit, and render every day of it cheerful and agreeable. It was impossible for any man to be more esteemed and admired than Mr Gibbon was at Lausanne. The preference he had given to that place, in adopting it for a residence, rather than his own country, was felt and acknowledged by all the inhabitants; and he may have been said almost to have given the law to a set of as willing subjects as any man ever presided over. In return for the deference shown to him, he mixed, without any affectation, in all the society, I mean all the best society, that Lausanne afforded; he could indeed command it, and was, perhaps, for that reason the more partial to it; for he often declared that he liked society more as a relaxation from study, than as expecting to derive from it amusement or instruction; that to books he looked for improvement, not to living persons. But this I considered partly as an answer to my expressions of wonder, that a man who might choose the most various and most generally improved society in the world, namely, in England, should prefer the very limited circle of Lausanne, which he never deserted, but for an occasional visit to M. and Madame Necker.

It must not, however, be understood, that in choosing Lausanne for his home, he was insensible to the value of a residence in England: he was not in possession of an income which corresponded with his notions of ease and comfort in his own country. In Switzerland, his fortune was ample. To this consideration of fortune may be added another which also had its weight; from early youth Mr Gibbon had contracted a partiality for foreign taste and foreign habits of life, which made him less a stranger abroad than he was, in some respects, in his native country. This arose, perhaps, from having been out of England from his sixteenth to his twenty-first year; yet, when I came to Lausanne, I found him apparently without relish for French society. During the stay I made with him he renewed his intercourse with the principal French who were at Lausanne; of whom there happened to be a considerable number, distinguished for rank or talents; many indeed respectable for both.

In the social and singularly pleasant months that I passed with Mr Gibbon, he enjoyed his usual cheerfulness, with good health. After he left England, in 1788, he had had a severe attack, mentioned in one of the foregoing letters,[4] of an erysipelas, which at last settled in one of his legs, and left something of a dropsical tendency; for at this time I first perceived a considerable degree of swelling about the ankle.

I must ever regard it as the most endearing proof of his sensibility, and of his possessing the true spirit of friendship, that after having relinquished the thought of his intended visit, he hastened to England, in spite of increasing impediments, to soothe me by the most generous sympathy, and to alleviate my domestic affliction; neither his great corpulency, nor his extraordinary bodily infirmities, nor any other consideration, could prevent him a moment from resolving on an undertaking that might have deterred the most active young man. With an alertness by no means natural to him, he almost immediately undertook a circuitous journey, along the frontiers of an enemy, worse than savage, within the sound of their cannon, within the range of the light troops of the different armies, and through roads ruined by the enormous machinery of war.[5]

The readiness with which he engaged in this kind office of friendship, at a time when a selfish spirit might have pleaded a thousand reasons for declining so hazardous a journey, conspired, with the peculiar charms of his society, to render his arrival a cordial to my mind. I had the satisfaction of finding that his own delicate and precarious health had not suffered in the service of his friend. He arrived in the beginning of June at my house in Downing Street in good health; and after passing about a month with me there, we settled at Sheffield Place for the remainder of the summer; where his wit, learning, and cheerful politeness delighted a great variety of characters.

Although he was inclined to represent his health as better than it really was, his habitual dislike to motion appeared to increase; his inaptness to exercise confined him to the library and dining-room, and there he joined my friend, Mr Frederick North, in pleasant arguments against exercise in general.[6] He ridiculed the unsettled and restless disposition that summer, the most uncomfortable, as he said, of all seasons, generally gives to those who have the free use of their limbs. Such arguments were little required to keep society, Mr Jekyll, Mr Douglass, etc., within doors, when his company was only there to be enjoyed; for neither the fineness of the season, nor the most promising parties of pleasure could tempt the company of either sex to desert him.

Those who have enjoyed the society of Mr Gibbon will agree with me, that his conversation was still more captivating than his writings. Perhaps no man ever divided time more fairly between literary labour and social enjoyment; and hence, probably, he derived his peculiar excellence of making his very extensive knowledge contribute, in the highest degree, to the use or pleasure of those with whom he conversed. He united, in the happiest manner imaginable, two characters which are not often found in the same person, the profound scholar and the peculiarly agreeable companion.

Excepting a visit to Lord Egremont and Mr Hayley, whom he particularly esteemed, Mr Gibbon was not absent from Sheffield Place till the beginning of October, when we were reluctantly obliged to part with him, that he might perform his engagement to Mrs Gibbon at Bath, the widow of his father, who had early deserved, and invariably retained, his affection. From Bath he proceeded to Lord Spencer's at Althorp, a family which he always met with uncommon satisfaction. He continued in good health during the whole summer, and in excellent spirits (I never knew him enjoy better); and when he went from Sheffield Place, little did I imagine it would be the last time I should have the inexpressible pleasure of seeing him there in full possession of health.

The few following short letters, though not important in themselves, will fill up this part of the narrative better, and more agreeably, than anything which I can substitute in their place.

Edward Gibbon, Esq., to the Right Hon. Lord Sheffield
October 2, 1793

The Cork Street hotel has answered its recommendation; it is clean, convenient, and quiet. My first evening was passed at home in a very agreeable *tête-à-tête* with my friend Elmsley. Yesterday I dined at Craufurd's with an excellent set, in which were Pelham and Lord Egremont. I dine today with my Portuguese friend, Madame de Silva, at Grenier's; most probably with Lady Webster, whom I met last night at Devonshire House; a constant, though late, resort of society. The Duchess is as good, and Lady Elizabeth as seducing as ever. No news whatsoever. You will see in the papers Lord Hervey's memorial. I love vigour, but it is surely a strong measure to tell a gentleman you have *resolved* to pass the winter in his house. London is not disagreeable; yet I shall probably leave it Saturday. If anything should occur, I will write. Adieu; ever yours.

To the same

Sunday afternoon I left London and lay at Reading, and Monday in very good time I reached this place, after a very pleasant airing; and am always so much delighted and improved, with this union of ease and motion, that, were not the expense enormous, I would travel every year some hundred miles, more especially in England. I passed the day with Mrs G. yesterday. In mind and conversation she is just the same as twenty years ago. She has spirits, appetite, legs, and eyes, and talks of living till ninety.[7] I can say from my heart, Amen. We dine at two, and remain together till nine; but, although we have much to say, I am not sorry that she talks of introducing a third or fourth actor. Lord Spencer expects me about the 20th; but if I can do it without offence, I shall steal away two or three days sooner, and you shall have advice of my motions. The troubles of Bristol have been serious and bloody. I know not who was in fault; but I do not like appeasing the mob by the extinction of the toll, and the removal of the Hereford militia, who had done their duty.[8] Adieu. The girls must dance at Tunbridge. What would dear little aunt[9] say if I was to answer her letter? Ever yours, etc.

York House, Bath, October 9, 1793.

I still follow the old style, though the Convention has abolished the Christian era, with months, weeks, days, etc.[10]

To the same

York House, October 13, 1793

I am as ignorant of Bath in general as if I were still at Sheffield. My impatience to get away makes me think it better to devote my whole time to Mrs G.; and dear little aunt, whom I tenderly salute, will excuse me to her two friends, Mrs Hartley and Preston, if I make little or no use of her kind introduction. A *tête-à-tête* of eight or nine hours every day is rather difficult to support; yet I do assure you, that our conversation flows with more ease and spirit when we are alone, than when any auxiliaries are summoned to our aid. She is indeed a wonderful woman, and I think all her faculties of the mind stronger, and more active, than I have ever known them. I have settled that ten full days may be sufficient for all the purposes of our interview. I should therefore depart next Friday, the eighteenth instant, and am indeed expected at Althorp on the twentieth; but I may possibly reckon without my host, as I have not yet apprised Mrs G. of the term of my visit; and will certainly not quarrel with her for a short delay. Adieu. I must have some political speculations. The campaign, at least on our side, seems to be at an end.[11] Ever yours.

To the same

Althorp Library,[12] Tuesday, four o'clock

We have so completely exhausted this morning among the first editions of Cicero, that I can mention only my departure hence tomorrow, the sixth instant. I shall lie quietly at Woburn, and reach London in good time Thursday. By the following post I will write somewhat more largely. My stay in London will depend, partly on my amusement, and your being fixed at Sheffield Place; unless you think I can be comfortably arranged for a week or two with you at Brighton. The military remarks seem good; but now to what purpose? Adieu. I embrace and much rejoice in Louisa's improvement. Lord Ossory was from home at Farning Woods.

To the same

London, Friday, November 8, four o'clock

Walpole has just delivered yours, and I hasten the direction, that you may not be at a loss. I will write tomorrow, but I am now fatigued, and rather unwell. Adieu. I have not seen a soul except Elmsley.

To the same

St James's Street,[13] November 9, 1793

As I dropped yesterday the word *unwell,* I flatter myself that the family would have been a little alarmed by my silence today. I am still awkward, though without any suspicions of gout, and have some idea of having recourse to medical advice. Yet I creep out today in a chair, to dine with Lord Lucan. But as it will be literally my first going down stairs, and as scarcely any one is apprised of my arrival, I know nothing, I have heard nothing, I have nothing to say. My present lodging, a house of Elmsley's, is cheerful, convenient, somewhat dear, but not so much as an hotel, a species of habitation for which I have not conceived any great affection. Had you been stationary at Sheffield, you would have seen me before the twentieth; for I am tired of rambling, and pant for my home; that is to say for your house. But whether I shall have courage to brave —[14] and a bleak Down, time only can discover ... Adieu. I wish you back to Sheffield Place. The health of dear Louisa is doubtless the first object; but I did not expect Brighton after Tunbridge. Whenever dear little aunt is separate from you, I shall certainly write to her; but at present how is it possible? Ever yours.

To the same at Brighton

St James's Street, November 11, 1793

I must at length withdraw the veil before my state of health, though the naked truth may alarm you more than a fit of the gout. Have you never observed, through my *inexpressibles*, a large prominency, *circa genitalia?* It was a swelled testicle which, as it was not at all painful, and very little troublesome, I had strangely neglected for many years. But since my departure from Sheffield Place, it has increased (most stupendously), is increasing, and ought to be diminished. Yesterday I sent for Farquhar, who is allowed to be a very skilful surgeon. After viewing and palping, he very seriously desired to call in assistance, and has examined it again today with Mr Cline, a surgeon, as he says, of the first eminence. They both pronounce it a *hydrocele* (a collection of water), which must be let out by the operation of tapping; but, from its magnitude and long neglect, they think it a most extraordinary case, and wish to have another surgeon, Dr Baillie, present. If the business should go off smoothly, I shall be delivered from my burthen (it is almost as big as a small child) and walk about in four or five days with a truss. But the medical gentlemen, who never speak quite plain, insinuate to me the possibility of an inflammation, of fever, etc.

I am not appalled at the thoughts of the operation, which is fixed for Wednesday next, twelve o'clock; but it has occurred to me, that you might wish to be present, before and afterwards, till the crisis was past; and to give you that opportunity, I shall solicit a delay till Thursday, or even Friday. In the meanwhile, I crawl about with some labour and much indecency to Devonshire House (where I left all the fine ladies making flannel waistcoats[15]); Lady Lucan's, etc. Adieu. Varnish the business for the ladies: yet I am afraid it will be public – the advantage of being notorious. Ever yours.

Immediately on receiving the last letter, I went the same day from Brighthelmstone to London, and was agreeably surprised to find that Mr Gibbon had dined at Lord Lucan's and did not return to his lodgings, where I waited for him, till eleven o'clock at night. Those who have seen him within the last eight or ten years, must be surprised to hear that he could doubt whether his disorder was apparent. When he returned

196

to England in 1787, I was greatly alarmed by a prodigious increase, which I always conceived to proceed from a rupture. I did not understand why he, who had talked with me on every other subject relative to himself and his affairs without reserve, should never in any shape hint at a malady so troublesome; but on speaking to his *valet de chambre*, he told me, Mr Gibbon could not bear the least allusion to that subject, and never would suffer him to notice it. I consulted some medical persons, who with me supposing it to be a rupture, were of opinion that nothing could be done, and said that he surely must have had advice, and of course had taken all necessary precautions. He now talked freely with me about his disorder; which, he said, began in the year 1761; that he then consulted Mr Hawkins, the surgeon, who did not decide whether it was the beginning of a rupture, or a hydrocele; but he desired to see Mr Gibbon again when he came to town. Mr Gibbon, not feeling any pain, nor suffering any inconvenience, as he said, never returned to Mr Hawkins; and although the disorder continued to increase gradually, and of late years very much indeed, he never mentioned it to any person, however incredible it may appear, from 1761 to November 1793. I told him, that I had always supposed there was no doubt of its being a rupture; his answer was, that he never thought so, and that he, and the surgeons who attended him, were of opinion that it was a hydrocele. It is now certain that it was originally a rupture, and that a hydrocele had lately taken place in the same part; and it is remarkable that his legs, which had been swelled about the ankle, particularly one of them, since he had the erysipelas in 1790, recovered their former shape, as soon as the water appeared in another part, which did not happen till between the time he left Sheffield Place, in the beginning of October, and his arrival at Althorp, towards the latter end of that month.

On the Thursday following the date of his last letter, Mr Gibbon was tapped for the first time; four quarts of a transparent watery fluid were discharged by that operation. Neither inflammation nor fever ensued; the tumour was diminished to nearly half its size; the remaining part was a soft irregular mass. I had been with him two days before, and I continued with him above a week after the first tapping, during which time he enjoyed his usual spirits; and the three medical gentlemen who attended him will recollect his pleasantry, even during the operation. He was abroad[16] again in a few days, but the water evidently collecting very fast, it was agreed that a second puncture should be made a fortnight after the first. Knowing that I should be wanted at a meeting in the country, he pressed me to attend it, and promised that soon after the second operation was performed he would follow me to Sheffield Place; but before he arrived I received the following letters:

Mr Gibbon to Lord Sheffield, at Brighton

St James's Street, Nov. 25, 1793

Though Farquhar has promised to write you a line, I conceive you may not be sorry to hear directly from me. The operation of yesterday was much longer, more searching, and more painful than the former; but it has eased and lightened me to a much greater degree. No inflammation, no fever, a delicious night, leave to go abroad tomorrow, and to go out of town when I please, *en attendant* the future measures of a radical cure. If you hold your intention of returning next Saturday to Sheffield Place, I shall probably join you about the Tuesday following, after having passed two nights at Beckenham.[17] The Devons are going to Bath, and the hospitable Craufurd follows them. I passed a delightful day with Burke; an odd one with Monsignor Erskine, the Pope's Nuncio. Of public news, you and the papers know more than I do. We seem to have strong sea and land hopes; nor do I dislike the Royalists having beaten the Sans Culottes, and taken Dol. How many minutes will it take to guillotine the seventy-three new members of the Convention, who are now arrested? Adieu; ever yours.

St James's St, Nov. 30, 1793

It will not be in my power to reach Sheffield Place quite so soon as I wished and expected. Lord Auckland informs me that he shall be at Lambeth next week, Tuesday, Wednesday, and Thursday. I have therefore agreed to dine at Beckenham on Friday. Saturday will be spent there, and unless some extraordinary temptation should detain me another day, you will see me by four o'clock Sunday the ninth of December. I dine tomorrow with the Chancellor[18] at Hampstead, and, what I do not like at this time of the year, without a proposal to stay all night. Yet I would not refuse, more especially as I had denied him on a former day. My health is good; but I shall have a final interview with Farquhar before I leave town. We are still in darkness about Lord Howe and the French ships, but hope seems to preponderate. Adieu. Nothing that relates to Louisa can be forgotten. Ever yours.

To the same

St James's Street, Dec. 6, 1793

16 du mois Frimaire.[19]

The man tempted me and I did eat[20] – and that man is no less than the Chancellor. I dine today, as I intended, at Beckenham; but he recalls me (the third time this week) by a dinner tomorrow (Saturday) with Burke and Windham, which I do not possess sufficient fortitude to resist. Sunday he dismisses me again to the aforesaid Beckenham, but insists on finding me there on Monday, which he will probably do, supposing there should be room and welcome at the Ambassador's.[21] I shall not therefore arrive at Sheffield till Tuesday, the 10th instant, and though you may perceive I do not want society or amusement, I sincerely repine at the delay. You will likewise derive some comfort from hearing of the spirit and activity of my motions. Farquhar is satisfied, allows me to go, and does not think I shall be obliged to precipitate my return. Shall we never have anything more than hopes and rumours from Lord Howe? Ever yours.

Mr Gibbon generally took the opportunity of passing a night or two with his friend Lord Auckland, at Eden Farm (ten miles from London), on his passage to Sheffield Place; and notwithstanding his indisposition, he had lately made an excursion thither from London; when he was much pleased by meeting the Archbishop of Canterbury,[22] of whom he expressed a high opinion. He returned to London, to dine with Lord Loughborough, to meet Mr Burke, Mr Windham, and particularly Mr Pitt, with whom he was not acquainted; and in his last journey to Sussex, he re-visited Eden Farm, and was much gratified by the opportunity of again seeing, during a whole day, Mr Pitt, who passed the night there. From Lord Auckland's Mr Gibbon proceeded to Sheffield Place; and his discourse was never more brilliant, nor more entertaining, than on his arrival. The parallels which he drew, and the comparisons which he made between the leading men of this country, were sketched in his best manner, and were infinitely interesting.

However, this last visit to Sheffield Place became far different from any he had ever made before. That ready, cheerful, various, and illuminating conversation, which we had before admired in him, was not now always to be found in the library or the dining-room. He moved with difficulty, and retired from company sooner than he had been used to do. On the twenty-third of December, his appetite began to fail him. He observed

199

to me, that it was a very bad sign *with him* when he could not eat his breakfast, which he had done at all times very heartily; and this seems to have been the strongest expression of apprehension that he was ever observed to utter. A considerable degree of fever now made its appearance. Inflammation arose, from the weight and the bulk of the tumour. Water again collected very fast, and when the fever went off, he never entirely recovered his appetite even for breakfast. I became very uneasy indeed at his situation towards the end of the month, and thought it necessary to advise him to set out for London. He had before settled his plan to arrive there about the middle of January. I had company in the house, and we expected one of his particular friends; but he was obliged to sacrifice all social pleasure to the immediate attention which his health required. He went to London on the seventh of January, and the next day I received the following billet; the last he ever wrote:

Edward Gibbon Esq. to Lord Sheffield

St James's Street, four o'clock, Tuesday

This date says everything. I was almost killed between Sheffield Place and East Grinstead, by hard, frozen, long and cross ruts, that would disgrace the approach of an Indian wigwam. The rest was something less painful; and I reached this place half dead, but not seriously feverish, or ill. I found a dinner invitation from Lord Lucan; but what are dinners to me? I wish they did not know of my departure. I catch the flying post. What an effort! Adieu, till Thursday or Friday.

By his own desire, I did not follow him till Thursday the ninth. I then found him far from well. The tumour more distended than before, inflamed, and ulcerated in several places. Remedies were applied to abate the inflammation; but it was not thought proper to puncture the tumour for the third time, till Monday the 13th of January, when no less than six quarts of fluid were discharged. He seemed much relieved by the evacuation. His spirits continued good. He talked, as usual, of passing his time at houses which he had often frequented with great pleasure, the Duke of Devonshire's, Mr Craufurd's, Lord Spencer's, Lord Lucan's, Sir Ralph Payne's, and Mr Batt's; and when I told him that I should not return to the country, as I had intended, he pressed me to go; knowing I had an engagement there on public business, he said, 'You may be back on Saturday, and I intend to go on Thursday to Devonshire House.'

I had not any apprehension that his life was in danger, although I began to fear that he might not be restored to a comfortable state, and that motion would be very troublesome to him; but he talked of a radical cure. He said that it was fortunate the disorder had shown itself while he was in England, where he might procure the best assistance; and if a radical cure could not be obtained before his return to Lausanne, there was an able surgeon at Geneva, who could come to tap him when it should be necessary.

On Tuesday the fourteenth, when the risk of inflammation and fever from the last operations was supposed to be over, as the medical gentleman who attended him expressed no fears for his life, I went that afternoon part of the way to Sussex, and the following day reached Sheffield Place. The next morning, the sixteenth, I received by the post a good account of Mr Gibbon, which mentioned also that he hourly gained strength. In the evening came a letter by express, dated noon that day, which acquainted me that Mr Gibbon had had a violent attack the preceding night, and that it was not probable he could live till I came to him. I reached his lodgings in St James's Street about midnight, and learned that my friend had expired a quarter before one o'clock that day, the sixteenth of January, 1794.

After I left him on Tuesday afternoon the fourteenth, he saw some company, Lady Lucan and Lady Spencer, and thought himself well enough at night to omit the opium draught, which he had been used to take for some time. He slept very indifferently; before nine the next morning he rose, but could not eat his breakfast. However, he appeared tolerably well, yet complained at times of a pain in his stomach. At one o'clock he received a visit of an hour from Madame de Silva, and at three, his friend Mr Craufurd, of Auchinames (for whom he had mentioned a particular regard) called, and stayed with him till past five o'clock. They talked, as usual, on various subjects; and twenty hours before his death, Mr Gibbon happened to fall into a conversation, not uncommon with him, on the probable duration of his life. He said, that he thought himself a good life for ten, twelve, or perhaps twenty years. About six, he ate the wing of a chicken, and drank three glasses of Madeira. After dinner he became very uneasy and impatient; complained a good deal, and appeared so weak, that his servant[23] was alarmed. Mr Gibbon had sent to his friend and relation, Mr Robert Darell, whose house was not far distant, desiring to see him, and adding, that he had something particular to say. But, unfortunately, this desired interview never took place.

During the evening he complained much of his stomach, and of a disposition to vomit. Soon after nine, he took his opium draught, and went to bed. About ten, he complained of much pain, and desired that warm napkins might be applied to his stomach. He almost incessantly expressed a sense of pain till about four o'clock in the morning, when he said he found his stomach much easier. About seven the servant asked, whether he should send for Mr Farquhar? he answered no; that he was as well as he had been the day before. At about half-past eight, he got out of bed, and said he was *plus adroit* than he had been for three months past, and got into bed again, without assistance, better than usual. About nine, he said that he would rise. The servant, however, persuaded him to remain in bed till Mr Farquhar, who was expected at eleven, should come. Till about that hour he spoke with great facility. Mr Farquhar came at the time appointed, and he was then visibly dying. When the *valet de chambre* returned, after attending Mr Farquhar out of the room, Mr Gibbon said, *'Pourquoi est-ce que vous me quittez?'* This was about half past eleven. At twelve, he drank some brandy and water from a teapot, and desired his favourite servant to stay with him. These were the last words he pronounced articulately. To the last he preserved his senses: and when he could no longer speak, his servant having asked a question, he made a sign, to show that he understood him. He was quite tranquil, and did not stir; his eyes half-shut. About a quarter before one, he ceased to breathe.[24]

The *valet de chambre* observed, that Mr Gibbon did not, at any time, show the least sign of alarm, or apprehension of death; and it does not appear that he ever thought himself in danger, unless his desire to speak to Mr Darell may be considered in that light.

Perhaps I dwell too long on these minute and melancholy circumstances. Yet the close of such a life can hardly fail to interest every reader; and I know that the public has received a different and erroneous account of my friend's last hours.

I can never cease to feel regret that I was not by his side at this awful period: a regret so strong, that I can express it only by borrowing (as Mr Mason has done on a similar occasion) the forcible language of Tacitus: *Mihi praeter acerbitatem* amici *erepti, auget maestitiam quod assidere valetudini, fovere deficientem, satiari vultu, complexu, non contigit.*[25] It is some consolation to me, that I did not, like Tacitus, by a long absence anticipate the loss of my friend several years before his decease. Although I had not the mournful gratification of being near him on the day he expired, yet during his illness I had not failed to attend him with that assiduity which his genius, his virtues, and, above all, our long uninterrupted and happy friendship sanctioned and demanded.

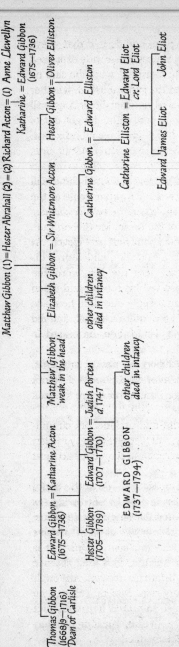

The Gibbon Family

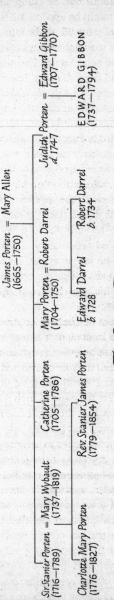

The Porten Family

Appendix 2

The Family Trees of Gibbon and Porten

Editor's Notes

NOTE TO INTRODUCTION

1 (p. 39). The arrangement of the text mainly follows that of Georges Alfred Bonnard, as do the chapter divisions. This short Introduction starts with the first paragraph of draft A, followed by the first of draft B, from 'A sincere and simple narrative ...'

NOTES TO CHAPTER I

1 (p. 41). Chapter I starts with two paragraphs taken from a separate sheet (now bound in with the drafts) in which Gibbon justifies his writing about his family. Then from 'A philosopher ...' down to '... neither glory nor shame' (p. 43) the text is that of draft A; from there to the end of the chapter the text is that of F, Gibbon's final draft.

2 (p. 42). *Colin Clout's Come Home Againe*, 536–8. The three ladies are the daughters of Sir John Spencer of Althorp, but the relationship between the Spencers and the poet Edmund Spenser is doubtful.

3 (p. 42). The supposed descent of the Earls of Denbigh from the Habsburgs is now proved false.

4 (p. 44). Pope, *Moral Essays III: To Lord Bathurst*, 287–8.

5 (p. 45). 'Ogress' or 'pellet' is the heraldic term for a roundel sable, which Edmund Gibbon probably substituted for scallop-shells to distinguish his own family from that of his cousins. It is difficult to believe that Gibbon did not know this standard term, meaning 'cannon ball', so he can hardly have believed his 'whimsical anecdote' about the female cannibals.

6 (p. 45). 'Now as to race and ancestry' (Ulysses in Ovid, *Metamorphoses* XIII, 140).

7 (p. 46). *2 Henry VI*, IV, vii.

8 (p. 46). At the time of writing Gibbon was anxious to believe that his great-grandfather Matthew was the younger son of the second Robert.

9 (p. 47). In 1786 or 1787 Gibbon was given a copy of the *Introduction to Latin Heraldry* published by John Gibbon, Bluemantle Poursuivant, who claimed descent

from the Lord Saye and Seale who was Lord High Treasurer to Henry VI. It was not until 1792 that Gibbon accepted that John the Herald was not his ancestor.

10 (p. 47). 'Up to this point I have corrected Roman heraldry; from now on may debased forms of words cease to be. If this book comes to be used as it deserves, it will be due witness of my diligence. Whatever carping critics may say, the coming age will admit that I showed skill in the art of self-defence.'

11 (p. 48). Capable.

12 (p. 48). The Actons intermarried with the Gibbons to a confusing extent. Richard Acton had a daughter, Katharine, from his first wife. A widower, he married in 1698 the widow of Matthew Gibbon, Gibbon's great-grandfather. Katharine married her stepmother's son Edward, Gibbon's grandfather, who thus became the nephew of Richard Acton's brothers and first cousin of their children. He was also the first cousin of Edward Acton, goldsmith, son of his uncle Walter. This Edward had two sons: Edward, a doctor, who married and settled in Besançon, and attended Gibbon's father, his second cousin (p. 52); and Richard, unmarried, chief officer in the navy of the Grand Duchy of Tuscany. Edward's eldest son (General Acton, p. 52) was minister to the King of the Two Sicilies (see Bonnard, pp. 238–9, and Gibbon Family Tree p. 203).

13 (p. 50). The Septennial Act of 1715 allowed a Parliament to continue for seven years before a general election had to be held. *Il serrar di Consiglio* (the 'Closing of the Council') was an episode in Venetian history of 1298.

14 (p. 52). Petersfield was evidently a 'burgage borough', i.e., a constituency in the unreformed parliament where the votes were held by the owner or by the tenants of lands held for fixed annual rents (burgage tenure).

15 (p. 53). 'Neighbourhood provided the first stages of their knowing each other; in time love grew between them, and they would have been joined by marriage ceremony, but their parents forbade it. One thing could not be forbidden: their hearts were held captive and they burned with equal passion' (Ovid, *Metamorphoses* IV, 59–62, of Pyramus and Thisbe).

16 (p. 54). 'Mrs' (Mistress) was the conventional title for an unmarried lady.

17 (p. 54). *A Serious Call to a Devout and Holy Life* (1728) was the most influential work of William Law.

18 (p. 55). Nonjurors were members of the established clergy (and their later followers) who refused to take the required oath of allegiance to William and Mary in 1689, on the grounds that it broke their oath to James II.

19 (p. 55). The dispute which arose out of the sermon preached by Dr Hoadly, Bishop of Bangor, in 1717 before George I, in which he argued that the Gospels gave no justification for any visible Church authority in matters of discipline or doctrine.

20 (p. 55). Bernard de Mandeville's verse satire of 1705 (*The Grumbling Hive*) was reissued in 1714 under the title *The Fable of The Bees, or Private Vices, Public Benefits*, and was attacked by William Law.

NOTES TO CHAPTER II

1 (p. 57). The text of Chapters II and III is that of draft F throughout.

2 (p. 57). The Gregorian Calendar (New Style) was not adopted in England until 1752, when eleven days between 2 and 14 September were dropped to correct the Old Style Julian Calendar. Gibbon is therefore updating the date of his birth. (Cf. p. 82.)

3 (p. 58). War between England and Spain broke out in 1739 over trade with the Spanish colonies and became part of the war for the Austrian Succession, which was ended by the Peace of Aix-la-Chapelle in 1748; in 1761 war broke out again when Spain joined France as her ally in the Seven Years' War, which ended in 1763 with the Treaty of Paris.

4 (p. 58). The Jacobite rising under the Young Pretender, Charles Edward Stuart.

5 (p. 60). Milton, *Paradise Lost* VIII, 253–73.

6 (p. 60). Cf. Descartes, *Le Discours de la méthode*: the famous phrase, *cogito ergo sum*.

7 (p. 61). For once Gibbon's memory is at fault: the registers of Putney Parish Church show that only one brother was called Edward James.

8 (p. 61). 'When one is torn away, a second does not fail.' This is adapted from Virgil, *Aeneid* VI, 143, Gibbon having substituted *uno* for *primo* ('the first').

9 (p. 63). The opening sentences of Kirkby's *Automathes*, the full title of which is *The capacity and extent of the human understanding, exemplified in the extraordinary case of Automathes, a young nobleman left in his infancy upon a desolate island*.

10 (p. 64). Edward Pocock's Latin version was called *Philosophus autodidactus* ('The Self-taught Philosopher').

11 (p. 65). Gibbon is vague about dates in his early life, and these were not corrected until Birkbeck Hill's edition of the Memoirs (see his Appendix 7). The registers of Putney parish and of Westminster School show that Gibbon's mother died in 1746, his grandfather absconded in 1747, and he entered the school in January 1748.

12 (p. 67). Gibbon's own note refers to 'a foolish novel of love and honour', i.e., the *Histoire d'Hipolite, Comte de Duglas* by Madame de la Mothe (1699), of which Prince Adolphus was the hero. An English translation had appeared in 1708.

13 (p. 68). Horace's *speciosa miracula* ('striking marvels') of *Ars poetica*, 144.

14 (p. 68). This should be 1747, his eleventh year.

15 (p. 69). Agesilaus; in his note Gibbon quotes the maxim in Greek.

16 (p. 69). Lionel Tollemache, Lord Huntingtower; see Index. Lord Sheffield omitted this incident.

17 (p. 73). A paraphrase of the third verse of Gray's 'Ode on a Distant Prospect of Eton College'.

18 (p. 73). 'Trifles affect light minds' (Ovid, *Ars amatoria* I, 159).

19 (p. 73). Xerxes' army were flogged as they worked to cut a channel through the isthmus of Mount Athos (Herodotus, VII, 22).

NOTES TO CHAPTER III

1 (p. 76). Built in 1733 and still known as the New Buildings.

2 (p. 78). Experts in canon (ecclesiastical) law.

3 (p. 78). Cf. Milton, *Comus*, 707: 'those budge doctors of the Stoic fur'. 'Budge' is lambskin with the wool worn outside as trimming for an academic hood.

4 (p. 78). *An Enquiry into the Nature and Causes of the Wealth of Nations*, Book V, Chapter 1, Article ii.

5 (p. 79). The thirty Demies, their allowance being half a Fellow's.

6 (p. 80). The headquarters of the Maurist scholars such as Mabillon and Montfaucon; see Index.

7 (p. 80). George Horne, later Bishop of Norwich, a follower of John Hutchinson's theory that Hebrew provided the key to all knowledge.

8 (p. 80). 'To be enrolled in the serene company of the gods' (Horace, *Odes* III, 3, 35–6).

9 (p. 82). See Chapter II, note 2.

10 (p. 82). In his *Chronology of Ancient Kingdoms* (1728), Newton had dated the earlier events of Greek and Roman history several centuries later than Marsham.

11 (p. 84). William Dodwell and Thomas Church; see Index.

12 (p. 85). 'The first path to safety open to you will start where you least expect, from a Greek city' (Virgil, *Aeneid* VI, 96–7). The Sibyl foretells that help will come to Trojan Aeneas from Greek Evander: so a Catholic Gibbon could have argued that the heretic Middleton first enlightened him.

13 (p. 85). Lord Sheffield gave his name as Molesworth; he is otherwise unknown.

14 (p. 85). The red dragon of Revelation 12, taken by Protestants to represent the Catholic Church.

15 (p. 85). Dryden, *The Hind and the Panther* I, 1ff.

16 (p. 86). Ibid., I, 141–5.

17 (p. 86). In draft C the bookseller is named Mr Lewis, and Lord Sheffield's note adds that that the priest was called Baker, a Jesuit chaplain to the Sardinian ambassador.

18 (p. 86). *Commentaries on the Laws of England* IV, 56.

19 (p. 87). Quoted from a conversation between Boswell and Johnson on 20 March 1776.

20 (p. 87). Milton, *Lycidas*, 128–9 ('whom' substituted for 'what').

21 (p. 88). 'I, William Chillingworth ... to all these articles and to the contents of each of them freely and willingly subscribe my assent and declare my agreement with them. 20th day of July, 1638.'

22 (p. 88). The old Comté de Foix, now the Département de Ariège.

23 (p. 89). From Plutarch's *Moralia; De superstitione*, para. 2.

24 (p. 89). Bonnard notes that this is quoted from Voltaire's *Lettre* VII, *Sur les Français* (1767).

25 (p. 90). In fact the profits were insufficient to do this.

26 (p. 91). Probably a reference to the sons of George III who had been sent to the universities of Hanover and Göttingen.

NOTES TO CHAPTER IV

1 (p. 92). Chapter IV gives the text of draft B, which continues through Chapter V. Two sentences are omitted, being nearly identical with two on p. 86; ll. 25–32.

2 (p. 94). There was in fact a tacit understanding between the Catholic and Protestant cantons not to proselytize.

3 (p. 94). See Gibbon's letters to his aunt Catherine Porten (*Letters* I, 3 and 5), D. M. Low, *Edward Gibbon* (1937), pp. 54ff., and Editor's Introduction, p. 22.

4 (p. 97). *Institutio oratoria* X, 1.

5 (p. 98). Published by Lord Sheffield in *Miscellaneous Works* IV, pp. 446–66, and dated by Gibbon 13 May 1757.

6 (p. 98). 'Study your Greek models by night and by day' (Horace, *Ars poetica*, 268–9).

7 (p. 98). Cf. 1 Corinthians 13:12.

8 (p. 100). Bayle's *Dictionnaire historique et critique*.

9 (p. 101). *Journal de mon voyage dans quelques endroits de la Suisse.*

10 (p. 101). 'Science' is generally used by Gibbon in the sense of 'learning'.

11 (p. 101). Gibbon's emendation (*otio* for *odio*) is generally accepted, and was subsequently confirmed by a single MS.

12 (p. 102). 'He is a humble country priest and misleads the peasants.' Quotation not traced.

13 (p. 102). Milton, *Paradise Lost* II, 561.

14 (p. 103). Frederick II (the Great) of Prussia, at whose court Voltaire lived from 1750 to 1752.

15 (p. 103). 'Virgil I only saw' (Ovid, *Tristia* IV, 10, 51).

16 (p. 103). 'O House of Aristippus! O Garden of Epicurus!' (Voltaire, *Lettre* XCI).

17 (p. 104). 'Love is the same for all' (Virgil, *Georgics* III, 244).

18 (p. 105). For the preceding ten words Lord Sheffield substituted the much-quoted passage from draft C: 'I sighed as a lover, I obeyed as a son; my wound was insensibly healed by a faithful report of the tranquillity and cheerfulness of the lady herself'.

19 (p. 105). The Swiss banker Jacques Necker became Minister of Finance in France in 1776, was dismissed by Louis XVI in 1781, and was recalled in 1788 when it was thought he could save France's financial collapse by introducing essential reforms. In the event his policy was a disaster, but Gibbon, writing in 1789, expresses the hopes of the time.

20 (p. 106). The Seven Years' War.

21 (p. 106). In Gibbon's Journals they are named as Daniel Lemaire and Jean-Louis Crousaz.

22 (p. 106). Luxemburg, originally a Habsburg duchy, had been seized by Burgundy in 1443 but returned in 1477 when the heiress Mary married Maximilian I; it remained part of the Holy Roman Empire.

23 (p. 106). Stanislaus Leszczynski had been given the duchy of Lorraine by Louis XV (husband of his daughter Marie) when prevented from occupying the throne of Poland by protest from Russia in 1735.

NOTES TO CHAPTER V

1 (p. 107). From the book of Common Prayer: 'A Collect or Prayer for all Conditions of men'.

2 (p. 107). Two sentences are omitted here; they are repeated in draft F, p. 62, ll. 15–19.

3 (p. 108). 'Fine' means *finalis concordia*, an agreement in court as a means of conveying land; 'levying a fine' or 'suffering a common recovery' are legal expressions used in order to break an entail.

4 (p. 109). 'For a stepmother enters as an enemy to the children of a previous marriage, no gentler than a viper' (Euripides, *Alcestis*, 309–10).

5 (p. 109). 'For indeed I have a father at home and a spiteful stepmother' (Virgil, *Eclogues* III, 33).

6 (p. 109). 'Drowning an audience's uproar, and by nature fitted for action' (Horace, *Ars poetica*, 32).

7 (p. 110). An omission mark in draft B is replaced in draft C by the word 'bagnio', the usual term for a high-class brothel at the time.

8 (p. 110). 'Domesticate yourself there while you stay at Naples' occurs in Lord Chesterfield's letter to his son of 29 March 1750.

9 (p. 110). 'Unforgiving enemy' is rather an exaggerated reference to Dr Johnson, though he is certainly highly critical in his *Life* of Mallet.

10 (p. 111). Gibbon lodged in Bond Street for the winter of 1758–9.

11 (p. 112). Scipio Africanus' words quoted by Cicero at the start of *De officiis* III.

12 (p. 113). From Chapter V of the *Essai sur l'étude de la littérature*: 'One of those societies which have done more to immortalize Louis XIV than an ambition often damaging to mankind was already starting on those researches which combined keen insight, elegance and erudition; where one finds so many discoveries and sometimes what is almost as important, an ignorance both modest and wise' (*Miscellaneous Works* IV, p. 19).

13 (p. 113). 'There was no book so bad that some good could not be got out of it' (Pliny, *Letters* III, 5, 10, quoting his uncle).

14 (p. 113). The passage in Livy deals with the tribute imposed by the Romans on Antiochus the Great of Syria after his defeat in 188 BC, and the discussion is about what is meant by '12,000 Attic talents of silver ... each talent to weigh not less than 80 Roman pounds' (cf. *Miscellaneous Works* V, p. 73).

15 (p. 115). The Académie française, Académie des sciences and Académie des inscriptions et belles-lettres.

16 (p. 115). Fontenelle (who died in 1757, aged nearly 100) had no specific 'school', but his sympathies were with the *'anciens'*. Racine and Boileau.

17 (p. 116). 'Keep it until the ninth year' (Horace, *Ars poetica*, 388).

18 (p. 116). The proposal in 1761, after five years of war, that a congress should meet at Augsburg to discuss peace plans fell through when Britain and France failed to agree on conditions.

19 (p. 116). Gibbon underlined these words; perhaps Dr Maty's comments irritated him as did the latter's delay in reading the MS.

20 (p. 118). Gibbon was writing draft B in 1789 and refers to the publication of the *Essai* in 1761.

21 (p. 118). 'I struggle to be concise and end by being obscure' (Horace, *Ars poetica*, 25–6).

22 (p. 118). For Newton's 'New Chronology' see Chapter III, note 10, and for 'specious' Chapter II, note 13.

23 (p. 119). Bentley had been attacked for coining the word 'vernacular', and defended himself in the preface to his *Works* by proving that it had been used before (in 1601, according to the OED).

24 (p. 120). Gibbon summarizes extracts from two of Cicero's letters to Atticus (I, 19 and II, 1: reference here corrected from his own confusing version).

25 (p. 120). 'Learned in the lore of either tongue' (Horace, *Odes* III, 8, 5, to Maecenas); quoted by Voltaire in the dedication of his tragedy *Brutus* to Lord Bolingbroke.

26 (p. 120). 'The first to bring to my country' (Virgil, *Georgics* III, 10).

27 (p. 120). 'I do not believe that you would pride yourself on being less easy to recognize as an Englishman than Lucullus was as a Roman'; and below, 'These striking features, these bold figures, this sacrifice of the rules to feeling and of rhythm to vigour ...'

28 (p. 121). The Seven Years' War (1756–63); the last one at the time of writing was the War of American Independence (1775–83).

29 (p. 121). Dryden, *Cymon and Iphigenia*, 399–408.

30 (p. 122). The Jacobite rising; cf. note 4 to Chapter II.

31 (p. 122). Hessian and Hanoverian regiments were brought over in 1756 to defend England against the threat of French invasion.

32 (p. 122). 'Who will break through the inertia of his fatherland and rouse to arms men grown idle' (Virgil, *Aeneid* VI, 814); prophesied of Tullus Hostilius.

33 (p. 122). Pitt had always opposed the subsidies to German troops and introduced his Militia Bill in 1756 and 1757.

34 (p. 123). At Quiberon Bay, where the greater part of the French Atlantic fleet was destroyed.

35 (p. 124). 'Specious' again in its Latin sense of 'striking, illustrious'.

36 (p. 124). George III, of the House of Brunswick, was born in England.

37 (p. 125). 'Foreign' in the sense of 'at a distance from home'.

38 (p. 125). The braggart soldier in a farce by Samuel Foote.

39 (p. 126). 'We should be ashamed of having come last' (Virgil, *Aeneid* V, 196): Mnestheus exhorting his rowers in the boat race.

40 (p. 127). 'The packs are on the ox. It is unbelievable how tired of the business I am ... It has put an end to my mental drive and industry and the work which was my pride. I miss the world, my books, the City, my house and you, my friends. But I'll put up with it as best I can so long as it's only for a year. If that's extended, I give up.' (Cicero, *Ad Atticum* V, 15, modified by Gibbon, who substitutes *libros* – books – for *forum*.)

41 (p. 129). That is, Cicero's *De natura deorum*.

42 (p. 129). 'The wind blew full on the sail and the dark wave swirled and hissed loudly as the ship went on her way, cutting a path through the waves' (Homer, *Iliad* I, 481–3). Gibbon's original Greek lacks accents and breathings.

43 (p. 130). Gibbon's comments on Bishop Hurd's edition of Horace were published by Lord Sheffield in *Miscellaneous Works* IV, 113–52.

44 (p. 130). 'The true genius is a mind of large general powers, accidentally determined to some particular direction' (Johnson's *Life of Cowley*).

45 (p. 130). This dissertation was included in *Miscellaneous Works* III, 206–22.

46 (p. 131). That is, *Memoirs of the Reign of Queen Elizabeth*; for Anthony Bacon, see Index.

47 (p. 133). Cosimo dei Medici is the correct form; Gibbon appears not to know that 'Medici' is plural.

48 (p. 133). 'A family apparently created by destiny to restore or cultivate learning' (Lipse, *Letters to the Germans and French* VII).

49 (p. 133). 'Matters sunk deep in earth and gloom' (Virgil, *Aeneid* VI, 266).

NOTES TO CHAPTER VI

1 (p. 134). Chapter VI continues to the end of draft B ('... my Italian journey', p. 140) and then carries on with draft C.

2 (p. 134). In Journal A and a letter to his father of 25 January 1763 Gibbon says that he crossed in a yacht with the Duke of Bridgewater, the Marquis of Tavistock and Lord Ossory.

3 (p. 135). The seats of the dukes of Argyll and the earls of Pembroke.

4 (p. 135). J. B. Languet de Gergy.

5 (p. 135). 'A famous and venerable name amongst men' (Cato to Pompey in Lucan, *Pharsalia* IX, 202).

6 (p. 136). 'Unbidden the worthy go to the banquets of the worthless' (Eupolis, *Fragment* 289 [Kock]).

7 (p. 136). The Comédie Italienne, afterwards the Opéra comique.

8 (p. 138). 'Assisted' in the French sense of 'attended'.

9 (p. 139). Gibbon reports only one such act in Journal B, pp. 31–2. Lord Sheffield omitted the passage.

10 (p. 139). Later the first Lord Sheffield and Gibbon's literary executor.

11 (p. 140). Put together by Lord Sheffield in *Miscellaneous Works* IV, pp. 157–328, under the title *Nomina gentesque antiquae Italiae*. *Insulae* were the apartment blocks of ancient Rome.

12 (p. 141). Virgil's *longo sed proximus intervallo* ('next, but at a long interval': *Aeneid* V, 320).

13 (p. 141). Italian *conversazioni*, i.e., social gatherings.

14 (p. 141). By his italics Gibbon probably refers to Livy, I, 12, 6, in which Romulus makes a stand and vows a temple to Jupiter Stator ('Stayer').

15 (p. 142). Ferdinand IV, King of the Two Sicilies, thirteen years old at the time.

16 (p. 142). From the *Lettres persannes*, 112: 'I have stayed more than a year in Italy and have seen only the remnants of the old Italy which was once so famous. Although everyone lives in the towns, these are quite empty and unpopulated.'

17 (p. 143). See Editor's Introduction, p. 16.

18 (p. 143). Gibbon was in fact peremptorily summoned home, and his allowance temporarily stopped, to his embarrassment (see D. M. Low, *Edward Gibbon*, 1937, pp. 188–90).

19 (p. 144). Horace, *Odes* III, 29, 12, translated by Gibbon immediately above.

20 (p. 144). 'Meagre resources at home' (Juvenal, *Satires* I, 3, 165).

21 (p. 146). Dated by Gibbon to 1307 (*Miscellaneous Works* III, pp. 260–65).

22 (p. 147). 'This hand, hostile to tyranny, seeks peace and quiet through the sword of freedom' (quotation as yet untraced).

23 (p. 147). Lord Sheffield added the footnote that Gibbon neglected to burn them, and he included the 43 folio pages left at Sheffield Place in the second edition of the *Miscellaneous Works* III, pp. 239–329.

24 (p. 148). *The New Bath Guide ... A Series of Poetical Epistles* by Christopher Anstey, 1766.

25 (p. 149). It is more likely that Gibbon himself wrote the refutation of Walpole's *Historical Doubts on the Life and Reign of King Richard the Third*, and it is included in the second edition of the *Miscellaneous Works* III, pp. 331–49.

26 (p. 149). The lines quoted from *Aeneid* VI are: 'They were walking in darkness through the shadows beneath the lonely night' (268); 'Here an ampler air clothes the plains with brilliant light' (640); '[But] the spirits send visions which are false in the light of day' (896).

27 (p. 150). *On the Delicacy of Friendship* was written by Bishop Hurd as an attack on Dr John Jortin who had criticized Bishop Warburton.

28 (p. 150). 'I will forbid one who has published abroad the rites of Ceres' (Horace, *Odes* III, 2, 26–7).

29 (p. 150). 'The learned Englishman, a master of fine style'.

30 (p. 151). 'His strictures are rather harsher than desirable'.

31 (p. 151). The *Lives* of the later Roman emperors by the *Scriptores Historiae Augustae*.

32 (p. 152). 'Read deeply, not widely' (Pliny, *Letters* VII, 9, 15).

33 (p. 152). Gibbon took the preceding 9 lines, from 'By the habit of early

rising' almost verbatim from draft B (p. 112), where they refer to an earlier period in his life.

34 (p. 153).   Happy he who far from business dealing
(like uncorrupted folk of yore)
and free from interest owing
works with his oxen his family land.

Horace, *Epodes* 2, 1–4
(translated by W. G. Shepherd)

35 (p. 153). Tacitus, *Histories* III, 54, where it refers to Vitellius; the word order should be *potius malorum*.

NOTES TO CHAPTER VII

1 (p. 155). Chapter VII continues to the end of draft C, and on p. 157 ('At the time of my father's decease') begins on draft E, which carries on through Chapter VIII to the end of the Memoirs.

2 (p. 156). According to vol. I of the *Letters* (223–4) he was an army horse contractor called Lovegrove.

3 (p. 156). His father's enjoyment of life, not his own.

4 (p. 157). In 1789 Gibbon had already chosen for his heir John Eliot, the younger son of his cousin Catherine Elliston, Lady Eliot; but in his last will of 1791 he left most of his property to the children of his mother's brother, Sir Stanier Porten, who had died in June 1789.

5 (p. 157). Gibbon added dates in the outer margins of draft E; following Bonnard's edition, these have been placed between dashes in the text.

6 (p. 158). Gibbon provided draft E with full notes; these are printed under separate heading on pp. 177–89 and marked in the text by numerals in brackets, starting at no. 27. (The first twenty-six notes refer to the pages of draft E not used in this edition.) Editor's notes to Gibbon's notes are on pp. 214–16.

7 (p. 159). See Chapter V, note 6.

8 (p. 161). *Decline and Fall*, Chapter XXI; the age of Constantine is in Chapters XVI–XX.

9 (p. 161). Chapters XV and XVI.

10 (p. 162). The *Mémoire justificatif pour servir de réponse à l'exposé de la Cour de France* was published in October 1779 (*Miscellaneous Works*, vol. V, pp. 1–34).

11 (p. 163). Lord George Germaine.

12 (p. 163). The Gordon Riots of 2–11 June 1780, named after the fanatical Lord George Gordon.

13 (p. 163). This refers to the words italicized in the following passage from 1 John 5:7–8: 'There are three that bear record *in heaven, the Father, the Word and the Holy Ghost, and these three are one* ...' These appear from 800 AD in the

Latin MSS, and were printed in the Authorized Version, but have been omitted since the Revised Version. See The *Oxford Dictionary of the Christian Church*, under 'Johannine Comma'.

14 (p. 164). Gibbon rented a house in Brighton from July to September 1781 and was lent a house near Hampton Court Palace from September to October 1782.

NOTES TO CHAPTER VIII

1 (p. 166). See Chapter VI, note 19.

2 (p. 166). Gibbon wrote draft E during 1791.

3 (p. 167). Gibbon and Deyverdun rented accommodation in Lausanne at first, and moved into La Grotte in spring 1784.

4 (p. 168). *Decline and Fall*, Chapter XLVII.

5 (p. 170). Lord Sheffield's town house.

6 (p. 171). Wilhelm de Sévery, the son of the family at Rolle: Saloman and Catherine de Sévery and their children, Wilhelm and Angletine, the 'respectable family' of p. 172.

7 (p. 172). 'Interval' here means 'interruption'.

8 (p. 173). The Pays de Vaud had been part of the republic of Bern since 1536: it was freed from dependency by the French in 1798.

9 (p. 173). 'Let this be your wall of brass, to have nothing on your conscience, no guilty pallor' (Horace, *Epistles* I, 1, 60–61).

10 (p. 174). Pope, *Essay on Man*, Epistle III, 3.

11 (p. 174). Gibbon allowed his stepmother £300 a year; the fact that there is no mention of her in his last will suggests that he did not expect her to outlive him. She died in 1796.

12 (p. 175). Horace's 'golden mean' (*aurea mediocritas*) of *Odes* II, 10, 5.

13 (p. 175). Gibbon took the end of this paragraph (from 'few books of merit . . .') from draft C (p. 157).

14 (p. 175). According to Buffon, at the age of eighty-five Fontenelle gave the twenty years between the ages of fifty-five and seventy-five as the happiest of his long life.

NOTES TO GIBBON'S NOTES
ON CHAPTERS VII and VIII

1 (p. 177). 'Teague', 'teg' or 'teigue', anglicized forms of Irish *tadhg*, is a nickname for an Irishman, first found in 1661 (OED).

2 (p. 179). Paul Philippe Gudin de la Brenellerie; see Index. The passage reads as follows:

'You were at M. de Foncemagne's, my dear Theodon, the day that M. l'Abbé de Mably and Mr Gibbon dined there among a large party. The conversation turned almost entirely on history. During dessert, the Abbé, a serious politician, directed it to administration and, as by temperament, disposition and admiration for Livy he thought well only of the republican system of government, he began to praise the excellence of republics, quite confident that the learned Englishman would fully approve and admire the depth of genius which had enabled a Frenchman to appreciate all these advantages. But Mr Gibbon had learned from experience the drawbacks of popular government, and did not share his opinion at all, but spoke warmly in defence of monarchy. The Abbé wanted to persuade him through Livy and certain arguments taken from Plutarch in favour of the Spartans. Mr Gibbon, blessed with an excellent memory and with all the facts at his fingertips, soon took command of the conversation; the Abbé was annoyed, lost his temper, and said harsh words. The Englishman kept the cool-headedness of his country, seized his advantages, and pressed them home with increasing success as the Abbé's rage threw him into greater confusion. The argument grew heated until M. de Foncemagne broke it off by rising from the table and moving into the salon, where no one attempted to renew it.'

3 (p. 180). 'Is there anything more tedious than a M. Guibbon in his interminable history of the Roman Emperors, who at every moment holds up the boring, sluggish flow of his narrative in order to explain the cause of the events you are going to read?'

4 (p. 180). *Miscellaneous Works* IV, pp. 575–95.

5 (p. 181). The Socinians were Anti-Trinitarian believers allied to the Unitarians and denying the divinity of Christ.

6 (p. 182). The nine-volume Italian translation published in Pisa from 1779 to 1786 is of the first three volumes of *The Decline and Fall*, all that had so far appeared.

7 (p. 183). See Chapter VII, note 13.

8 (p. 183). Bishop Newton had wrongly accused Gibbon of misquoting Burnet's *De statu mortuorum* in a note to Chapter XXVIII of *The Decline and Fall* (p. 144 of vol. 3, Everyman edition). The English translation is: 'According to the accepted language of Holy Scripture, death is called sleep, and the dying are said to fall asleep, which seems to me to suggest that the state of death is a state of quiet, of silence, and of rest from toil.'

9 (p. 183). In Chapter XXXVIII of *The Decline and Fall* Gibbon first used the phrase 'while Arcadius and Honorius again slumber on the thrones of the House of Bourbon'. In the 1789 and subsequent editions this was changed to 'thrones of the South' (p. 109 of volume 4, Everyman edition).

10 (p. 184). Gibbon substituted 'a demon' for 'Mirabeau', who was known to have written these memoirs, published anonymously after his death.

11 (p. 185). 'It is right to learn even from an enemy' (Ovid, *Metamorphoses* IV, 428).

12 (p. 185). The palladium was a sacred statue of Pallas Athene, believed to protect the city which preserved it, and brought from Troy by Aeneas to ensure the foundation of Rome.

13 (p. 186). The Rev. Joseph Warton, headmaster of Winchester College, had

written more explicitly about Abelard's castration than Gibbon, who has only one reference to 'the famous and unfortunate lover' in Chapter LXIX of *The Decline and Fall* (p. 471 of vol. 6, Everyman edition).

14 (p. 186). 'The Latin language flies in the face of propriety: [But the French reader must be respected]' (Boileau, *L'Art poétique*, chant II, line 175). Gibbon misquoted '*ses*' for '*les*'.

15 (p. 187). For Johann Georg Meusel, see Index. The passage reads as follows:

'Gibbon must undoubtedly be counted amongst the greatest historians of our day. He conceived the idea of writing this work as he stood amidst the ruins of the Capitol, and spent the best years of his life assembling and working on his material. From this was created a "monument more lasting than brass"; and though here and there passages may appear less happily expressed, unpolished or insufficiently accurate, nearly everywhere we are aware of the highest concern for investigating and expressing the truth. Even so, where our author lacks Tillemont's guidance, as the latter's history ends, he falters and goes astray more often; this is especially so when he handles Church affairs or Roman jurisprudence (Volume IV), though it also appears elsewhere. But minor blemishes of this kind in no way diminish the warmth of our admiration for the supremely organized arrangement of the work, the wise selection of subject-matter which can also show great subtlety, the language and style which is equally suitable for the historian and the philosopher and has not been surpassed by any other English writer, Hume and Robertson not excepted. We congratulate our age on a history of this kind ... Gibbon has found hostile critics both at home and abroad for having explained the propagation of the Christian faith not in the usual manner of the theologians, but in a way suitable to a historian and philosopher.'

16 (p. 187). Swift is the 'long-sighted friend' whose imitation of Horace, *Satires* II, 6, was referred to in Pope's *Second Satire of the Second Book of Horace paraphrased* (1734); lines 163–6 are quoted here.

17 (p. 189). 'Strait is the gate and narrow is the way which leadeth into life, and few there be that find it' (Matthew 7:14).

NOTES TO LORD SHEFFIELD'S
CONTINUATION OF THE MEMOIRS

1 (p. 190). Taken from *Miscellaneous Works* I, pp. 277–8, 329–31, 404–28, following George Birkbeck Hill's edition of the Memoirs (1900). The pages omitted from Hill contain letters, all of which are included in J. E. Norton's *Letters of Edward Gibbon*, vol. III. The passages omitted by Lord Sheffield from the quoted letters are not important.

2 (p. 190). cf. Chapter VII, p. 158.

3 (p. 190). The Sheffield family stayed with Gibbon from July to October 1791.

4 (p. 191). Letter in answer to Sheffield's, dated 5 February 1791.

5 (p. 192). Lady Sheffield died on 3 April 1793; Gibbon left for England on 9 May,

arriving on 1 June. England was already at war with France and he had to travel via Basel, Karlsruhe, Frankfurt and Ostend.

6 (p. 192). cf. Chapter IV, p. 95.

7 (p. 194). She was then nearly eighty.

8 (p. 194). The bridge tolls at Bristol had been extended after a promise to discontinue them, and were finally abandoned after three days of rioting, during which the Militia's fire had killed fifteen people.

9 (p. 194). Lord Sheffield's sister, Sarah Martha Holroyd, the 'Aunt Serena' of her niece Maria Josepha's correspondence.

10 (p. 194). The French Convention had changed the names of the months on 20 September 1793.

11 (p. 194). The Allied Army under the Duke of York and the Prince of Coburg had recently been defeated in the Low Countries.

12 (p. 195). The Althorp Library assembled by the second Earl Spencer was sold complete in 1892 to the widow of John Rylands, and since 1972 has provided the main part of the John Rylands University Library of Manchester.

13 (p. 195). Gibbon lodged over Peter Elmsley's bookshop at 76 St James's Street.

14 (p. 195). The name omitted is that the Prince of Wales, who was at Brighton in command of the troops.

15 (p. 196). For the soldiers of Flanders (Lord Sheffield's note).

16 (p. 197). That is, up and about.

17 (p. 198). At Eden Farm, home of Lord Auckland.

18 (p. 198). Lord Loughborough; see Index, under Wedderburn.

19 (p. 199). See note 10.

20 (p. 199). A parody of Genesis 3:13.

21 (p. 199). Lord Auckland, Ambassador at the Hague.

22 (p. 199). Dr John Moore, Lord Auckland's brother-in-law.

23 (p. 201). His Swiss valet, Dussaut.

24 (p. 202). For Gibbon's death from streptococcic peritonitis, see Editor's Introduction, p. 10, and de Beer, *Gibbon and his World*, pp. 118 ff., and Appendix, p. 129.

25 (p. 202). 'But apart from the pain of losing a friend, my own sorrow is increased by being unable to sit by his sick-bed, support his failing strength and satisfy my longing for his fond look and embrace' (*Agricola* XLV; *amici* is substituted for *parentis* and *filiaeque* omitted).

INDEX

MORE ABOUT PENGUINS, PELICANS
AND PUFFINS

For further information about books available from Penguins please write to Dept EP, Penguin Books Ltd, Harmondsworth, Middlesex UB7 0DA.

In the U.S.A.: For a complete list of books available from Penguins in the United States write to Dept DG, Penguin Books, 299 Murray Hill Parkway, East Rutherford, New Jersey 07073.

In Canada: For a complete list of books available from Penguins in Canada write to Penguin Books Canada Ltd, 2801 John Street, Markham, Ontario L3R 1B4.

In Australia: For a complete list of books available from Penguins in Australia write to the Marketing Department, Penguin Books Australia Ltd, P.O. Box 257, Ringwood, Victoria 3134.

In New Zealand: For a complete list of books available from Penguins in New Zealand write to the Marketing Department, Penguin Books (N.Z.) Ltd, P.O. Box 4019, Auckland 10.

In India: For a complete list of books available from Penguins in India write to Penguin Overseas Ltd, 706 Eros Apartments, 56 Nehru Place, New Delhi 110019.